Panther Gorge

Kevin B. MacKenzie

Upper Jay, NY

Copyright © 2019 Kevin B. MacKenzie

All rights reserved. No part of this publication may be reproduced, distributed, or transmitted in any form or by any means, including photocopying, recording, or other electronic or mechanical methods, without the prior written permission of the copyright holder, except in the case of brief quotations embodied in critical reviews and certain other noncommercial uses permitted by copyright law.

First Edition

Editor: Tony Goodwin
Proofreader: Deb MacKenzie
Designer: Kristen Taylor
Pen and ink drawings / pencil sketches: Nolan Huther
Cover photograph: Panther Gorge Aerial Autumn 2013
Back cover: Panther's Pinnacle
Photographs by author unless otherwise noted.

Library of Congress Control Number: 2019902719
ISBN 13: 978-0-578-48061-9

Dedication

In loving dedication to my wife, Deb – my soulmate and inspiration for learning to climb. Your love, unwavering support, proofreading, humour, pre-dawn rides, post-midnight pickups, loaves of "bushwhacker's banana bread," advice, patience, and understanding bless my life. Thank you for everything. Without you, I'd be incomplete.

In memory of:
Blanche MacKenzie,
Perley Smith MacKenzie, Sr.,
Owen Taylor

Contents

DEDICATION 3

ACKNOWLEDGEMENTS 6

READ THIS FIRST 7

FOREWORD 8

LEAVE NO TRACE / WILDERNESS ETHICS 11

PREFACE 13

INTRODUCTION 14
    Description 15
    Marcy Brook 18
    Cliff Overview 19
    Remote Perspective 19

GENERAL HISTORY 20
    Alfred Billings Street 1865 20
    Orson Schofield Phelps 21
    Verplanck Colvin 25
    A Railroad? 30
    First Winter Ascent 1893 31
    Newell Martin & Wesley Lamb: Six Summits on August 5, 1894 31
    William James 1898 32
    James A. Goodwin 1925 33
    Gerald D. Murray's Solo Bushwhack of 1934 35
    The Panther's Fang (1965), Panther Gorge's First Named Rock Climbing Route 36
    The Phantom Trail 38
    Robert W. Carroll, Jr.: Discovering Mount Marcy Cavern 1975-76 39
    Search, Rescue, and Recovery Incidents 42

CLIMBING HISTORY 47
    The Early Years and the Great Void: 1936-81 48
    Dawn of the Ice Age 49
    A New Age of Stone: 2003-04 50
    The Golden Age of Rock and Ice: 2012-2017…and Beyond? 50
    Rock 50
    Ice 51
    The Future 52
    First Ascent List 52

THE CHRONICLES OF PANTHER GORGE ... 54
- General Approach for Context ... 54
- Learning the Terrain: In the Beginning, There was Grand Central Slide ... 56
- Two Marcy Slides and a Skylight Bushwhack ... 60
- The Great DeRanged Traverse ... 64
- Circumnavigating Marcy's East Face: A Day with a Forest Ranger ... 68
- Marcy's East Face ... 72
- Haystack's Conjoined Slides: Day 3 of 3 in Panther Gorge ... 77
- All Things Holy on Haystack ... 81
- South on Marcy and Climbing the Gorge's Largest Free-Standing Pillar ... 84
- A Climbing Trilogy: CrazyDog's Halo, Watery Grave, and the Panther's Fang ... 88
- A Winter Bushwhack: Attempting Marcy's Chimney ... 91
- 3.1415 ... 94
- Racing the Storm: Misty Climbing on Haystack and a Flash Flood ... 97
- Climbing Like a Cat on a Wet Tin Roof ... 101
- Rumours of War on Marcy ... 104
- The Kitten's Got Claws, and so does Marcy ... 107
- Hunting with the Pride ... 110
- Finding the Promised Land ... 114
- Tour de Gorge: Exploring Marcy and Haystack with a Night Exit over Marcy ... 118
- A Blustery Winter Ascent by Tooth and Claw ... 123
- Mt. Haystack's First Ice Routes: Orson's Tower and Fly By ... 127
- Pioneer Anomaly and Belshazzar's Fate ... 131
- Embracing our Predatory Instincts ... 135
- Lost in a Galaxy of Tears ... 139
- Sometimes it Takes a Woman to Put up One for the Boys ... 143
- Persistence Leads to a Tail of Redemption ... 146
- Climb After Slime and You Moss be Kidding Me! ... 149
- Stunning Revelations on the Slabs of Marcy ... 153
- On the Wind with a Prayer: Psalm 23 and Windjammer ... 159
- A Birthday Celebration on Kitty Cake and a Second Ascent of By Tooth and Claw ... 163
- A Mythical Melting Beast: Chimæra ... 167
- Time to Ride the Lightning on Haystack ... 171
- All Ryled Up About Marcy's Great Chimney & Slacker Cracker ... 175
- Anorthofright: Breaking Through the East Face Roof System ... 180
- The Panther's Pinnacle ... 185
- Dragon's Breath ... 189
- Between Scylla and Charybdis ... 194

ENDNOTES ... 198

REFERENCE PLATES ... 205

EPILOGUE ... 217

INDEX ... 218

ABOUT THE AUTHOR ... 226

Acknowledgments

The insight and support of many generous people have made this project a reality.

I wouldn't have made it this far in life without Jesus Christ. He walks with me every step of the way and His Word is my core inspiration. There's no outing on which I don't have a Psalm in mind. My ability to explore is a blessing.

My family: Deb MacKenzie, Lois & Mac MacKenzie, Janice Taylor, and Ed Tuttle. The support of one's family is a blessing. Thank you!

Special thanks to Don Mellor for writing the Foreword, Jim Lawyer for the advice and support over the years, Tony Goodwin for editing, Nolan Huther for the line drawings, Kristen Taylor for the design work.

One develops skills in a number of ways, one if which is through mentors who happen to be friends. Rich McKenna – if there's blame to be placed for my off-trail slide climbing obsessions, it belongs with you! Jean-Luc Michaud – I stumbled onto the ice with improper gear and little technique. Your teachings opened up a new world as we soloed the icy Adirondack faces. Don Mellor, Adam Crofoot, Bill Schneider – your technical rock and ice climbing skills are inspirational. I learned more during a day of watching you than I can possibly describe.

Thanks to the following individuals for their contributions, knowledge, advice and/or help with research: Jeff Chiarenzelli, Adam Crofoot, Emilie Drinkwater, Will Roth, John Sasso, Richard E. Tucker, Scott van Laer.

This journey belongs to all whose name appears in the narratives. Listed in trip order:

Mark Lowell, Greg Kadlecik, Scott van Laer, Anthony Seidita, Adam Crofoot, Allison Rooney, Bill Schneider, Hunter Lombardi, Justin Thalheimer, Dan Plumley, Devin Farkas, Nolan Huther, Alan Wechsler, Dustin Ulrich, John Pikus, Loren Swears, Jaryn DeShane, Doug Ferguson, Walker Wolf Bockley, Matt Dobbs, Jace Mullen, Steven St. Pierre, Ken Hebb, Laura Duncan, Brent Elliott, and Aaron Courain.

Thanks also to the following: Neal Burdick, the Adirondack 46ers, the Adirondack High Peaks Foundation, the Kelly Adirondack Center (Union College), and the Adirondack Mountain Club.

Read This First

This publication is not a guidebook. It is instead a history of Panther Gorge accompanied by narrative accounts of our experiences therein. The information in this book is for general informational purposes only. Trekking or climbing in Panther Gorge is serious business. The Gorge is a dangerous environment for all but the most experienced and prepared hiker or climber as one can easily become disoriented or injured there. In fact, one can, quite literally, disappear without a trace in the talus fields as the reports herein on search and rescue efforts clearly document. Any search and rescue operation in this setting is necessarily complex and response time is long. There is no cell phone reception. The author/publisher assumes no liability or responsibility for the safety or actions of those who enter Panther Gorge.

The Promised Land. Pencil sketch by Nolan Huther.

Foreword

This fall I've been thinking a lot about Fred Beckey, who died recently after an almost nine-decade career in the mountains. His realm was mainly the Canadian Rockies and the Cascade Range of Washington State. Fred would trek just about everywhere, and where other climbers saw impenetrable wilderness, Fred saw potential routes. Beckey's list of first ascents is probably longer than anyone else's in climbing history, the Alps included. He also leaves behind a dozen or so publications, mainly guidebooks marked by scholarly research and crisp writing.

What made me think of Fred when I was reading through Kevin MacKenzie's *Panther Gorge* wasn't the comparison between the Canadian Rockies and Panther Gorge. That's a stretch. What made me think of Fred was the exploratory passion of Kevin MacKenzie and the encyclopedic depth of his documentation. This isn't a simple how-to-get-there guidebook. It's an attempt to tell the story, the whole story, of the most mysterious and remote pocket in the High Peaks.

Beckey was a quirky guy, obsessive, some would say. So is Kevin. Like Beckey, the self-described Adirondack MudRat began his climbing career without any guidance and without a lot of gear. He just wanted to be up early enough to see the sunrise, and he wanted to see that sunrise not from a window but through a canopy of trees. He wanted to be off the regular trail scribed by humans and out on a real path laid out by nature. God's trail, he'd say. The slide tracks, the stream beds, the slippery vertical gullies – these are more than just lines on a mountain to Kevin. They are callings.

And, man, did Kevin MacKenzie ever answer.

The book in your hand is the product of that calling. It's a look at the when and the how and even the why behind the explorations of Panther Gorge. If you don't know yet, Panther Gorge is the most eerily legendary place in all of the East's mountains. If you were to take a map and stick a push-pin into the center of New York's high country, that pin would stab Panther Gorge.

But it isn't just the remoteness that sets it apart. It's the downright difficulty of getting there and back. Legendary guide Orson "Old Mountain" Phelps said that the wilderness peaks of the Adirondacks gave him a sense of Heaven Up-h'istedness! Yet a lot of early trekkers to Panther Gorge came back claiming a sense of Pain In-the-Arse'edness. They'd lug a climbing pack back there, thrash around for endless hours, and stagger back with a new appreciation for the ease and civility of roadside climbing areas like the Gunks, that rock-climber's playground visible from the New York Thruway.

So a lot of people just wrote it off. They did so because, in a lot of minds, Panther Gorge was better as a concept than a real place. "It was there," as Everester George Leigh Mallory might have said. Just knowing this was good enough for most people. Like wondering about the dark side of the moon, we need to know that trackless terrain still exists.

With *Panther Gorge*, the Gorge is now a place. It has edges and dimensions. Where once there were ghosts there are now some real people. Many of the rock faces have been measured and climbed. The ice drips, too. The big features have been given names. Thus, the shroud has been lifted. But only partly.

My guess is that this book will grab you. An eighteen-hour round trip can't be *that* bad, you'll tell yourself from the comfort of your reading chair. You'll see the photographs, the lines on the big rock walls, and you'll read the story, as told by the MudRat himself. Then a few of you will actually make the trip. Yet despite all the excellent journaling, the meticulous research, the delineations, and the definitions, you will discover that Panther Gorge still protects most of its secrets.

Kevin MacKenzie's *Panther Gorge* has cracked the door open a bit and let in some light. But the Gorge is a big place, and a book such as this one is just a start.

— Don Mellor *Lake Placid, November 2017*

Tamarack on a Marsh. Pen and ink by Nolan Huther.

Leave No Trace / Wilderness Ethics

Panther Gorge's remoteness and difficult access routes mean that the area has not been affected by the recent surge of hikers. Nevertheless, where 20 years ago virtually no one (save lost hikers) traversed this area, now there are multiple named climbing routes and regular visitation throughout the year. All visitors must remember that we are but guests in a unique wilderness resource. I, therefore, hope that future visitors will carefully practice leave no trace (LNT) principles so that the wild and challenging allure of the area is not lost. As the author of this book that will undoubtedly spark greater interest in the area, I feel a particular responsibility to instill a powerful sense of stewardship in each potential visitor.

LNT principles are vital in order for Panther Gorge to remain one of the wildest places in the Adirondacks. We practice these principles during our trips and ask anyone who visits the area to do the same. Those principles can be found at the organization's website, lnt.org. Most people find it easier (and safer on account of rock or ice falls near the cliffs) to camp at the Slant Rock Lean-to area.

For rock climbing, we ascend the cracks and faces as we find them. Because ice scours the vegetation from most cliffs annually, the cracks are generally clean of all but the occasional plug of moss or lichen. The fragile alpine vegetation of environmental concern is not damaged as it is not present on the routes. Likewise, the glades below most of the cliffs where peat mosses, ferns, false hellebore, bluets, closed gentian, and blackberries are often found are disturbed much more by annual ice-falls than by careful climbers.

Panther Gorge is a dynamic natural environment. Its steep walls annually shed large chunks of ice that affect the vegetation at the base of the cliffs. Additionally, frequent rockfalls and landslides create freshly exposed rock. Compared to these natural events, the impact that one person can make on the land might seem trivial. Nevertheless, I hope that visitors will take care to ensure that the only visible changes are natural ones.

Rappelling down the southern side of the Chimney Wall. No Man's Land, the V Wall, and Little Haystack are in the background.

Preface

We wander, climb, hike, and ski, each of us seeking that special activity or wilderness area that touches our soul. We pursue a niche specific to our abilities and personality. What draws us? The answer may be simple or complex. Some find retreat in the Adirondacks where, away from the hustle and bustle of "real" life, one can find adventure be it on the shore of a small mountain pond or off-trail in the most remote recesses of the park. Enter Panther Gorge.

I looked across this dizzying void during my first visit to Mt. Haystack in 2004. The slide torn flank of Mt. Marcy met my stare. I had no thoughts of climbing or bushwhacking nor did I consider that others may have done so, but I felt awe and respect for the wilds before me as I contemplated my existence. How very small humans are when compared with the designs of nature. That was the genesis. That experience planted seeds that would take root and grow throughout the years, but I didn't realize that this remote chasm would one day be the focus of my ambitions. Since then, Panther Gorge has grown into a refuge where I could shed the tensions of life, discover unknown parts of myself, commune with nature, and feel close to Christ. I experience His presence in the heart of creation as much as in church though there is certainly less of a congregation!

My relationship with Panther Gorge is nothing if not an epic adventure, a collection of diverse excursions spread over years that evolved from climbing hundreds of Adirondack slides. This exploration has always been and continues to be a labor of love. It evolves each season and the new discoveries seem virtually endless. The more I visit, the more my curiosity grows. Panther Gorge offers roughly 200 forested and anorthositic acres below 3,800' in elevation where there is much to explore for the tenacious bushwhacker, photographer, scrambler, or technical climber. Little did I know that the area would become my backcountry home and sanctuary. Some of my closest friends have been an integral part of the journey. What a blessing.

The following text contains a physical description, history of the region, climbing history, and personal narratives. The Chronicles are abridged accounts of our visits to Panther Gorge from August of 2009 through the winter of 2018 – approximately 42 trips. I began writing these accounts, or trip reports as they're known online, during the early 2000's in order to describe the backcountry experience to my father, a Type 1 diabetic. The disease limited his range for hiking, hunting, and similar activities. The intent of the Chronicles section is similar. They document the area and share our experiences with those who want to vicariously visit the Gorge via text and photographs. If the reader takes away an appreciation for the area's beauty, gains respect for the region, or shares in the excitement, then its purpose has been served.

The initial outings involved bushwhacks and slide climbs that built the foundation for more technical endeavors on rock and ice. The logistics of most trips are similar (approach route, times, elevation gain/mileage), so the introductions are truncated unless there are details worth mentioning. Each chapter represents a successful outing. We've enjoyed a particularly high success rate as things go in the mountains. There have been so called failures, days when unforeseen or uncontrollable variables necessitated a retreat. We've hauled 65-pound winter climbing/camping packs into the Gorge only to carry them out hours later without anything to show for the effort except sore muscles. Yes, we grumbled, then laughed as we found humour in the situation (and ourselves) while contemplating lessons learned. There is value in failure, never doubt that. If you're one to explore, expect days where the wind is at your back and the sun shines on your goals, but be ready to suck it up and pay the mountain every now and again.

Distance is noted in miles (or feet), elevation in feet, and temperature on the Fahrenheit scale. The Yosemite Decimal System (YDS) is used for rock climbing routes and the Water Ice (WI) grading system is used for ice climbing routes. The overall journey will continue after this book is published whether by us or parties yet unknown. Personal post-publication reports may be found on the internet at adirondackmountaineering.com.

May your ambition for the goal allow you to be a student of the journey.

Introduction

Two thousand feet deep and lined with broken cliffs rising above a remote forest lies one of the last great Adirondack enigmas – Panther Gorge. It seems fitting that it lies between New York's first and third highest peaks, Mts. Marcy and Haystack. The area has exuded an air of mystery and adventure since the first pioneers ventured to the foot of Mt. Marcy, long before the Gorge itself was named. Early accounts in the purple language of the period attribute words such as "terrible" and "awful" to the chasm. These adjectives stoke romantic visions and contribute to its reputation even if modern day technologies have rendered the area slightly less mysterious. Still, when the hanging vapors cling to the mountains like a gray shroud and the winds tear through its northern pass, it's difficult not to feel a sense of humility, respect, and curiosity for what lies within. A newspaper article from the eighteen-hundreds relays the author's impression of the Gorge:

> *You look upward and see three immense black domes (Marcy, Haystack and Skylight) hovering so near together that they darken even the midday sun. It is altogether, the wildest spot that can be found in the whole northern wilderness, a fitting place it would seem for the grim old Monarch of the mountains to hold his court, while his vassals bow their heads thickly around, as if to vie with each other in crowding near to do him homage.*[1]

Most Adirondack hikers pursuing the 46 High Peaks are familiar with the Gorge if just by name. They rub shoulders with it en route to Mt. Marcy, Mt. Skylight, or Mt. Haystack – the latter offering the best summit perspective of the chasm. The majority of Marcy's cliffs and slides – God's creative hand at work in nature – can be viewed from Haystack's ridge. One can sense the rugged power born from the combination of sheer slabs, curving slides, shadowy crags, concealing forest, and Mt. Marcy's summit. There is no easy access and no trail to its innermost recesses. But it is not entirely untouched by man. Search parties have looked for lost hikers. Regional pioneers – Phelps, Stoddard, Colvin, Hopkins, Goodwin – once tramped through its forest on their respective pursuits. Traces of their passage didn't last long, however. Their backcountry marks have faded with the exception of Phelps who cut several of the area's trails and Colvin who inset the copper survey bolts into many a mountain's summit.

The Gorge is a place of solitude – nature in the raw. There are no buzzing cell phones or signs of the "civilized" world. Here lies remote Adirondack wilderness. Boreal chickadees, warblers, and thrushes sing at dawn and the close of each spring day while rills gurgle under moss-covered talus in a watery symphony. Winter is punishing in contrast. Frigid winds whip to and fro carrying sounds that raise the hair on one's arms – the shotgun blasts of cracking ice.

The majority of those who have visited the Gorge proper usually trek to its southern end near Panther Gorge Lean-to. The "open camp" was constructed in 1940[2] and rebuilt in 1989[3]. It is worth noting that there has been a "camp" in the vicinity since Verplanck Colvin's first visits to the Gorge with O.S. Phelps in the early 1870's. E.R. Wallace also noted a "log camp within 6 rods of where Elk Lake Trail diverges from 'Panther Gorge Trail,' about .75 m. below the camp near Lake Tear."[4] Access to this area is usually via the Elk Lake to Marcy Trail which ascends from Elk Lake before it splits at Panther Gorge; west to Four Corners between Mts. Marcy and Skylight and east up the Bartlett Ridge to Mt. Haystack or the Ausable Lakes. The lean-to and several nearby campsites offer excellent jump-off points for trips up any of these High Peaks. It seems even from here, the allure of the Gorge spawns tales of adventure. Stories of the hardships of climbing

Haystack from the south or linking the three aforementioned mountains in a rugged loop are common modern-day themes. Add winter into the mix and the stories nearly always involve trail breaking through deep snow to the ice-entombed summits. The south end offers a tranquil setting, but the true jewels of the Gorge can only be seen by venturing into the jaws of the north end.

Photo collections, text and videos of bushwhacks and rock and ice climbs have now been taken of many locations in the Gorge; search "Panther Gorge" on the internet to open that door. Anyone with a computer can vicariously explore in two dimensions. True appreciation and understanding is experiential; one must contribute blood, sweat, and tears; hear the birdsong, feel the wind, and drink the mountain water. Am I suggesting that anyone who reads this text should venture into the Gorge? No. Only experienced bushwhackers and climbers familiar with all the complexities of a rugged backcountry outing should explore it without a licensed guide – there are dangers hidden amongst the beauty.

Description

A physical description of Panther Gorge is in order before we venture into its heart. The last of several ice sheets that covered the Adirondacks was the Laurentian ice sheet of the Wisconsin glacial period. The lobe of the ice sheet relevant to the Gorge flowed southwest and accounts for many of the characteristics of Panther Gorge. Looking from the north end, the characteristic "U" shape of a glacial valley is obvious. While rockfall explains some of the talus and cliff features in the Gorge, the southwestern moving glacier plucked pieces of stone from the southern aspects of the mountains depositing them downstream. Glacial erratics, stones of a different type from the local bedrock, riding in the great raft of ice were also deposited throughout the region. Other features such as the free-standing spires were likely the result of physical and chemical weathering – cracks weathered to create a gap between the feature and the mountain. Even the large spires of the Gorge are transitory, however. The same processes that created them will continue until they structurally fail.

The Gorge is a north-northeast trending glacial valley located in the township of Keene between Mts. Marcy and Haystack, New York's first and third highest peaks. The elevation differential is over 2,000' from Marcy's summit (5,344') to Panther Gorge Lean-to at the south end. The height of the Marcy/Haystack col (the north pass) sits at roughly 4,175' where the Phelps Trail skirts its northernmost border. One can see the smaller cliffs of Haystack a few hundred feet south of a small marshy area of the trail though the most inspiring views begin about one eighth of a mile away where the slope falls away amidst a host of large cliffs.

Here begins a variety of diverse geologic features: gullies, dikes, free-standing pillars, fins of anorthosite, and weathered slabs. Noteworthy trap dikes can be found on both sides. A dike is simply an intrusion in the bedrock. A trap dike is a general name for a dark, fine-grained igneous rock. A dominant dike forms the right-hand border of Haystack's *V Wall* though the most significant dike is a nearly vertical chimney slightly north of Marcy's *East Face*. Additional gullies split the cliffs on both sides and tend to be more inset on Mt. Marcy.

The pieces of talus are chaotic stacks of natural artwork. Walk through and you will find intriguing sights: hanging spears of stone, acute chiseled patterns on the ceilings of talus caves, laser-cut cracks that disappear from sight, and balancing pancakes. The passages between or under the blocks are too numerous to count though a description

Acres of talus covered with moss sit below every cliff.

or two may provide context and scale. A corridor near *Grand Central Slide* led under a 90-foot long boulder perched on "smaller" pieces. Subsidiary passages led to the sides and downward. I didn't explore the full extent. This, however, is minor compared to a talus cave reported by caver Robert W. Carroll, Jr. in 1976. "Mt. Marcy Cavern" was reported to have 440' of passages.[5] Deposits of ice are not uncommon even in June. Mature trees and thick carpets of moss adorn the tops of the upper blocks. One might think I'm describing the famed talus fields of Indian Pass!

There are myriad cascades in Panther Gorge. Some are obvious and high on the flanks of the mountain while others are hidden under the forest canopy along the edges and center of the valley. Text from a *Plattsburgh Republican* article describes them as follows: "[...] in the spring, streams pour from both sides, rivalling the falls of the Yosemite Valley."[6] They are not only present during the spring snowmelt, but after each rainstorm or on warm winter days when the sun heats the dark bedrock and punishes the ice formations. Even minor showers quickly augment the volume of small rivulets flowing into Marcy Brook.

While none of the waterfalls rival those of Yosemite, the tallest is roughly 100' high and sits along the northern edge of the *East Face* of Marcy. It may be heard and seen from Mt. Haystack if its volume is sufficient. The cascade was mentioned by several early pioneers though it may be more of a landmark in modern times since it lies at the base of a relatively recent addition to the area – the 1,400 foot long *Grand Central Slide*. The majority of the water tumbles down a near vertical cliff while the remainder flows down a leaning cleft in a huge corner. Edwin R. Wallace's *Descriptive Guide to the Adirondacks* refers to this as "Panther Gorge Falls."[7]

Natural processes have modified the terrain over both the millennia and via single violent events. Ice and heat weather the cliffs, loosening blocks that add to the underlying talus fields and storms ravage the forests. Jim Goodwin, a local guide of the

1900's, described the Gorge as a "pleasant 'herd path' route"[8] and author Alfred B. Street described the forest as "pathless but by no means tangled."[9] The chasm was home to stands of large spruce trees.

One of the most abrupt post-settlement events occurred on November 25, 1950. A hurricane – a.k.a. the Big Blow – decimated over 800,000 acres of timber in the Adirondacks.[10] Areas of the Gorge were transformed into dense fields of crosshatched trees and unearthed root-balls pointing skyward. The days of easy bushwhacking ended overnight. Patches of deadfall from the Big Blow still remain though most can be avoided if one knows the terrain. Subsequent storms have made their mark as well. Torrential rain and flooding from Tropical Storm Irene in 2011 likely damaged the beaver ponds. They were pristine glistening jewels before the storm, but empty shortly afterward. Nearly all the dams had holes in them. The first signs of new beaver activity reappeared in 2015.

Panther Gorge Falls at the bottom of Grand Central Slide.

A rock-fall in 2010 or 2011 scraped a white strip down the top right of Marcy's *East Face* and leveled nearly 200' of the forest below. Minor rock-falls are common. We only await the next storm or the subtle workings of ice and water to make additional alterations. The valley may be more rugged now than a century ago, but modern-day access to its borders became easier with the advent of trail-cutting in the 1800's.

The grade of the forest floor from the north pass near the Phelps Trail is initially gentle, but drops steeply for roughly .25 mile. Here, the cliffs of Mt. Marcy and Haystack are only a couple hundred feet apart. It's little wonder that most of the forest floor is choked with overgrown talus. The slope eases considerably at 3,600' in elevation and remains moderate for almost a mile to the south.

Conditions in the center of the Gorge might be considered serene if not for several blowdown fields. Glacial erratics are strewn about Marcy Brook. The summits of Marcy and Haystack are 1.25 miles apart. For locational context, drawing a line from summit to summit crosses near the northern edge of several beaver ponds. Farther south and free of the cliffs, Marcy Brook meets the Elk Lake to Marcy Trail where the elevation is approximately 3,280'. The south end couldn't be more different than the north.

Marcy Brook

Marcy Brook, sometimes mistakenly called Panther Brook, is part of the Champlain Watershed. Not surprisingly, the sound of its rushing waters has been romanticized by likening it to the roar of a panther. It flows south from the north pass and shouldn't be confused with the Marcy Brook flowing northwest toward Marcy Dam. Runoff high in the north end begins as a low gurgle, or purr if you will, that builds during its descent. It is, at first, largely subterranean beneath the talus, but intermittently emerges downslope.

Roughly 600' lower, the rills that feed the brook from gullies on Mts. Marcy and Haystack are more obvious as they meander through the mossy forest floor. Marcy Brook is about six feet wide at 3,500' in elevation where the drainage stream from Marcy's *Grand Central Slide* joins. Additional gullies feed the brook as it winds down the center gaining volume and width. Faint herd paths and beaver slides weave serpentine patterns on the sphagnum moss along the brook near the beaver ponds at roughly 3,420' in elevation. Spectacular views of the Gorge's north cul-de-sac can be viewed from the edge of the ponds. The brook grows wider and rockier until the next major stream enters from

The ragged cliffs of No Man's Land. Notice the balancing block.

the west. This is the drainage from the historic *Old Slide* facing Mt. Skylight. Farther downstream, the brook becomes more rugged with deep pools and small cascades until it crosses the Elk Lake to Marcy Trail. It then flows between the Bartlett Ridge on the east and Skylight, Little Nippletop, and McDonnel on the west. Miles to the south the brook feeds Stillwater Inlet, the Ausable Lakes, the east branch of the Ausable River, and finally Lake Champlain.

Cliff Overview

E. R. Wallace described Panther Gorge as follows. "Its walls, in some places, tower aloft ten or twelve hundred feet," and, "Its gloomy depths are completely veiled from the sun except during a small portion of the day."[11] The guidebook overstates the cliffs' scale unless we take it to mean the elevation differential between the valley and summit (in which case it's understated). The words do, however, drive the point home – the area is dramatic and cliffs sheer.

The highest concentration of cliffs is in the north end. Notable exceptions are intermittently scattered down the Gorge on Mt. Marcy. The northern crags host some of the highest elevation climbing routes in the Adirondacks. The cliff bases generally begin between 3,600' to 4,000' in elevation. As such, the rock climbing season is shorter than for the lower crags; they hold moisture late into spring and begin to collect ice early in autumn or even late summer.

Specific cliff details precede the Chronicles section. In a nutshell, Marcy's northern cliffs – the *Panther Den, Feline Wall, Agharta Wall,* and *Huge Scoop* – are high, broad, and delineated by a buttress. From the north, they form a 1,600' southwest trending arc. Smaller cliffs and slides lie to their south before the *East Face,* the primary slab in the Gorge. The *Agharta Wall* and *East Face* are the tallest cliffs with roughly 400' of vertical gain.

Mt. Haystack's cliffs, in contrast, are generally less than 100' tall. Exceptions that reach nearly 200' in height include an obvious slab, *No Man's Land,* and the *V Wall,* the latter of which is the last large cliff on Haystack before the forested terrain becomes more dominant. In the far north, the cliffs tend to be tiered and separated by horizontal bands of forest. Set on multiple aspects ranging from southwest to northwest, Haystack's cliffs also tend to retain moisture whereas many of Mt. Marcy's slabs dry quickly in the sun. Unique to Haystack is a trio of free-standing pillars with historic significance and a large fin of rock connected to the Haystack massif on its northern end. Several technical slides lie to the south.

Remote Perspective

Discussions regarding the Gorge often lean toward how difficult it is to access given its remote location. One needs context to understand. This isn't in a part of the Alaskan wilderness where access is best accomplished via aircraft. One can reach the north end at the Haystack/Marcy col after about four hours of steady albeit rugged hiking. None-the-less it is listed among the Adirondacks' most remote areas.[12]

Comparative distances including alternative routes to Panther Gorge should illustrate the point for those familiar with the High Peaks. We'll use trail distances as opposed to "as the crow flies" distances from nearby roads. Wallface is 4.4 miles from the trailhead at Upper Works or about 5.5 from Adirondak Loj. Gothics' North Face is roughly 6.5 miles from the Garden in Keene Valley. Each venue involves less elevation gain than visiting Panther Gorge. The Gorge lies roughly 7.8 miles from the Garden in Keene Valley though the shortest distance to the north pass of Panther Gorge is 7.5 from Adirondak Loj via the Van Hoevenberg Trail. This option involves climbing to within .6 mile of Marcy's summit before descending down a steep .7 mile section of the Phelps Trail to the col. One would then need to re-ascend the Phelps Trail after the climb. This may be the best option for backcountry skiers. The south end is nine miles via the Elk Lake to Marcy Trail or 10.7 miles from Upper Works via Lake Colden. Either involves an additional mile of bushwhacking to access the north-end.

General History

The history of those exploring Panther Gorge is drawn on a canvas which relatively few have made their mark. Fewer have returned multiple times. Alfred Billings Street, Orson Schofield Phelps, Verplanck Colvin, and Jim Goodwin are the most notable players though a few others have logged trips worth mentioning. The area touched each in a unique and sometimes spiritual way. The paths and time-periods of the pioneers sometimes intertwined; especially Phelps and Colvin. Detailed writings of the first explorers are sparse yet descriptive; each unique to his respective personality. Alfred B. Street ascribes a dark presence to the area while Verplanck Colvin's writings are more quantitative in nature. Thanks to their accounts, the modern-day adventurer can tour the Gorge and identify some of the features described 150 years ago. Each contribution adds another piece to the puzzle. In the end we see that much has changed, but much remains the same including the spirit of adventure.

Alfred Billings Street 1865

Our walk through history begins with the wanderings of author Alfred Billings Street. Detailed descriptions interwoven with dramatic prose make his book, *The Indian Pass*, a must-read for Adirondack history and backcountry aficionados. His account of Panther Gorge, though only a small part of the book, is poetic and memorable. Street embarked upon a great tramp led by guides Loyal A. Merrill and Robert Scott Blin in 1865.[13] His purpose was, in part, to visit four of the great Adirondack gorges including a then unnamed gorge between Mts. Marcy and Haystack.[14] Here he would carve a name in the annals of Adirondack history, "The Panther Gorge."

The sojourn took them from Indian Pass up Marcy's summit, down the *Old Slide* facing Mt. Skylight "and along a 'recent' trail upon its border."[15] This was four years after Orson Schofield Phelps cut the first trail up Mt. Marcy. The slide is a persistent theme in the early climbs of the mountain. They descended through the forest until reaching Marcy Brook. The party then bushwhacked north to "track the rill to its source in the gorge."[16] The character of the forest during the 1800's was different than today – comparatively easy walking. They walked .5 mile through "a pathless but by no means tangled woods"[17] to where the view of Marcy and Haystack is both ominous and inspiring. This distance placed them near the present day beaver ponds and nearly centered between the summits. Street describes the area with dark prose; two anorthositic foes seem locked in an ancient war.

Grim and threatening stood the two mountains, scowling at each other, as if summoning their energies for the dreadful strife. The loftier Tahawus soared, the loftier towered Haystack. Awful stillness reigned. My heart almost ceased its beatings. It seemed as if a stone, rattling from either mountain, would be the signal to hurl one against the other. The brook hid itself, as if in fear, under a rock. And now the two dread crags drew closer and closer. In the black, frowning cleft, for it was now merely that, enormous crags, green with moss and crowned with trees, were piled in every shape, as if the two mountains had in old days clutched vast fragments from their breasts and dashed them against each other. Gloomier scowled the ravine and narrower it grew, while the rocks completely filled it. Yet above and through them I could see that the tortured mountains had at last locked themselves in a Titan struggle, falling upon their sides to do so. The gorge was at an end, a majestic cul de sac.[18]

Street's description of the stacked tree-covered talus and the fact that they "repassed the two tangled miles"[19] back to the south suggests that they stopped after about a mile somewhere in the north end, probably where the slope increases. His depiction as a whole is dramatic yet accurate. Fallen rocks, glacial erratics, and broken crags make this appear to be a tortured landscape especially as the Gorge narrows. Marcy's tallest cliff is crumbing at the top and bottom. House-sized blocks have tumbled or been plucked from the walls leaving great voids in their stead. Other massive pieces are still in place, but clearly separated from the mountain. He would have been able to see these. Haystack looks sheer and broken – cracked walls abound and obvious dikes slash the mountainside.

The party tried to peer over the north pass from a tall stone. Here Merrill chiseled their names into its surface. If this is fact, could it have stood the test of time and weather? Street continued his description after exiting south, "I looked toward the terrible gorge. It seemed as if a mighty horror brooded over it; as if some demon made within it his black and scowling lair."[20] He seems to relate demons to great passes and likened a wind gust from Indian Pass to the shout of a demon.[21] One might agree if they've been in the area during a violent storm.

Street's final words named the Gorge. "As for the rocks, they seemed the very home of panthers, and I immediately named the chasm The Panther Gorge."[22] The name instilled an air of mystery that endures today. Shadows obscure the details of the cliffs and the forest canopy hides the myriad streams and talus fields – only the occasional crest of a large stone hints at the secrets hidden beneath. Whether the Gorge was actually home to panthers or not, they were reported in the area before their extirpation. He could not have labeled the terrain between Marcy and Haystack more aptly.

Orson Schofield Phelps

O. S. Phelps aka "Old Mountain Phelps" stands among the most famous Adirondack guides of the 1800's and was "probably the most active guide from 1850 through the early 1870's."[23] His colorful anecdotes and naming of several High Peaks is widely known. Perhaps less known is that he was a philosophical thinker that contributed regularly to local newspapers and wrote a series of essays now known as the *Orson Schofield Phelps Collection*. Details on precipitation, the slides, the Adirondacks in general, poetry, and even religion are included in his papers. His writings also scribed Panther Gorge into the annals of Adirondack history. In fact, he likely visited the Gorge more than any other person of his time; a result of his great love for Mt. Marcy or "Mt. Mercy" as he called it. On the mountaintop, he experienced the self-described feeling of "heaven up-h'isted-ness." He climbed the mountain for the first time in 1849[24] and claimed to have visited Panther Gorge nearly 100 times[25] as noted in both *The Adirondacks: Illustrated* and *Adirondack Cabin*. This number may be conservative since he purportedly guided over 500 people to Mt. Marcy's summit.[26] Included in this number are several notable figures such as surveyor Verplanck Colvin and photographer Seneca Ray Stoddard. Artist Frederick S. Perkins, Mary Cook, and Fannie Newton (two of the first women to climb Marcy) accompanied Phelps to the summit on August 19, 1858.[27] Almon Thomas, one of the owners of Township 48 which included most of Panther Gorge, along with several others made the trek on September 17, 1870.[28]

Phelps made a tangible and lasting mark in Panther Gorge and on the nearby mountains via trail cutting. This cutting may not have, in some cases, involved fully "bushing out" the trail so much as marking it. Old Mountain Phelps cut the first trail up Mt. Marcy in 1861. Marked with ax blazes on trees and piles of rocks (cairns), the 1861 trail led from Upper Ausable Lake over the Bartlett Ridge, into the center of Panther Gorge then diagonally up to Marcy's summit ridge via the "great slide" on its southern flank facing Mt. Skylight. Jim Goodwin stated that the trail took Phelps about three weeks to complete with a third of that time spent in the Gorge.[29] Guiding up the slide was a clever yet obvious move; any seasoned bushwhacker knows that slides offer the way of least resistance even if they are comparatively precarious. It also added to the overall adventure for his clients. Phelps noted in *The Rivers and Brooks of the Adirondacks*, part of the *Orson Schofield Phelps Collection*, that the slide array was created by a storm in 1856, though due to a slide's propensity to re-avalanche over the years, it is likely that some of the tracks existed beforehand. Photographs indicate that the most recent slide activity was slightly before 1985.

The section of the 1861 trail from Upper Ausable Lake over Bartlett Ridge seems to have fallen out of favor during subsequent years. Verplanck Colvin reported it as "disused" in 1875.[30] In fact it disappears completely from the USGS topographic map of 1895 (Mt. Marcy Quadrangle). Colvin suggested they "essay a new route" around the south end of Bartlett Mountain in October of 1875 during his "levelling" of Mt. Marcy.[31] In the process, they intersected the trail that, by 1871, extended from Mud Pond (aka Elk Lake) to Panther Gorge. Phelps reported that this trail was "done mostly by the hotel proprietors at Schroon River and Schroon Lake"[32] though Phelps has been credited with cutting a portion of it.[33]

Fourteen years after cutting the 1861 trail from Upper Ausable Lake, in 1875, Phelps cut the trail from Panther Gorge Camp at the mouth of the Gorge up to what is now known as Four Corners between Mts. Skylight and Marcy. The year is sometimes thought to be 1873 when Colvin explored the route, but Phelps' words and those of the Tahawus Club of Plattsburgh date the event. ***Note:*** this shouldn't be confused with the Tahawus Club associated with Tahawus, NY which was formed in 1897.[34] Phelps wrote the following on July 8, 1875 in "New Trails to the Summit of Mount Marcy":

> On Monday, June 21st, O.S. Phelps, L.S. Lamb and E. Phelps, went to Mount Marcy for the purpose of laying out new trails on an easier grade to the summit. Their efforts resulted in a new and better trail, which starts from the old Camp at the south base of Marcy – or Panther Gorge – and follows up the south side of the Skylight pass Brook to the summit of the pass between Mt. Marcy and Skylight, where [sic] is a large, new camp. From this camp two trails leave the main pass-one for Marcy and one for Skylight.

Phelps noted at the end of the article that George Sawyer met them on the twenty-second and helped with both the trails and the camps. This effectively extended the trail west to "within thirty or forty rods of the main Opalescent stream and old trail."[35]

These trails would aid Colvin's party in taking further measurements of Mt. Marcy as well as all the hikers who would one day approach from the south. Phelps cites the Tahawus Club of Plattsburgh as the catalyst for cutting the trail as they paid "$12 or $15 dollars" in combination with other donations.[36] They committed the funds to Phelps' trail improvement idea during an outing of the Round Trip, a multi-day hike beginning at the Ausable Lakes that touched upon Panther Gorge, Marcy, Lake Colden, the Deserted Village, Indian Pass, Lake Placid, and Whiteface, during August of 1874. They climbed up the southern slide of Marcy "in a fog so thick that a man 10 yards away looked like a spectre."[37] Obviously the trail had not been created yet. Their trip down the west side of Marcy prompted the club members to ask if there was a better way up (or down) the western aspect. Phelps contended that there was and he had been talking about it for some time, but could garner no help – funding for the venture soon followed.[38]

Phelps' began writing about his interactions with Colvin as their paths overlapped. The *Plattsburgh Sentinel* published Phelps' article called "Among the Adirondacks" on

September 19, 1873. One of the most notable sections relates to Phelps' sojourn with Verplanck Colvin a month earlier. We'll see Colvin's perspective below, but Phelps wrote, "Mr. Colvin gave it up when he got on Haystack, and looked down into Panther Gorge, that there was no other gorge or pass in the Adirondacks that would compare with that, being so narrow he could talk with his assistant from the summit of Haystack to the summit of Marcy, and their words passing over a vacuum of more than 2000 feet deep, and a clear view of the tree tops standing in the very bottom of it."[39] Most visitors to Mt. Haystack have likely not been able to talk back and forth from Marcy to Haystack. The conditions must be nearly perfect. In contrast I'd fathom that many of us recall Haystack as being among the windiest peaks where one often has to shout to those nearby in order to be heard.

Three free-standing pillars on Mt. Haystack. For Whom the Lichen Tolls follows the crack up the left-hand tower.

The Tahawus Club, commissioners of the 1875 trail from the Gorge to Marcy, published "The Stroll of the Tahawus Club" in the *Plattsburgh Republican* on September 4, 1875. It describes a six-day trip at the end of August, 1875. Their guide was none other than O.S. Phelps who they refer to as the "Guide, Philosopher and Friend of the club" without whom they didn't undertake their annual hiking trips. The members included a photographer and a botanist. As a whole their purposes were focused on pleasure, research, and photography. Their arrival at Panther Gorge Camp, a "little open space" at 3,342' in elevation, begins the relevant section of an article well worth reading in full.

They followed the trail to Marcy's summit and described the dramatic views which included new slides on Giant (likely caused by the freshet of 1856)[40] and Lake Perkins a.k.a. Lake Tear of the Clouds. The group returned to camp (likely what they call Tip-Top camp [aka Junction Camp or Summit Camp] in the saddle of Marcy and Skylight) that evening before splitting up the following morning. Some climbed Skylight via the freshly cut trail while others re-ascended Marcy before descending to the head of Panther Gorge where they recorded a descriptive account of their bushwhack back to camp. Some details may sound familiar to those who have visited the Gorge. My comments are in brackets.

A blind trail leads down to the head of the gorge; it winds around to the right, and here we find the very buttresses of the old mountain. First we come to a wall of rock some 50 feet in height which increases rapidly as we go winding around to the right [the Panther Den]. Huge cracks are seen in this rock wall, which seem to divide it into regular columns, and away up on the summit mighty masses of rock seem ready to tumble down at any moment. But soon the attention is directed towards the left of what is now a narrow gorge, to where Haystack shuts down in an almost perpendicular wall. Here we see three huge columns ten feet square and one of them at least 50 feet high, standing out some ten or twelve feet from the side of the mountain, one of them supporting upon its top a massive rock apparently loose, as if it were a capital.[41]

The account describes a series of pillars south of the modern day Phelps Trail, the largest of which climber Adam Crofoot and I measured at about 40' high. There are several free standing pinnacles on both Marcy and Haystack, but the rest are markedly smaller. Phelps describes the same pinnacles below in the S.R. Stoddard text. Given his description as well as his strong connection to the Tahawus Club as their regular guide, it seems likely that Phelps suggested that they watch for the features during their trip. The article continues:

> What strange freak of nature has left these immense columns standing here like the pillars of some ancient temple? Still passing onward and downward we discover to the right that the wall is receding and soon find that there is an immense amphitheatre, flanked by perpendicular walls upwards of 1,000 feet high and measuring some half a mile across the front – while back in the centre is a square rift in the rock, apparently where a column has once stood which has been shaken down by some convulsion [Likely describes the Agharta Wall – the tallest cliffs of Marcy though the walls are only about half the height and a fraction that wide. The square rift is part of a roof system that crosses part of the lower wall.] Huge masses choke the narrow gorge, and in the interstices which have been formed as rocks have fallen in promiscuous heaps there is plenty of room for a man to walk upright as we demonstrated by actual experiment.[42]

It seems that they appreciated the grandeur of even the talus fields. The group rejoined their comrades at Panther Gorge Camp likely following Marcy Brook. They professed that Panther Gorge "surpasses in sublimity anything we have seen in the wilderness – even the far famed Indian Pass falls below it, inasmuch as there is there a wall of rock only upon one side while here on one side the wall is perpendicular and higher than that of Wallface, while upon the other side of Haystack looms up at a sharp angle almost 2,000 feet."[43]

While Phelps often guided up the southern slide, he wasn't restricted to it. He led distinguished photographer S. R. Stoddard north through the Gorge. In the text, Phelps detailed a bushwhack that led up the Haystack side where they viewed the Marcy cliffs from the east and the pinnacles of Haystack from the west. They then exited and climbed to Marcy's summit. Stoddard noted landmarks and details ranging from large obvious features to minutiae such as the deeply pocketed anorthosite indicative of the area. At the risk of being redundant, it's interesting to read Phelps' description of the north end of the Gorge. Again, my notes are in brackets.

The blocky columns at the top of the Panther Den. Phelps' "Castle Column" is among the blocks.

Well, I guess I kin show you the way, fur I've been up there near a hundred times, I s'pose. Let's see, we're in Panther Gorge now, I believe, and, before we go up Marcy, I want to show you a sight up here, from the side of Haystack, that is worth seeing, where we can look right down into the gulf below. See that precipice on the Marcy side? It is one continuous wall of rock, a mile in length, circling around to the head of the gorge, with Castle Column at its head [The north end of the Panther Den on Mt. Marcy is angular and divided by chimneys and cracks. One buttress stands out among the rest. This is assumedly Castle Column]. That is one of the wildest places in the Adirondacks, where, after a heavy rain or in the spring, streams pour down it from all sides. You see that water-course over there in the centre? I have seen an almost unbroken sheet of water, six feet wide, pouring over that to the bottom of the gorge, almost a thousand feet below. Now we will pass on up the trail once more, just stopping to notice those shafts of rock across on the Haystack side. There are three of them, entirely detached from the wall nearby, about ten feet square, and one of them near fifty feet high, with a loose cap-stone on top of it. The soft rock must have crumbled away between them and the main ledge while they were left standing.[44]

Phelps wasn't restricted to trail blazing in the Panther Gorge area from the south. For those unfamiliar with the area, the Phelps Trail begins at the present day Garden Trailhead in Keene Valley, passes Johns Brook Lodge and Bushnell Falls before crossing Johns Brook on its way to Slant Rock and finally up to the head of the Gorge and Marcy's summit. *Peaks and People of the Adirondacks* by Russell Carson noted that Ed Phelps, Orson Phelps' son, and Seth Dibble cut the trail up via Johns Brook to the northern pass of Panther Gorge in 1871. Others note that Old Mountain Phelps may have marked the trail over a decade earlier. In any case, accounts indicated that it was difficult to follow during the late eighteen hundreds, but was popular by the early twentieth century.

The intimacy with which O.S. Phelps knew Panther Gorge and Mt. Marcy left an indelible mark on those he guided as well as the history of the High Peaks. Phelps' guiding, anecdotes, quirky phrases, articles, trail cutting, High Peak first ascents, naming of several peaks, and written papers in the Adirondack Research Library of Union College all contribute to his legacy. His writings continue to inspire and inform. They open a unique window into the past that shows that, while some things in the Gorge have changed, much of the area remains as it was over a century ago. Moreover it demonstrates that Phelps' interest was not entirely unique. Curiosity and appreciation for the backcountry wilderness is as strong among many modern-day hikers as it was during the 1800's.

Verplanck Colvin

Verplanck Colvin was superintendent of the Adirondack Survey, the first extensive survey of the region. The survey not only measured much of the area's topography, but also determined the correct location of county and township boundaries. The breadth of his work encompassed exploring countless Adirondack summits, valleys, and lakes from 1872 to 1900. Colvin was a tenacious explorer who loved the region as well as his vocation. Detailed maps, illustrations, and data were included in his annual reports to the state. The reports not only detail the specifics of his survey work, but also provide an extraordinary window into the logistics of his party's work along with descriptions of the wilderness and the hardships he and his party endured as they worked through all manner of storms and harsh weather. Like today, uncooperative weather was a common part of venturing into the wilderness. Shut your eyes and imagine a thunderstorm or winter whiteout. Remember the challenges you faced then contemplate hiking without the aid of modern clothing or equipment. This was Colvin's reality.

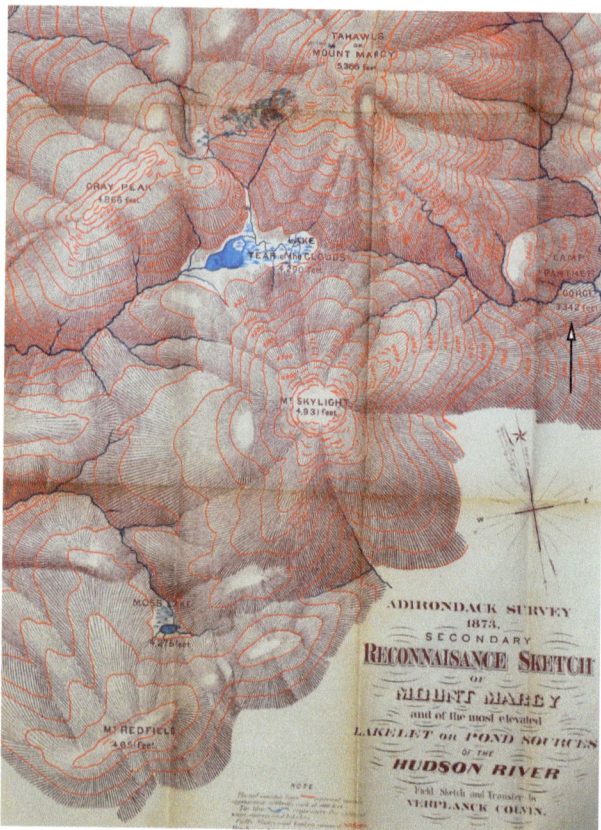

Figure 1: Portion of Verplanck Colvin's 1873 sketch of Mt. Marcy and the surrounding area. The arrow points to the location of Camp Panther Gorge.[i]

Panther Gorge's location at the foot of Mt. Marcy made it an ideal basecamp for visiting Marcy and the surrounding peaks. As a result, his sojourns to the Gorge are the most quantitatively detailed of this area's historic accounts. Colvin and his party visited Mt. Marcy multiple times from various directions, but the trips during 1872, 1873, 1875, and 1877 are the most notable visits involving the Gorge. This time period coincided with the years that O.S. Phelps was guiding so their paths often merged. He became one of Colvin's most trusted guides though the annual reports generally refer to him as "my old mountain guide" or "the guide."

1872

Colvin's trip in 1872 left a tangible reminder of his visit: copper bolt #1 that he inset into Marcy's summit. This also marked the first recorded measurement of Marcy since 1839,[45] when Professor Farrand Benedict measured the elevation at 5344.69'; it was the first of several taken by Colvin using various methods that successively increased the accuracy of his measurements. In coordination with barometric readings taken at a lower observation station, 72 barometric readings were taken on Marcy in 1872[46] while 591 readings were taken in coordination with the Panther Gorge station the following year.[47]

He arrived at the summit on September 14 by way of Indian Pass and Lake Colden. Burdened with his usual gear including a theodolite and barometers, his party met rain, strong winds, and cold temperatures. Such conditions were nothing new to Colvin, but were not conducive to survey work. Stormy weather plagued them for days. Colvin wrote, "We descended the slippery rocks down and across the great slide on Marcy, toward the spot, two miles distant, where I had encamped last year, and where we hoped to find the bark huts still standing. Meanwhile the rain did not cease to fall, and it was dusk when, trembling from fatigue and exposure, we stumbled into the old camp in Panther Gorge."[48]

The following day he noted signs of a panther, or chat de montagne as he sometimes referred to the large feline. He also found the prints of one tracking a rabbit in the pass between Mts. Marcy and Skylight as he reported in "Winter Fauna of Mount Marcy."[49] The party re-ascended Marcy, worked throughout the day and spent the night on the summit. Using the average of a series of barometric measurements, he ascertained the height of Mt. Marcy at 5,333.64' above sea level.[50] The party left the summit the following morning to retreat from an approaching storm, but not before measuring "Summit Water" (aka Lake Perkins or Lake Tear of the Clouds) and determining that it was the highest pond source of the Hudson River. The bad weather delayed an attempt at the then unclimbed Mt. Skylight – that would have to wait.

1873

Colvin returned on August 23, 1873; this time from the east for a longer duration. Colvin and company climbed Marcy on the 24th, but left an assistant in the Gorge to take "barometrical observations at intervals of five minutes" in correspondence with observations taken at the Dudley Observatory in Albany. They'd taken 591 readings by the week's end, the average of which placed the elevation of the Panther Gorge camp at 3,378.71' above sea level.[51]

He also measured the elevation of a series of mountains by barometer and level including Macomb, Gray, Dix, Skylight, Haystack, and Mt. McIntyre (which was previously measured and subsequently renamed Algonquin). Measurements were taken from exposed rocky slopes on Marcy with unimpeded views. Considering that he ascertained each measurement as they reached the relative height of the inferior mountain, most calculations must have been measured from the southern ridge of Mt. Marcy as opposed to the slide. Colvin seemed especially enthusiastic that Haystack and Skylight proved to be the third and fourth highest peaks in New York. Once on the summit, high winds beset the group and they descended to the bark hut at Panther Gorge Camp.

August 25 was clear so Colvin re-climbed Marcy. He was able to use a theodolite telescope to establish contact with the signals on both Bald Peak and Hurricane Mountain, which served as primary triangulation stations for the Adirondack Survey. This provided the angles necessary for his trigonometrical computations. In combination with a series of barometric readings from his assistants, he determined the altitude above the "level of mean tide in the Hudson River" to be 5,402.65' – another step toward determining the true height of the mountain. He wrote, "We now added to our previous adventures the first descent of Mt. Marcy in the night. Down the ledges and the oozy 'slide' path of an avalanche, we groped our way, and once in the forest, lighting our lanterns, we went easily down to our camp."[52]

August 26 was another day of clear weather though it didn't last. Colvin hoped to measure Mt. Haystack, which he also called the "Matterhorn of the Adirondacks,"[53] by barometer and to "occupy it as a trigonometrical station."[54] As if the adventure of climbing Marcy's slide wasn't enough, he wrote of Haystack, "No trail no mark of axe on tree, here indicated that man had ever ventured before even on the lower steeps of this proud mountain; though one or two have claimed to have scaled it [...] and clambering amidst cliffs, slowly found our way, and cut a trail up the southern end."[55] Modern hikers still speak of hiking the steep trail up Mt. Haystack's southern flank; some with disdain and some with pride.

Colvin's aspirations to measure Haystack weren't over; he re-climbed it with two guides including O.S. Phelps during clear weather on August 27. Colvin wrote, "I took two guides and re-ascended Mount Haystack, answering across the deep chasm the faint, distant shouts of the assistant now climbing Mount Marcy."[56] Phelps describes the same experience in his 1873 article detailed in the Phelps chapter. The progress on Mt.

Haystack included setting survey bolt #11. He also measured the height of Basin and Gothics (which he noted as previously unmeasured) as well as "Saddle Mountain" or Saddleback Mtn.

August 28 found Colvin accomplishing a previously unfulfilled task – ascending and directly measuring Mt. Skylight for the first time. Descending in the late afternoon, he explored "Moss Lake" (now called Moss Pond), which is slightly southwest of Skylight's summit. Colvin's zoological interest is evident when he describes a pond containing bivalve shells and bordered by sphagnum moss. He then struck northeast to "lake Tear-of-the-clouds." He ended the day under waning daylight by scouting a new trail back to Panther Gorge Camp, one that would "avoid the necessity of climbing Mount Marcy."[57] This may be why some people erroneously believe that the trail from Panther Gorge to the Marcy-Skylight col was cut in 1873. As noted above, Colvin's work did lay the groundwork for Phelps and company to cut the trail in 1875.

The party exited over the summit of Marcy the next day having surpassed Colvin's original goals – a dramatic difference from the previous year. He intended to return the following spring, but could not until 1875 due to "accumulated office business, with reductions in appropriations."[58]

1875

Phelps' 1875 trail was completed only months before Colvin's return to measure the height of Marcy with rod and level (a more accurate method to determine altitude than barometric leveling). The new trail would be the key to the success of this endeavor while Panther Gorge would be the primary camp through November 6. Phelps was one of many in the party that accompanied Colvin on this sojourn.

October 22-23: The party ascended from a camp at the south end of the Bartlett Ridge after bypassing Phelps' 1861 trail over the ridge to attain Marcy's summit by a continuous slope – Colvin's idea.[59] With clear weather, Colvin ascended Marcy by the "new trail" (Phelps's trail from the Gorge to the Marcy/Skylight col) to pick a route for the leveling party. He noted disturbing two eagles and found that his old signal was destroyed, something that he'd remedy in 1877 by erecting larger more durable towers. The next day Colvin wrote, "The guides carried forward more of the supplies to the gorge camp, and I with one aid re-ascended Marcy."[60] Clear weather turned hazy and he spotted several ravens flying out of the Gorge – still a common avian in the area.

October 25-26: Good weather prevailed until noon before a cloud enveloped the summit. The leveling party reached a height of 3,635' in elevation; the most accurate measurement of Mt. Marcy's altitude was progressing. Meanwhile a guide was sent for provisions and returned with bear meat; the guide's narration of killing the bear provided the evening's entertainment while around the campfire in the Gorge – the perfect setting for such a tale. Despite the clouds that clung to Marcy the following day, Colvin again climbed to the summit.

October 27-28: Snow storms deposited 8" of snow while the team continued to toil in harsh conditions. The twenty-eighth was clear so Colvin climbed Marcy again while the leveling party reached the east end of "Lake Tear notch" (Four Corners area) at 1:00 p.m. Colvin wrote, "[…] our old mountain guide – weather-wise by experience, calls our attention to the depth of snow, the lateness of the season, and prophesies against us."[61] The snowpack and ice-encrusted evergreens would have made progress and navigation arduous.

October 29-30: Undeterred, Colvin re-ascended Marcy to measure angles, but eventually turned back to join the leveling party which was working up through the ice-encased krummholz. Colvin again makes note of the wildlife – an owl flew close to them as they descended after dusk. One benchmark of consequence was the height they reached since it provides the general location of the old route's exit. "We have passed the junction of the old 'slide trail' [Phelps' 1861 trail] to Marcy to-night [sic] and have reached an altitude of 4,799' above tide – already the highest point so far reached by any regular leveling work in New York."[62] He was not shy about reveling in their accomplishments.

Colvin continued the narrative by describing the humbling beauty of the encroaching winter in Panther Gorge. His words also exemplify his dedication to the survey work before deteriorating weather conditions halted the effort.

Icy cliffs on Mt. Haystack.

The morning of the 30th, showed the mountains wrapped in dense fog streaming down into the deep gorge, ghostlike over the black yet icy ledges or slides on the inclosing peaks. The black cliffs of Haystack are grim with monstrous yellowish icicles. We are unable to do any leveling, and our old mountain guide counsels me to desist, and asks leave to return, fearing least we may be entrapped in the deep snows in the gorge. I resolve, however, to carry the line forward to the summit at all hazards.[63]

Phelps' wrote about the same day in an article entitled "Finding the True Height of Tahawus" published in the November 20, 1875 issue of *The Plattsburgh Republican*. He refers to himself as the "Old Pioneer" throughout – "The next morning Panther Gorge was enveloped in a thick fog, with howling winds sweeping over Tahawus, and Haystack."

November 1-2: Colvin didn't give up leveling, but noted that he "reluctantly abandoned all hope of completing angular measurements on Marcy."[64] The weather was not cooperating. The theodolite, however, needed to be retrieved and two guides risked exposure (one froze both ears) in estimated winds of 70 m.p.h. with temperatures of 0 degrees Fahrenheit.[65] Colvin noted that the guide departed or in Phelps' own words, "The

Old Pioneer got leave to go home, as there was no more bush-hook work."[66] Colvin called this a "brush hook" and had the guides use it to clear limbs interfering with the line of sight surveying instruments.[67] The following day was similar – strong winds and harsh temperatures.

November 3-4: Clear weather found the party re-ascending Marcy which was "deeply drifted with snow, and aglare with ice."[68] Regardless of the brutal conditions, they measured to within 200' of the summit – an exposed area well above treeline. The long days of working in challenging conditions were taking an obvious toll as they descended in the dark: "[...] worn out with exposure and exhaustion, we make our way down, slipping and falling constantly from very weariness [sic]."[69] The next day also found them laboring in harsh conditions. Colvin wrote, "A dense fog, or frost, now enveloped us – the sunlight illuminating it with mysterious splendor."[70] This lack of visibility certainly slowed the leveling process, but they persevered and completed their final measurements at 4:50 p.m. when they measured the summit at 5,344.311' above sea level.[71] They celebrated with joyous yelling and revolver shots before descending into the inky darkness of Panther Gorge with a storm approaching. They knew that they had made history with a measurement that is still used today.

1877

The season of 1877 saw Colvin erecting heavy timber pyramid-shaped "tower signals" on several High Peak summits including Mt. Marcy. These replaced smaller more fragile ones built during previous years. They approached from the Ausable Lakes and entered Panther Gorge earlier than the previous season. The Gorge was not used as a basecamp, however. Instead, they used a shelter at the Lake Tear Camp between Marcy and Skylight. Colvin wrote, "The erection of such a signal on the barren, wind-swept crest of Marcy was a work of difficulty. It required almost a week's labor of half a dozen guides to transport the lumber from below the timber-line nearly a thousand feet up the ledges."[72]

Colvin's collective writings describe survey work throughout the Adirondacks. His efforts on Mount Marcy were significant, but only a part of his overall accomplishments. The Adirondacks would have been a different landscape today if not for his contributions. Though Panther Gorge didn't play an exclusive role, it was a key position and hotbed of activity during their visits. The trails we use to ascend Haystack, Skylight, and Marcy from the south today are a direct result of this era in Adirondack history.

A Railroad?

Some saw the Adirondack passes as a means to an end. The proposed use would make most of us balk from a wilderness advocacy perspective. The *Plattsburgh Republican* published "Adirondack Railroad Facts and Fancies" on April 25, 1891. The article discussed a "through line" rail from New York to Montreal. Distance and altitude were obvious considerations in planning the line and the great passes were only natural to consider. Imagine our most remote regions disrupted by a railway. Panther Gorge, Ouluska Pass, Hunters Pass, Caribou Pass, Ampersand Pass, Elk Pass, the Ausable Pass, and Indian Pass were listed as viable options. Even Verplanck Colvin noted that various parties including the railroad industry would be interested in his survey data.[73] I can feel you shuddering. Thank God for Article XIV of the New York State Constitution or the Adirondack landscape might have been much different.

First Winter Ascent 1893

March 18, 1893 marked the first winter ascent of Mt. Marcy by Adirondack Mountain Reserve forester and game warden, John W. Otis and Benjamin S. Pond. This was from the east by way of Panther Gorge. An article by Russell Carson in the January, 1932 issue of *High Spots* called "Snow Climbing in the Adirondacks" includes a letter by Pond that recounts the tale.

The temperatures were cold – negative 18 Fahrenheit – when they departed from Otis' camp on the Upper Ausable Lake. The snow was two or three feet deep in the woods at this elevation. The text notes that they didn't strictly follow a trail so much as "rounded Bartlett Ridge" to Marcy Brook and followed it to Panther Gorge Camp which was buried in snow. Higher at the Marcy/Skylight col they estimated the snow to be at least 10' deep since no trees could be seen. Under a windless blue-bird sky, they then climbed to the summit cone on a hard crust where they encountered heavy ice on the summit proper. They finished the climb at roughly noon and were able to return to their camp about dusk "claiming the distinction of being the first to climb Mount Marcy in winter."[74] It is notable, especially for hikers who know the rigors of winter climbing, that they managed to complete the venture without taking food along!

Newell Martin & Wesley Lamb: Six Summits on August 5, 1894

Peak bagging and arduous bushwhacks aren't new concepts though they usually don't include routes across three trailless peaks of the Great Range with Panther Gorge in the mix. The Range Trail from Gothics to Haystack was cut in 1905 by Ed Phelps, Ed Isham, and Charlie Beede[75] thus the feat of Newell Martin and guide Wesley Lamb was especially difficult in terms of route finding and endurance. Martin led the way even though he traveled with guide Wesley Lamb who volunteered to bear the burden of the gear needed for the day. Guide Charlie Beede served as support and hiked emergency overnight gear to a camp partway up the trail between Skylight and Marcy via a different route. He waited and prepared dinner for their arrival.

Martin noted that others of his time were stronger and faster, but it "never occurred to any of them, before 1894 to take those six summits at once."[76] It should, however, be noted that Walter Lowrie, a theologian and explorer of the region, and Malcolm MacLaren, his classmate at Princeton, connected five summits during July of 1892 in the following order: Marcy, Haystack, Basin, Saddleback, and Gothics.* Martin's article "Six Summits" notes, "The forests have been tamed. Modern boys and girls equal our old records and modern athletes easily surpass them. But for this they will not get due credit, because trails have been cut through all the woods, and paths cleared over all the summits traversed in that walk."[77] His comment isn't bragging so much as noting that such alterations change the accessibility of mountain summits as well as the difficulty of multi-peak traverses including the modern day Great Range Traverse.

The route climbed Gothics from St. Huberts and then went "without a trail and without even a blazed line"[78] over Saddleback, Basin, and Haystack. The connector trail from Little Haystack to the Phelps Trail wasn't cut until 1919.[79] Thus they bushwhacked

---

* Like Newell, Walter Lowrie also embarked upon ambitious hikes including multiple peaks of the Great Range and other areas. During one documented outing, he used Slant Rock as a base camp, ascended to the head of Panther Gorge. Pages 9 and 12 of his untitled journal in the Keene Valley Library note that he then went "down gorge to skirt base of Haystack to Little Brook [sic]." This brook does not appear to be formally named, but based on his hand drawn map, it may have been one of the drainages between Haystack and Little Haystack. He then climbed to Haystack's summit.

down Haystack "by big rocks and slides and a brook"[80] into Panther Gorge, hung a left, and aimed straight for the Alderson Camp where Beede awaited their arrival. This camp, long gone, was a lean-to built by Charles Alderson in 1889.[81] It was located about halfway up on the trail from Panther Gorge to Four Corners and is marked only as "Camp" on the 1902 Mt. Marcy Quadrangle topographic map.[82] Unfortunately, Martin doesn't describe the details of Panther Gorge. Since he left Haystack at 2:50 p.m. and arrived at the camp at 4:20 p.m., it's safe to say that the Gorge was easier to travel through than today and they were in phenomenal physical condition. He even reported that they were not very tired or sore after the trip.

Martin changes the pronoun from "we" to "I" after taking a 10-minute break at the Alderson Camp which suggests he hiked the last leg alone. He left camp and arrived at the Marcy/Skylight col after 10 minutes. After that, he climbed Skylight and Marcy which marked the end of the peak bagging portion of the trip. They then hiked back to the Ausable Lakes and St. Huberts where they arrived at 11:00 p.m. after 16 hours and 10 minutes. Martin was 40 at the time of his endeavor, at "an age at which one excels in diligence rather than speed."[83] Some of us might beg to differ based on the rate at which he finished his trip given the logistics!

William James 1898

Most of the names thus far have belonged to rugged Adirondack explorers. There was another notable figure that visited the Keene Valley area during the 1800's and early 1900's: William James, born in 1842. He visited the valley often and was a pioneer of the mind whose intellectual contributions touched upon the fields of psychology, philosophy, religion, and literature. He is perhaps best known for the book *The Varieties of Religious Experience* which developed from a series of twenty lectures called The Gifford Lectures that he presented at the University of Edinburgh.

William James also wrote detailed correspondences to family and friends including his wife Alice. These comprise the 1926 book *The Letters of William James*. Two letters, one written to Alice on July 9, 1898 and the other to his protégé and long-time friend Pauline Goldmark on September 14, 1907, touch upon Panther Gorge. The first letter speaks volumes about a night in Panther Gorge which was a catalyst that helped him move forward to develop the Gifford Lectures. While the trip helped on the intellectual plane, it did not on the physical. Visiting the Gorge was and continues to be an arduous affair that many people underestimate.

When James visited the region in 1898, he was fatigued after a semester of teaching at Harvard University and contracted a cold en route to Lake Placid.[84] He spent the latter part of June recovering and hiking various peaks while staying at the Adirondack Lodge (the spelling had not yet been changed to "Loj") with his host Henry Van Hoevenberg. Here he hoped to work on problematic aspects of the lectures.

James had written Pauline Goldmark asking her and her sister to meet him in Panther Gorge. She, along with several others, obliged and was waiting at "Panther Lodge Camp" when he arrived with his guide after climbing Mt. Marcy. Writings of his experience are among of the most spiritually descriptive accounts written regarding the Gorge. The following excerpts are from a letter written to his wife in 1898.

I was in a wakeful mood before starting, having been awake since three, and I may have slept a little during this night; but I was not aware of sleeping at all. My companions, except Waldo Adler, were all motionless. The guide had got [sic] a magnificent provision of firewood, the sky swept itself clear of every trace of cloud or vapor, the wind entirely ceased, so that the firesmoke rose straight up to heaven. The temperature was perfect either inside or outside the cabin, the moon rose and hung above the scene before midnight, leaving only a few of the larger stars visible, and got into a state of spiritual alertness of the most vital description. The influences of Nature, the wholesomeness of the people round me especially the good Pauline, the thought of you and the children, dear Harry on the wave, the problem of the Edinburgh lectures, all fermented within me till it became a regular Walpurgis Nacht. I spent a good deal of it in the woods, where the streaming moonlight lit up things in a magical checkered play, and it seemed as if the Gods of all the nature-mythologies were holding an indescribable meeting in my breast with the moral Gods of the inner life. The two kinds of Gods have nothing in common—the Edinburgh lectures made quite a hitch ahead. The intense significance of some sort, of the whole scene, if one could only tell the significance. [...] It was one of the happiest lonesome nights of my existence, and I understand now what a poet is. He is a person who can feel the immense complexity of influences that I felt, and make some partial tracks in them for verbal statement. In point of fact, I can't find a single word for all that that significance, and don't know what it was significant of, so there it remains, a mere boulder of impression. Doubtless in more ways than one, though, things in the Edinburgh lectures will be traceable to it.[85]

Christopher Shaw noted in his article "At Panther Gorge with William James" that the night spent in Panther Gorge was only one of several variables that enabled this breakthrough. A variety of other factors likely preconditioned James to this response.[86] In any case, this single visit helped unlock thoughts that enabled him move forward with the lectures.

James was 56 at the time of his visit to Panther Gorge and, according to his son, was not in shape for this degree of exertion. Day two of the trip, a bushwhack over the summits of Basin, Saddleback, and Gothics, was especially rugged though the trip as a whole was also a serious undertaking. As noted in *The Letters of William James*, "The intense experience had consequences that were unforeseen at the time."[87] The exertion caused an untreatable vascular lesion and he suffered symptoms throughout the summer.

In 1907, a few years before his death, James wrote Pauline Goldmark and reminisced about their trip during 1898. By that time he was limited to visiting more accessible locations in the Keene Valley area. In reference to the Gorge, he wrote that a large group intended to visit the area and trek back over the Great Range which, by then, had a trail (cut in 1905) and was therefore easier than the tree blazes that he followed nearly a decade before. James eventually succumbed to heart disease in 1910.[88]

Most hikers don't go into the Gorge seeking spiritual awakenings, but the wilderness experience does touch some more deeply than others. Its primal beauty, remoteness, and geographical position amidst three High Peaks allows, or perhaps forces, us to disconnect from our normal routines. The mountains are humbling, the nights are uninterrupted by the lights of towns and villages. It allows a chance for reflection without distraction and a chance to find parts of ourselves that might otherwise remain forever hidden.

James A. Goodwin 1925

Jim Goodwin, born in 1910, is among the most well-known local guides and the first person known to rock climb in Panther Gorge. Like Phelps, he cut several trails in the area around Keene Valley. He also likened the Gorge to a miniature Yosemite Valley[89] and recalled large spruce trees and the waterfall on Mt. Marcy.[90] An early trip through Panther Gorge in 1925 with Will Lewis led to further outings through the area. He recalls in his memoires, *And Gladly Guide*, that the trip was "a practical, glorious trip."[91] The pleasant bushwhacking inspired him to use it as a "return route to Slant Rock from Marcy and Skylight" with several clients. He noted that the area was "a magnificent spruce forest until the 1950 hurricane funneled into it."[92] Indeed the storm changed the character of many Adirondack slopes.

Of all the trips Goodwin took to the Gorge, two were particularly significant – a technical climb up the highest cliffs on Marcy and a scramble up the *Old Slide* to commemorate the Forest Preserve centennial. The first was an historic rock climb on Mt. Marcy during 1936. His climb was the first recorded technical ascent in Panther Gorge, and is infinitely inspirational from a climbing and backcountry aficionado's perspective. Though Jim described it as slightly unsafe in hindsight, the climb is equally bold given the location, his young age, and the level-headed demeanor with which he led his young clients. Why did he choose such a remote location? Ironically, the reason was because it was conveniently located near their camp at Plateau Lean-to high on Mt. Marcy. He also thought it offered some "interesting possibilities"…to say the least.[93]

The specific line he climbed remains a mystery to this day, but it may have been somewhere on or near the *Agharta Wall* based on his description of the location as "about three-quarters of the way to the floor of the Gorge, to the base of the highest cliffs on the Marcy side."[94] This prospect is daunting in its exposure, but makes sense in that there are ways with good holds to break through the initial cliff. Joining him on the ascent were two 12-year old boys. Two counselors who accompanied them, but didn't initially join in the climb since they were only supposed to observe, snickered at Goodwin during two unsuccessful attempts up the first pitch. He succeeded on the third try. He said, "The cliffs above looked ferocious and I would have called it quits right there, but having no belay point from which I could rope down, I decided that all we could do was to go on to the cliff top."[95] Thus he led the boys up the following pitches using a manila rope to keep them safe. Meanwhile, the counselors tried to follow, but got stuck and hopefully learning a lesson in humility. Goodwin led the boys back to the lean-to, ran down the trail to the Gorge and bushwhacked back down to help the counselors. They had partially down-climbed before Goodwin talked them the rest of the way to safety.

The age of rock climbing in Panther Gorge had begun. Though it's always possible that a tenacious climber ventured into the Gorge between Goodwin's ascent and that of the first named route in 1965, it seems that the area remained unclimbed in between. A simple statement by P.F. Loope in a 1955 newspaper article called "Marcy via the Ausable" notes, "A trip up the gorge is worthwhile. There is interesting rock climbing on both sides."[96] His words were prophetic.

Goodwin's next well publicized outing into Panther Gorge was in 1985. As the Adirondack Trail Improvement Society's (ATIS) president, he led five hikers up Mt. Marcy via the original "slide trail" route of O.S. Phelps. He organized the hike to celebrate the Forest Preserve centennial (1885-1985). They paddled up Lower Ausable Lake, hiked to the Warden's Camp, over the Bartlett Ridge, and into the southern end of the Gorge. The original entrance and exit trails to the slide had obviously disappeared, but like Phelps, they used the *Old Slide* (including a new slide track along the east side) to access the ridge and finally the summit. Ed Hale portrays the feel of the slide and outing perfectly including various historical facts recounted by Goodwin. One can almost feel the burning muscles of the climbers as they scramble up the steep slide avoiding flaky weathered rock and push through the stiff dwarf spruce. Then as now, a day-hike of this magnitude is a serious commitment of time and energy. Their outing took roughly 13.5 hours from the time they put the canoe in Lower Ausable Lake to the time they finished at the same location. Three and one half hours was spent bushwhacking and slide climbing.

Jim Goodwin's contributions to society and climbing reach far beyond Panther Gorge and indeed beyond the Adirondacks. The spirit of adventure that Goodwin instilled as a climber, pioneer, trail-cutter, explorer, leader, and guide lives on today through his accomplishments and via people that knew him.

Gerald D. Murray's Solo Bushwhack of 1934

Gerald Murray isn't a name often associated with the Adirondacks, but he did record a notable bushwhack through Panther Gorge in the July 1934 issue of *High Spots*. If nothing else, it proves that, though certainly not widespread, the intrigue of the Gorge was alive. His article simply called "Panther Gorge" has overtones of a modern day trip report. It focuses on a solo bushwhack down the center of the north pass – one of the most difficult non-technical ways to enter from the north since it leads through a steep span of overgrown talus. Descriptions of the adventure are filled with vivid imagery.

I stumbled upon Murray's account after my first exploration of Marcy's talus fields in 2013 and read his descriptions with interest. The following quote is from one of his more eloquent descriptions as he descends the north pass:

> Behind the pool, great clapped-together fragments of stone formed a cave. In wilder days Algonquins from Canada, found hunting away from their fellows by Iroquois, may have hidden there. The portico-floor was a Gulliver-step below the pool level. A boulder, its biggest furniture, gave me purchase for a leap up to the darkened inner room, where small rounded stones made movement in the dimness an adventure. The heavy walls leaned over me, as a malignant blind threat of crushing death or lonely starved imprisonment, if I should stir a fundamental bit of the structure. A light lacking, the low black chamber behind kept its mystery. I clambered out of the cave.[97]

His account and my personal experiences continue to inspire me to seek additional hidden sculptures of talus on both sides of the Gorge. The conclusion – there are more passages in the area than can be counted. Robert W. Carroll's 1976 report of the 440' "Mt. Marcy Cavern" adds further context and is discussed in detail below.

Murray would have encountered typical bushwhacking conditions like this.

The article struck another resounding chord with the following text, "In the springtime birds create a multitude of variations to the hidden brook's [Marcy Brook] gentle melody."[98] Spring and summer mornings and evenings are filled with a cacophony of birdsongs – thrushes, dark-eyed juncos, cedar waxwings, vireos, boreal chickadees, and a variety of warblers.

Murray only makes passing comments regarding the cliffs. He's obviously impressed, but his focus lies on the details underfoot. Tenacity paid off and he reached deer paths that crossed the "long gentle slope" – a perfect description for the valley floor. He noticed a porcupine and "two frames of lean-tos for hunters each with a hearth of piled stones in front."[99] While these have disappeared, one can take heart that every trip to the Gorge is one of discovery. It is this simple reality that occasionally draws the adventurous hiker off the beaten track.

General History **35**

The Panther's Fang (1965), Panther Gorge's First Named Rock Climbing Route

Mt. Marcy's Panther Den. The red circle marks the start of Panther's Fang.

An Interview with Craig Patterson and Ronald Dubay

The following information on Panther Gorge's first named rock climbing route is from telephone interviews with first ascensionists Ron Dubay on December 5, 2016 and Craig E. Patterson on December 20, 2016.

Panther Gorge fell off the radar of climbers after Jim Goodwin's climb in 1936; there were countless roadside crags to develop as climbing became more popular. Craig Patterson and Ronald Dubay, two young men in their early twenties, put Panther Gorge in the books when they climbed a plumb line up a vertical crack on the northernmost cliff of Mt. Marcy during August of 1965. This was a bold line for this era. Craig was the hut master at Johns Brook Lodge and Ron worked part time for New York State as an Interior Wilderness Campsite Caretaker at what is now known as the Johns Brook Interior Outpost.

They were situated in the perfect location to visit the Gorge, but first hiked to Mt. Haystack's summit to reconnoiter the area below. The details of the Gorge were a mystery to them, but the cliffs looked appealing. Meanwhile, Trudy Healy was writing her *Climber's Guide to the Adirondacks*, the region's first rock climbing guidebook. Ron credits this as an inspiration for some of their climbing.

The pair embarked early one morning and walked 4.5 miles to the north end of the Gorge. Ron describes the initial bushwhack as "scary" on account of the huge boulders and crevasses in combination with not being able to see where he was stepping. An eighth of a mile from the trail they reached the base of the cliff now known as the *Panther Den*. They chose the best looking crack roughly halfway down the wall and began their ascent at about 9:00 a.m. Fair weather was on their side.

Their gear included a 120 foot long 7/16" Goldline three-strand spiral wound nylon rope. These did not have the strength or stretch of modern dynamic ropes. Ron joked, "If you did a summer's worth of climbing with a Goldline, it was NOT a climbing rope thereafter...you just discarded it." They used 5/16" Goldline rope as slings. Thin soled climbing boots of the day, a light piton hammer, and pitons were also in their arsenal. Craig wore his caving helmet. Chalk and most of the gear associated with modern climbing – cams, chocks, quickdraws, etc. – were noticeably missing.

Craig, who Ron describes as "very good and very cautious," took the lead as usual. Ron said, "You really need to be able to trust someone to climb with them in a place like Panther Gorge." Meanwhile, Ron dynamically belayed from below. Dynamic belaying as they practiced it means that Ron had the rope around his back and would arrest a fall by allowing the rope to slip through his hands. This mitigated the forces placed on protection, the rope, the belayer, and the lead climber. Leather gloves protected the belayer's hands while a denim jacket protected the back. Ron's strongest memories of the climb revolve around belaying; Craig remembers the feeling of remoteness.

They split the route into two pitches. Craig protected himself with a few pitons and hammered the final one in a crack at the top to belay. The highest piton remains to this day, but the lower two pitons rusted to the point of failure – they fell out when Adam Crofoot, Bill Schneider, and Nic Gladd climbed the route in 2003. During the first ascent, Ron followed and they finished the *Panther's Fang* around 3 p.m. and bushwhacked to the Phelps Trail rather than rappelling. Once on the trail, they rushed back to Johns Brook Lodge since Craig had to do the dishes that evening!

The *Panther's Fang* was most likely named by Craig and listed in Trudy Healy's 1967 guidebook. Interestingly, it was removed from her subsequent books. The route reappeared in 1983 when Don Mellor published *Climbing in the Adirondacks*. It was removed again before finally being printed with a handful of other Panther Gorge routes in the first edition of *Adirondack Rock* by Jim Lawyer and Jeremy Haas.

The *Panther's Fang* wasn't Craig and Ron's only contribution to Adirondack rock climbing. One of the best known may be *Teddy's Trauma* on the *Rainbow Slide* of Gothics' eastern aspect, a friction route that Ron says may have taken the longest of any of their first ascents. They took Ron's dog, Teddy, along for the trip. Ron describes him as a patient animal, but at some point during the climb he decided that he'd had enough. "The dog barked twice when we were partway up the route and when I looked he was at the top."

Ron laughed as he continued, "That made us feel really good." Apparently, Teddy got frustrated and ran around the slide to wait at the top. Another notable undocumented mention is an unfinished line on Big Slide Mountain that crested the dominant overlap on the face. They ran out of time to finish the route and never returned.

As for Panther Gorge, neither visited again. Craig moved out west and became

Rusted pitons from the first ascent of the Panther's Fang.

a climbing instructor in Yosemite; this led to a ranger job. He then became a climbing ranger in the Tetons. He also authored the book *Mountain Wilderness Survival* (alternately called *Surviving in the Wilds*). As of 2016, he was still climbing. Ron was involved with the mountains and mountain rescues for many years to come, but only climbed during 1965.

The Phantom Trail

The 1953 USGS topographic map (Mt. Marcy Quadrangle) includes a trail that bisects Panther Gorge from the Elk Lake to Marcy Trail to the Phelps Trail in the north. A circa 1920 survey map included a trail down the northern pass of the Gorge. I found this interesting and searched in vain for remnants of this trail during several visits to the Gorge. I only noticed intermittent game trails near the beaver ponds in the center and a faint herd path along the Marcy side in the north. So where was this "phantom" trail? Was it simply destroyed by a storm? The answer to this question lies in the past. A brief history of the landownership of Panther Gorge sets the stage.

The land was in the hands of the "Native Indians" prior to one of the most important historic land sales relative to this region – the Totten and Crossfield Purchase. This passed ownership from Indian hands to Great Britain in 1772.[100] The transaction was complicated by the Revolutionary War and ownership of the lands eventually passed to New York State. "A few years after the close of the war, the state made an effort to dispose of its wild lands."[101] This was long before the existence of the State Forest Preserve and before anyone realized the true value of the region. The land of the Totten and Crossfield Purchase was then subdivided into townships which were sold to various parties. Panther Gorge lies primarily in Township 48 with a fraction of its southwestern acreage in Township 45. Our focus is upon Township 48. Both were owned by Zephaniah Platt who purchased Township 45 in 1786 and Township 48 in 1791. Sylvanus Wells, a lumberman and a State Canal Commissioner, bought most of Township 48 before selling it to the Thomas and Armstrong Lumber Company in 1866.[102]

The "first legalities" of a key landownership transaction took place in December of 1886 when William G. Neilson and William C. Alderson purchased most of Township 48 from Almon Thomas and Thomas Armstrong.[103] Neilson and Alderson, with other members, created the Adirondack Mountain Reserve (AMR) in 1887. This effectively protected most of Panther Gorge and many of the High Peaks from lumbering. A.S. Hopkins was hired in 1922 to survey the AMR lands for a proposed land sale to New York State.[104] The state purchased Mt. Marcy's summit and eastern aspect as well as the "northern slopes of the Great Range from Little Haystack to the summit of Lower Wolf Jaw" among other areas.[105] A small amount of acreage in the southwestern area of the Gorge and several High Peaks including Skylight (not owned by the AMR) were also purchased by the state in the early 1900's.[106] The entire Gorge, however, was not under state ownership until the AMR sold an additional 9,100 acres in 1978 which included the remainder of its stake in Panther Gorge, most of Mt. Haystack, and the tops of a variety of other High Peaks of the Great Range as well as other mountains.[107] In the end, when it comes to the complex history of land ownership, the most important detail to note is that Panther Gorge was not always part of the Forest Preserve, but in private hands and environmentally unprotected.

Back to the phantom trail…Tony Goodwin, guidebook editor and son of guide Jim Goodwin, asserts that the trail on the 1953 USGS topographic map likely never existed. He noted, "When Hopkins was surveying the new boundaries of the AMR, his crews had to travel between the Johns Brook Valley, Indian Falls, and Panther Gorge. At some

Figure 2: *Section of Hopkins' survey map. Note the "trail" into Panther Gorge. Courtesy of Tony Goodwin.*[ii]

point his survey crew apparently laid out some sort of route through Panther Gorge." Tony surmised, "While the surveyors may have blazed a line for their own use, no one stepped in to make it a formal trail. The result was that the blazed line quickly returned to its natural state."[108]

Jim Goodwin drew many of the AMR boundary maps[109] in addition to his aforementioned guiding through the Gorge. Tony recalls that his father could not remember seeing a trail (or a cut boundary line) in the area. Jim's own words in his memoires further attest to this. One of his ventures led him up Mt. Haystack via a line that he described as between the Marcy and Haystack summits. He stated, "I was sure no line was cut across the face of Haystack above Panther Gorge after the AMR-State sale of 1921 because Will Lewis, Pop Anderson and I saw no trace of such a line on our Haystack ascent from the gorge in 1926."[110]

The only way to reach the Panther Gorge Lean-to via trail from the Phelps Trail is over either Mt. Marcy or Haystack. Thankfully the phantom trail never became a reality as it would dampen the remote ambiance of one of the wildest places in the High Peaks. It would also retain some of the dangers involved in bushwhacking through the area. The terrain away from the cliffs involves navigating through talus fields while walking close to the cliffs holds the danger of ice-falls during early fall through late spring.

Robert W. Carroll, Jr.: Discovering Mount Marcy Cavern 1975-76

The following quotes and map are largely taken from the notebooks of Robert W. Carroll, Jr., 1941-2005, which are archived with the Northeastern Regional Organization of the National Speleological Society and graciously provided by Chuck Porter, editor of

The Northeastern Caver. Carroll published extensively in *The Northeastern Caver* including "Mount Marcy Cavern" which appeared in the January-February 1977 issue. I've left Carroll's wording exactly as it was written to retain the feel of the original work.

A computer programmer at Clarkson University, caver Robert W. Carroll, Jr. was a pioneer of a different nature. He explored and mapped the Northeast's most remote talus caves including the Touchy Sword of Damocles (TSOD) cave below Wallface Mountain. To put his accomplishments in perspective, he "found and documented well over a thousand caves in remote areas of the Northern Forest."[111] He also "wrote 132 articles for *The Northeastern Caver* since 1969, most of them on significant new finds."[112] Carroll made several trips into Panther Gorge during 1975-76, some in harsh weather conditions. He described the Gorge as "one of the most diabolically difficult places to reach in the Adirondacks."[113] He would awaken at around 3:00 a.m. and drive from Potsdam, NY to either the South Meadows or Elk Lake trailhead. He'd then trek into the Gorge and systematically search below the cliffs and around the summits of Marcy and Haystack. His efforts led to the documentation of over a dozen caves varying from small to one of the largest high-elevation talus caves in the northeast, Mount Marcy Cavern.

Carroll's first trip was during June 7-8, 1975. He approached from South Meadows and embarked on his first trip up Marcy. In "poor visibility and rain," he located a small cave near the northeastern snowfield.[114] He then took the trail down to the Marcy/Haystack col and bushwhacked south into the central drainage stream where he mapped a series of small caves located between 3,800' and 4,000' in elevation. They varied in size from 10'-40' of inclusive passages. He described them as the "most remote to date in the Adirondacks," and named them Upper Panther Gorge Caves 1-5.[115] They are, in all likelihood, among the caves that Gerald D. Murray noted during his 1934 trip through the same area.

Carroll's next exploration was during June 26-27, 1976. The trip led to his most significant discovery in Panther Gorge, the details of which he recorded in his journal. He approached from Elk Lake noting a couple of small caves en route to Panther Gorge Lean-to. He bushwhacked north and wrote that he "veered toward Marcy cliffs near large waterfall a mile north of lean-to. In a brush-masked talus cluster near the falls, I made the best find of the day."[116] The description seems to place this near *Panther Gorge Falls* at the base of *Grand Central Slide*, though Carroll's map places it farther south. The

Map of Marcy Cavern. Courtesy of Chuck Porter. iii

cave's on-map location could simply be an error of scale since the symbols marking the cave were not drawn on a topographic map but a 1.5" section of a larger hand-drawn map encompassing an area from Marcy to Elk Lake. Carroll noted that there was "a large talus cluster with large openings, behind which was an impressive 300+ footer, complete with 30-foot wide rooms, gravelly stream, numerous unchecked leads and small impurity speleothems."[117] Speleothems are secondary minerals found in caves. Though he only estimated the distances during this trip, he wrote, "Marcy Cavern has a good chance of being the most remote cave of its size in the Northeast, if not the East!"[118]

He continued up the west side of the Gorge noting other caverns including one with 100' of passages – Marcy Cavern II-III. There are innumerable small talus caves under the large Marcy cliffs at various elevations, but Carroll must have exited lower and linked up with the "main gorge talus channel" (aka the central drainage stream of the north pass). Here he found other talus caves including some that he did not count because he feared double-counting his 1975 discoveries. A notable finding included the following: "A huge cracked boulder at ~3,800' on Haystack side yielded a rather impressive 100-footer (Haystack Boulder Cavern) with [sic] 15-foot high entrance."[119]

Anthony Seidita exploring one of the large talus caves on Mt. Marcy during a trip in 2013. We assumed this was Mount Marcy Cavern based on its size.

Carroll returned during the following August 7-8 with his sights set on mapping Mount Marcy Cavern. Bad weather almost thwarted his trip, but he endured as tenacious explorers tend to do. He wrote the following. [...] "Measured special 'measuring stick,' a sturdy 4 ⅝ - foot branch found in the woods, then proceeded to map out cave system. Noted more 'impurity-nodule' flowstone and crumbly nature of some of anorthosite. June 26 visit had covered most of system, but 3.5 hour mapping session uncovered a few new leads, put everything 'in perspective,' and set cumulative length at 440' and relief at about 25'. Cave is by far most remote and highest elevation in NE for its size and impressiveness."[120]

Carroll's contributions not only encompass the sense of adventure intrinsic to Panther Gorge, but provide a degree of structure within an otherwise chaotic series of moss-covered talus mazes. The preceding map is one of several of Robert W. Carroll's hand-drawn maps of Mount Marcy Cavern. Ceiling heights, entrances, notable boulders, subterranean passages, and even a "porkie" den are noted.

Mt. Marcy from Mt. Haystack.

Search, Rescue, and Recovery Incidents

There is a dark side to Panther Gorge where "awful," "terrible," and "gloomy," descriptors used by authors Street and Wallace, are appropriate. The very attributes that make the Gorge intriguing can also make it dangerous. The proximity of the Gorge in relation to Mt. Marcy and the prevailing winds make it a potential snare for those who become disoriented and wander eastward. It stands to reason that hikers setting their sights on climbing this particular mountain are usually the victims. Marcy has inspired climbers since the 1800's; there is no decline in its popularity during modern times. People tend to underestimate the ruggedness of the terrain as well as the severity and unpredictability of Adirondack weather. Whiteouts, bullet-ice, gale force winds, deep unconsolidated snow, and sub-zero temperatures are normal conditions during many months of the year. Low-visibility makes the aspects of Marcy's summit cone look similar to one another. An indistinct ridge-line, markers (cairns and blazes on the stone) that are often obscured by snow and ice, and a meandering trail complicate navigation. Even experienced hikers can get turned around on a tree-less summit. Wander below tree line and the snow can be well above head-height. Take the wrong direction and there's little possibility of climbing back up. Spruce traps, voids in the snow created by evergreen branches, make it even more treacherous. Descend far enough east and the cliffs become a hazard.

Rescue logistics are complicated by the remote position, weather, cliffs, talus, blowdown, falling ice, and strong winds that often funnel through Panther Gorge. It takes time to organize a rescue once a hiking party is reported overdue and helicopters can only be used when the weather cooperates. Dense tree growth on the upper slopes make grid searching nearly impossible. Searches often call upon state and local resources, but have involved national resources as well. The Department of Environmental Conservation (DEC) Rangers, police, Bureau of Criminal Investigations (BCI), rescue dog teams, various military assets, local search and rescue teams, and civilian volunteers are among those who have been involved searching from helicopters, on snowmobiles, and on foot.

Each hiker has his or her own reasons for climbing and reasons for the gear they carry. While it's easy to form armchair opinions regarding the how's and why's of an incident, accidents are a reality. The point of this section isn't to cast judgment (especially since the individuals involved were often tenacious and resourceful), but present the situation as it was reported.

October 25, 1875: The following is one of the earliest documented search and rescue accounts in the area. Verplanck Colvin's survey team was measuring Marcy by rod and level. They arose early in the morning to scout a way to the base of Mt. Skylight. According to Colvin, "The second growth of evergreen was very dense, and we failed to find a favorable route. The leveler attempting to return alone along the trail to the nearest benchmark, lost his way."[121] Colvin's party searched the nearby woods, trails, and fired pistols to signal to the lost man who was eventually located on the Bartlett ridge.

October 4, 1883: Three men departed from the Ausable Lakes to summit Mt. Marcy. They passed through about 6" of snow in Panther Gorge; there was a foot by the time they reached the Skylight/Marcy col. They didn't have the gear to overnight, but had the prudence to seek help from Mills Blake (of the Adirondack Survey) who had a camp near Marcy's summit. Battling up through waist deep snow they found the camp occupied and were "hospitably entertained by Mr. Blake."[122]

March 14, 1973-1976: A man hiked from Adirondak Loj to Marcy Dam where he signed in at the trail register. He was alone and last seen at Indian Falls. His family reported him missing on March 16, but "particularly foul weather was reported" the weekend following his entry into the High Peaks.[123] He was reportedly prepared for inclement conditions, something that would prove true years later. An intense 10-day search involving a variety of teams and vehicles was implemented following his disappearance. "Foul weather and deep snow conditions discouraged a longer effort."[124]

Three years later, on June 13, 1976, his personal effects were discovered in Panther Gorge. Another search was conducted along the Marcy side of the Gorge on June 15, 1976 which led to the discovery of a sleeping bag, boots, a hat, jacket, glasses, and wallet on a ledge.

A volunteer who was involved in previous searches was asked by the subject's father if he would revisit the area in light of the recent findings. He agreed and, with the help of another volunteer, scoured the west side of the Gorge on July 25, 1976. Part of the search involved the slopes above the ledge. The searcher said, "I came to a spot where I had to stoop down to get underneath a low fallen tree. I bent down and when I looked down, there it was."[125] He'd found a human skull. The author continues, "He said that the person was apparently headed-uphill and had fallen and tried to continue crawling upward."[126] The remains were recovered the following Monday thus ending a three year mystery.

January 12-13, 1976: Two brothers were reported overdue on January 12. They overnighted in a tent at Indian Falls lean-to on the night of the tenth before attempting the climb. Temperatures plummeted to negative 24 degrees Fahrenheit[127] the first night, but they had the proper gear. The next morning, they hiked the last few miles to the summit, but they left most of their gear behind. One of them said, "We expected to be back at Indian Falls by noon. All we took were snowshoes, ski poles, and a camera. When we got to Plateau [lean-to], we dropped off the snowshoes because we thought we could make better time without them."[128] By the time they located the summit, darkness was closing in.

The next decision placed them among those who have been caught off-guard by the strong winds and tried to descend along a protected aspect of the ridge. Their dilemma was compounded by deep snow as they descended off-trail. They eventually gave up and dug a snow-cave to ride out the bitter night and exercised to stay warm. Temperatures bottomed out near negative 10 Fahrenheit. In the morning they knew they needed to find the trail and tried to climb up to the ridge – 30 feet took an hour's time.[129] With that strategy out of the question, they consulted a map and determined that they would run into a stream or another trail below. They descended into the Gorge and packed down an "SOS" in the snow hoping it would be seen from above. Exhausted, they built another snow shelter and hunkered down to spend another evening in below zero temperatures. The brothers tried to exit the Gorge again on Tuesday morning. They again stopped before becoming exhausted and presumed rescuers would find them during the clear weather. They made another SOS and lined it with pine boughs.

The combination of footprints in the snow and the SOS caught the eye of a ranger searching from a helicopter. Due to high winds and the boys' position, the ranger was lowered with snowshoes for the boys. He pushed through deep snow, found them and escorted them to a nearby clearing where they were hoisted to safety. They were treated for "severe frostbite on their feet and frost nip on their hands."[130]

April 12-, 1976: The following account has been called "the most extensive search ever conducted on Marcy."[131] Six hikers trekked to Lower Plateau Lean-to where they set up camp. At roughly 3:30 p.m. on April 12, 1976, one of the hikers left his gear and walked off on a firmly packed trail wearing a "blue bandana, yellow Bulkflex jacket, blue wool sweater, red-and-white checked shirt, white wool long underwear, blue jeans and Herman boots with Vibram soles."[132] The subject's brother later noted that he did not mention going to the summit.[133] This would explain the lack of gear.

Though it was mid-April, the temperatures were around 10 degrees Fahrenheit and windy – not uncommon for this time of year, but harsh to say the least. By the time his companions searched for him later that evening, strong winds were blowing ice and snow into their faces and temperatures were well below zero with the wind-chill. They found no trace of the lost hiker and looked again in the morning before notifying authorities. An intensive search began that involved Department of Environmental Conservation, state police and Air Force helicopters, search and rescue dogs. and volunteers. They combed the nearby areas including Panther Gorge. The "intensive effort" of the search ended on April 21,[134] but other searches took place; he was still not found.

The subject's brother walked thousands of miles over the decades, climbed Marcy more than 600 times as of April 1982[135] and participated in multiple rescues and recoveries in subsequent years. As a result, he may have visited Panther Gorge more than anyone. We may never know what became of the lost hiker, but those of us who visit the Gorge regularly are always on the lookout for personal articles that could have endured through the ages.

January 2-5, 1987: A father and son as well as the son's friend camped at Indian Falls. The forecast called for heavy snow. Though they left snowshoes behind, they did take a single sleeping bag; something that would save their lives. Sixty mile-per-hour summit winds and whiteout conditions forced them east off the trail and down into the Gorge. They used a fallen tree for shelter during the first night. The two boys squeezed into the sleeping bag; the father slept only in his clothing while the temperatures fell to nearly zero degrees Fahrenheit.

The next day, the boys left to find help. The senior member of the party remained in the sleeping bag with food. The boys plunged farther into the Gorge through waist deep snow. Due to the conditions, it took them the day to reach the bottom (this would normally take an hour or so) where they overnighted in Panther Gorge Lean-to. During the process, one of them stepped into a brook; something that would add to the severe frostbite he suffered.

January 4 was the day of saving grace. Both boys made their way up to the now dismantled lean-to at Four Corners between Marcy and Skylight where they met other hikers who escorted them to Uphill Lean-To located to the west. The rescue effort moved into high gear when the Lake Colden caretaker found the two boys and radioed the forest rangers. The team included several rangers and volunteers. They arrived and found one of the boys with frostbitten feet; he was packaged in a toboggan and taken to Adirondak Loj and then the hospital. The *Press Republican* reported that it "took an hour for one boot to be cut off his foot. There was a quarter inch of ice between his foot and his boot."[136]

The next day, the helicopter transported the other boy to the hospital and dropped off forest rangers in the Gorge. They followed the boys' tracks and found the third member of the party alive and well in the sleeping bag.[137] This is but one of several rescues that occurred during the same multi-day period.

March 4-7, 1989: Two men began skiing to Mt. Marcy from Adirondak Loj on Saturday, March 4; a day-hike that started in a light mist. They left with little more than the clothing they were wearing, a little food and no compass, map, or lamp. The outing became a four-day fight for survival during a brutal combination of weather conditions. Upon nearing the summit cone on the north side, they took off and propped their skies in the snow. Crampons were better on the icy terrain. Once on the summit and like many others, they got turned around in strong winds and clouds that limited visibility.

Instead of heading north, they exited south which was likely protected from the encroaching weather, but opposite of their skis. They stopped somewhere in the trees and bivouacked near Lake Tear of the Clouds. The following day brought rain, but they side-sloped around Marcy and ended up spending the night "in the open below the summit."[138] They re-summited the following day in hopes of a rescue. The weather was clear, but this marked a cold front after a day of rain. They descended into Panther Gorge via a "steep gully" when no one arrived and as evening approached. Ambient temperatures dropped below negative 20 degrees Fahrenheit during the night. It was the perfect combination for frostbite especially after falling in a stream several times. They dug a snow-cave and lined it with pine boughs for insulation.

It was Tuesday when they located and followed the Elk Lake to Marcy Trail to Marcy Swamp. They then bushwhacked down to the Upper Ausable Lake and made it to the safety of a camp shortly before being rescued. Rangers in a helicopter spotted and followed tracks along the streambed. They found one of the lost subjects waving a bright flag.

The pair had gotten wet, but one of them outlined several factors that helped save them. He noted that they dug the snow-cave and consciously worked as a determined pair to stay alive – e.g. they crouched to retain core heat and used body heat to re-animate cold feet. They were unable to remove their boots after falling into the stream, however. Ranger Gary Hodgson said being a pair helped save their lives.[139] They kept moving during the day which Ranger Fred LaRow noted was also a factor that contributed to their survival given their particular situation.[140] At Lake Placid, "A half-inch of ice was found inside their cross-country skiing boots, which had to be cut off at the hospital."[141] After all was said and done, they suffered frostbite.[142]

April 8-9, 1991: Two Australian hikers, a man and a woman, were on the last leg of a world tour when they hiked from Keene Valley over Marcy and to Panther Gorge. Their clothing included summer-weight cotton gear and no snowshoes, likely a result of "being deceived by unseasonably warm weather"[143] before a cold front accompanied by rain moved into the region. They initially overnighted at a lean-to past Johns Brook Lodge. The next day they climbed over Marcy and found deep snow being undermined by runoff in the higher elevations near Four Corners, between Marcy and Skylight. The man succumbed to hypothermia as they were descending into Panther Gorge. The woman spent the night in the Gorge then post-holed west to the Colden Interior Outpost and called for help. She was airlifted from the area and suffered "bruises and abrasions."[144] The body was recovered a couple days later due to bad weather and the rugged terrain.

January 19-20, 2015: Two hikers began hiking from Adirondak Loj on January 19. They reached Mt. Marcy's summit, but lost their way in strong winds and whiteout conditions. The pair found a single cairn, but couldn't find a second. One of the pair stated that they "got to a point where we could no longer progress due to lack of grips or points of anchor, and we were forced to take some sort of natural slide."[145] They were on the southeastern flank of Marcy and bushwhacked into Panther Gorge.

Deep snow and the dense vegetation slowed progress especially since they didn't have skis or snowshoes which, on the onset of the trip, they didn't believe they needed since the trail was hard-packed. They also did not have a map or compass, but packed a survival kit, extra layers, a knife, and food. This equipment, in combination with a snow hole and pine boughs to block the wind, enabled them to start a fire and spend a safe night on the side of Marcy. The pair avoided the *Old Slide* during the descent and, the next morning, followed a drainage stream to an unbroken Elk Lake to Marcy Trail. They were found by rangers and accompanied to Elk Lake. They were tired, but uninjured and asserted that they would have been able to make it down and back to their vehicle had rangers not found them.

Winter rescue on Mt. Haystack. Photo taken during the first ascent of Fly By.

Adam Crofoot on the Agharta Wall.

Climbing History

The ultimate guidebook for rock climbing in the Adirondacks is *Adirondack Rock* by Jim Lawyer and Jeremy Haas; Don Mellor's *Blue Lines 2* is the go-to ice climbing guide. The books contain a few of our routes, but dozens of others were added after their publication. New rock climbing routes in the Gorge are listed on the *Adirondack Rock* "new routes" page at www.adirondackrock.com. New ice routes are located at www.mountainproject.com. Detailed information may also be found at adirondackmountaineering.com.

Climbing is a team-oriented discipline. This statement cannot be overemphasized. Hubris and competition were not components of our trips as such traits can be deadly in the backcountry. Inspiring and sometimes unexpected things happen when like-minded people join in the pursuit of a common goal. The individual trips and journey as a whole belong to each person involved. Everyone contributes. Many of the routes wouldn't be as aesthetic, diverse, or exciting without the skills, intuition, and ideas of the lead climbers. The objective of each outing was to explore the unexplored and immerse ourselves in the wilderness experience.

There are single and multi-pitch rock and ice climbing routes on Mt. Marcy and Mt. Haystack though many parts of Haystack trend toward single pitch options. In either case, the anorthosite of Panther Gorge is surprisingly clean despite such route names as *Climb After Slime* and *You Moss be Kidding Me!* This isn't what one might expect of the stone in such a wet environment. Sharp feldspar crystals in the anorthosite often aid in climbing even where the rock is less than pristine. Thus the route development philosophy has been to climb "as is" without cleaning. A bottom-up climbing strategy has also been employed thus far. While a few first ascendants climbed with packs and bushwhacked to the Phelps Trail, most leave their packs at the base, climb, and rappel. There is no fixed gear on any of the routes.

The rock climbing grades currently range from 5.3 - 5.11d YDS with the majority in the 5.7 - 5.9 YDS range. There are countless unclimbed options for stiffer lines. Many of the harder routes tend to be cracks prone to holding moisture – one needs a multi-day window of clear weather before climbing such lines. Ice routes presently vary from WI2 - WI5-; again there are challenging options that remain unclimbed. Why haven't we pushed the grade on rock or ice? The obvious natural lines were the most sensible options with which to start – and there were many. The finicky Adirondack weather has also influenced our decisions. Being on location at the right moment to climb them is sometimes a matter of luck. Then there's the location; climbing hard routes so far from help tends to awaken one's conservative nature.

Ice climbing is a completely different beast. The logistics are more complex. Adam Crofoot may have encapsulated it best during a conversation about a trip gone awry, "This is exactly why ice in Panther Gorge is the mystical, mythical thing that it is. Sometimes the stars have to align perfectly to swing a tool." A deep snowpack, frigid temperatures, unpredictable precipitation, fickle ice, and heavy winds are always wild cards. Everyone in the party must have the proper gear, layering, food, water, and skill set dialed in. In short, when a day goes well it's a beautiful thing, but when it doesn't, there's often a lesson to be learned. It's important to note that only specific lines, usually ones without pitches on the dark slabs prone to baking, remain reliable throughout the season.

Route names reflect the personalities of each climber. Depending on the group, we usually take turns choosing names or spend time during the exit tossing ideas back and forth. I tend to select route names with Christian themes. Bill Schneider leans toward names with feline allusions. Adam has a battery of ideas ranging from cerebral names to lichen-based puns. In any case, route appellations usually have a more profound meaning than face value.

Note: Piecing together an accurate history of first accents is complicated. Some climbers have methodically reported their route(s) to guidebook authors while others climb without so much as a whisper to another soul. Even the most diligent researcher can't uproot these accounts unless the climber volunteers the information. Someone may come forth, however rarely, to set the record straight regarding a past climb. Thus it is standard practice to document a route as a first ascent unless there's compelling information to the contrary. As such, the trips below (with a couple of exceptions noted in the respective chapter) represent what I believe to be first ascents based on available information. If this publication prompts someone to step forward to validate a historic climb, then I'd certainly welcome the information. Updates will be posted to adirondackmountaineering.com.

The Early Years and the Great Void: 1936-81

Jim Goodwin's 1936 climb, discussed earlier in detail, is the first known technical ascent in Panther Gorge – it is unnamed, and its exact location remains a mystery.

Craig Patterson and Ron Dubay entered the scene while Trudy Healy was writing the Adirondack's first rock climbing guidebook. Theirs was the first named route in Panther Gorge, the *Panther's Fang* circa 1965. Technical climbing activity then went dark on Mts. Marcy and Haystack, assumedly as climbers focused on developing more accessible crags or other backcountry areas with a less fearsome reputation.

It was thought that climbing in the Gorge ceased for 34 years until new information came to light in 2017. Climber Dave Jackson responded to an online article on climbing in Panther Gorge and noted that he and his partner Scott Olsen visited the area four times between 1978 and 1981. They climbed the largest chimney in the Gorge, Marcy's *Great Chimney* (aka *Empty Tomb*), during mid-September of 1978.[146]

Dawn of the Ice Age

Adirondack surveyor Verplanck Colvin described what, from his perspective, must have seemed like a hostile wilderness when he penned, "The black cliffs of Haystack are grim with monstrous yellowish icicles," on October 30, 1875.[147] The same words describe a limitless playground to an ice climber, however.

Christian Fracchia and Charlie Dickens added what remains the premier ice line, *Agharta*, in 1999. The multi-pitch route, rated at WI4-, ascends the highest wall in the Gorge. Delamination can make the center pitches unnerving. It was a bold milestone that marked the Gorge's first named ice climbing route. Miles Davis' *Agharta* album inspired the name (sometimes misspelled as Agartha). The alternate meaning is a Buddhist reference to a mythical subterranean world. This reference "also fit with how the Gorge felt," noted Fracchia during a 2014 email exchange. It took years for additional ice lines to go up.

Winter climbing isn't all about highly technical ice. Adventure also takes the form of endurance-based outings with semi-technical overtones. The late Joe Szot, a notable Adirondack rock and ice climber, and Willard Race completed the *Adirondack Trilogy* on March 13, 2009. Local guide, Will Roth commented that Joe envisioned this as a way to create a single big route in the Northeast and as a way to train for larger objectives in higher mountain ranges. It included the following stipulations: Climb Gothics' North Face direct, Marcy via *Grand Central Slide* (and *Panther Gorge Falls*), and Colden's Trap Dike during calendar winter with no backtracking in under 24 hours.[148] One must, of course, climb over Saddleback, Basin, and the shoulder of the Haystack massif to access *Grand Central*. Szot's path from Marcy continued down the south side to the Opalescent River then to Colden. Weather and other logistics made this a long-standing project requiring more than one attempt.

International Federation of Mountain Guides Associations/local guide Emilie Drinkwater repeated the *Trilogy* solo on Monday, March 16, 2009 – the only differences being that she skied (vs. using snowshoes) and connected Marcy to the Trap Dike via the Van Hoevenberg Trail instead of descending the south side of Marcy. Emilie graded *Panther Gorge Falls* below the slide as a pitch of WI4- ice in spring conditions that would unlikely hold an ice screw if she'd had a partner. She recalls the Panther Gorge leg as, "the most desperate part of the day." Her skis, strapped to her pack, caught on almost all the trees and she regularly fell into waist-deep spruce traps until the slide base.[149] Online articles and conversations regarding the *Trilogy* shined a light on Panther Gorge for the first time among northeastern climbers – not that there was a conga line waiting to repeat the feat. Descriptions of the route logistics added to the Gorge's infamous reputation for heinous bushwhacking and navigational challenges.

A New Age of Stone: 2003-04

Tenacious rock climbers with modern equipment entered the remote heart of the High Peaks during the dry summers of 2003 and 2004. Local climber, Bill Schneider partnered with several others to add five rock climbing routes on several walls on Mt. Marcy with grades up to 5.10a YDS. The routes included *Cloudsplitter*, one of the longest in the area. They expected grungy, overgrown cliffs. Instead, they found vast tracts of rock that didn't need cleaning. Bill was the driving force during this era though he humbly downplays his role, "I wanted to explore the unknown. I was just the match that started the fire; it's all of us that have made it burn brightly."[150] Local climber, Adam Crofoot was also a part of this era; both would return over a decade later to pioneer routes during the heaviest period of route development in Panther Gorge.

The Golden Age of Rock and Ice: 2012-2017...and Beyond?

A couple of rock climbing routes were put up during 2009 and 2010, but new routes were added with increasing frequency beginning in 2012 when Kevin MudRat MacKenzie focused his sights on Panther Gorge. The rugged backcountry setting inspired dozens of trips over the coming years. His interest in technical climbing spiked when he met Adam Crofoot and Bill Schneider. They understood the risks and rewards of combining high-mileage days, technical climbing, and route development. Other adventurous souls joined as the years passed and routes started going up regularly.

Rock

The first few climbs between 2012 and early 2014 were easy by technical climbing standards; adventure climbs with the requisite Adirondack challenges – gnarly bushwhacks enduring the onslaught of blackflies and midges, explorations of various talus fields, night exits over windy summits, and camping in hailstorms. The initial trips laid the groundwork for more difficult ascents during subsequent years when all the stops came out. Cliff development didn't follow a particular pattern, but rather sought obvious natural features on whatever stone happened to be dry at the time. Meticulous research using online technology and hundreds of beta photos collected during previous trips created a collection of potential routes.

Haystack saw its first long route added in 2014 as well as a 5-star fingercrack up the largest free-standing pillar (noted by Orson Phelps in the 1800's) – *For Whom the Lichen Tolls* – with Crofoot leading and MudRat following. The lines on Marcy pushed south to the *Agharta* buttress with its high-quality line, *Wreck of the Lichen Fitzgerald*. The year of 2015 continued similarly. Adam, hard-climber Allison Rooney, and MudRat snuck in an early season climb during May of 2015 and opened a new cliff on Haystack called the *Ramp Wall* during a wet, misty day that preceded powerful electrical storms. Flash floods ravaged the region while they were camping and, sadly, killed a woman in Feldspar Brook on the opposite side of Marcy. The rest of the summer saw the opening of the intimidating *Huge Scoop*, the southernmost of the large north-end walls. The premiere route on this wall is *The Pride* led by Bill Schneider and followed by Crofoot and MudRat. New climbers to the Gorge joined during other trips when routes were added to the *Feline Wall* and *Panther Den*.

The 2016 rock climbing season exploded at the end of May and lasted through September with a total of 11 routes during eight trips. *Galaxy of Tears*, led by local guide Dustin Ulrich, and *Predatory Instincts*, led by Schneider, were highlights of the season with such characteristics as diverse cracks, airy traverses, sharp-edged technical slabs, roof systems, and uniquely weathered faces. A particularly grueling day-trip with MudRat leading Nolan Huther and Loren Swears up *Revelations*, an appealing yet runout route on Marcy's *East Face*, lasted nearly 22 hours – a new time threshold that they vowed to avoid in the future. The following season saw a few new lines go up, but wet weather hampered substantial route development. By autumn of 2017, options for new multi-pitch natural lines were noticeably tighter, but the overall vision for the area was materializing. There were 39 named rock climbing routes, a sharp rise compared to the nine added between 1965 and 2010. Articles on Panther Gorge were limited to regional magazines until it made its national debut during November of 2017 when *Climbing Magazine* published an article by journalist/climber Alan Wechsler.

Ice

Doug Ferguson leading By Tooth and Claw on the Panther Den.

Several first ascent parties added ice climbing routes during the winters of 2015-17. The first new route, *Pi Day* (by Crofoot, Anthony Seidita, and MudRat) was located deep in the Gorge and put up during a drizzly day at the end of the 2015 season. One of the most diverse and reliable lines is arguably *By Tooth and Claw* on Marcy's *Panther Den*, put up in 2016 by Schneider, MudRat, and Devin Farkas. Other notable routes included *Just Nickel and Iron*, a high-quality line adjacent to *Agharta* that was first climbed by Charlie Beard, Jesse Colangelo-Lillis, and Matt Dobbs. Dobbs and MudRat returned in 2017 to squeeze in an elusive smear on the *Feline Wall*. *Chimæra* melted significantly under the climbers when temperatures spiked and the sun heated the underlying anorthosite.

Mt. Haystack also saw new route development; not all the attention was devoted to the long lines on Marcy. Haystack's westerly exposure and incut gullies guard reliable ice. MudRat picked away at appealing single pitch routes high in the north end with various compatriots including Nolan Huther who accompanied him for the first named routes on the eastern massif. *Orson's Tower*, near the aforementioned free-standing pillar, offers interesting, accessible climbing. A few routes were also added during the snowy winter of 2016-17. AMGA guide Doug Ferguson and Walker Wolf Bockley added Haystack's first multi-pitch ice line, *Needle in a Haystack*. A trip in 2017 with Alan Wechsler on lead saw the addition of one of the Gorge's most challenging named routes, *Ride the Lightning*. A perfectly timed freeze-thaw cycle thickened the ice on a wall that frequently holds only a thin smear. One of the most aesthetic ice climbing routes, *Charybdis*, was added in 2018 by MudRat, Laura Duncan, and Brent Elliott. Laura became the first known woman to put up a route in the Gorge as they followed the ice-encrusted chimneys in *Twin Fracture Gully*.

The Future

How will the next years of the Panther Gorge development look? Will interest turn in a different direction? I've asked these questions at the end of other journeys. The answers always resolve themselves in unexpected and exciting ways. It's doubtful that the area will attract any but the most adventurous souls that are willing to put in a full day and even bleed a bit. Access will always be via a long approach and requisite bushwhack. No matter how it evolves, there is room for further ice and rock development – a new era – in this rugged Eden. The following chart lists the history of known first ascents in Panther Gorge as of the publication of this book.

YEAR/DATE	NAME	AREA	GRADE	FIRST ASCENSIONISTS
1936	n/a	unknown	n/a	Jim Goodwin & Kids
1965 Aug	Panther's Fang	Marcy-Panther Den	5.8+	Craig Patterson, Ronald Dubay
1978 Sept	Marcy's Great Chimney (aka Empty Tomb)	Marcy-Chimney Wall	5.8	Dave Jackson, Scott Olsen
1999	Agharta	Marcy-Agharta Wall	WI4-	Christian Fracchia, Charlie Dickens
2003	Cloudsplitter	Marcy-Agharta Wall	5.9	Bill Schneider, Nic Gladd
2003	Le Chat Noir	Marcy-Panther Den	5.8+	Bill Schneider, Adam Crofoot, Nic Gladd
2003	The Cat's Meow	Marcy-Feline Wall	5.7+	Bill Schneider, Adam Crofoot, Nic Gladd
2003	Toma's Wall	Marcy-Agharta Wall	5.8	Bill Schneider, Chad Kennedy
2004	Puma Concolor	Marcy-Panther Den	5.10a	Colin Loher, Bill Schneider
2009 Sep 19	Kat Nap	Marcy-Agharta Wall	5.9+	Josh Josten, Conor Murphy, Andrea Hoffman
2010 Jul 4	Bushy Pussy	Marcy-Feline Wall	5.9+	Mark Toso, Willow Toso
2012 May 12	The Margin Slide	Marcy-East Face	5.3	Kevin MudRat MacKenzie, Greg Kadlecik
2013 Sep 6	Ranger on the Rock	Marcy-East Face	5.6	Anthony Seidita, Kevin MudRat MacKenzie
2014 Jun 1	Haycrack	Haystack South End	5.4	Kevin MudRat MacKenzie, Anthony Seidita
2014 Jul 12	All Things Holy	Haystack-V Wall	5.7	Adam Crofoot, Kevin MudRat MacKenzie
2014 Aug 16	Wreck of the Lichen Fitzgerald	Marcy-Agharta Wall	5.8+	Adam Crofoot, Kevin MudRat MacKenzie
2014 Aug 16	For Whom the Lichen Tolls (pillar)	Haystack-Pillars	5.9	Adam Crofoot, Kevin MudRat MacKenzie
2014 Sep 27	CrazyDog's Halo	Marcy-Agharta Wall	5.8	Adam Crofoot, Kevin MudRat MacKenzie
2014 Sep 27	Watery Grave (Top Rope)	Marcy-Agharta Wall	5.10a	Adam Crofoot
2015 Mar 14	Pi Day	Marcy-Overhang Slide	WI3+	Adam Crofoot, Kevin MudRat MacKenzie, Anthony Seidita
2015 May 30	All Battered Boyfriends	Haystack-Ramp Wall	5.7	Allison Rooney, Adam Crofoot, Kevin MudRat MacKenzie
2015 May 30	Less Than Zero	Haystack-Ramp Wall	5.5	Adam Crofoot, Kevin MudRat MacKenzie, Allison Rooney
2015 May 30	Eye for an Eye	Haystack-Ramp Wall	5.8	Allison Rooney, Kevin MudRat MacKenzie, Adam Crofoot
2015 Jun 14	Cat on a Wet Tin Roof	Marcy-Panther Den	5.8	Bill Schneider, Kevin MudRat MacKenzie
2015 Jul 11	Rumours of War	Marcy-Huge Scoop	5.9	Hunter Lombardi, Kevin MudRat MacKenzie
2015 Aug 1	Kitten's Got Claws	Marcy-Feline Wall	5.7+	Kevin MudRat MacKenzie, Justin Thalheimer
2015 Aug 30	The Pride	Marcy-Huge Scoop	5.9-	Bill Schneider, Adam Crofoot, Kevin MudRat MacKenzie
2015 Sept 19	Promised Land	Marcy-Panther Den	5.8	Kevin MudRat MacKenzie, Dan Plumley
2016 Jan 30	By Tooth and Claw	Marcy-Panther Den	WI4	Bill Schneider, Kevin MudRat MacKenzie, Devin Farkas
2016 Feb 27	Just Nickel and Iron	Marcy-Agharta Wall	WI4	Charlie Beard, Jesse Colangelo-Lillis, Matt Dobbs

YEAR/DATE	NAME	AREA	GRADE	FIRST ASCENSIONISTS
2016 Feb 28	Sorry, Kevin	Marcy-Feline Wall	WI4	Charlie Beard, Jesse Colangelo-Lillis, Matt Dobbs
2016 Mar 5	Orson's Tower	Haystack-Near Pillars	WI3+	Kevin MudRat MacKenzie, Nolan Huther
2016 Mar 5	Fly By	Haystack	WI3+	Kevin MudRat MacKenzie, Nolan Huther
2016 May 28	Pioneer Anomaly	Marcy-Agharta Wall	5.8	Adam Crofoot, Alan Wechsler, Kevin MudRat MacKenzie
2016 May 28	Belshazzar's Fate	Marcy-Panther Den	5.8	Adam Crofoot, Kevin MudRat MacKenzie, Alan Wechsler
2016 June 4	Predatory Instincts	Marcy-Huge Scoop	5.9	Bill Schneider, Kevin MudRat MacKenzie, Nolan Huther
2016 June 17	Galaxy of Tears	Marcy-Feline Wall	5.9	Dustin Ulrich, Kevin MudRat MacKenzie
2016 June 25	One for the Boys	Marcy-Panther Den	5.9	Allison Rooney, Kevin MudRat MacKenzie, Bill Schneider, Adam Crofoot
2016 July 30	Tail of Redemption	Marcy-Agharta Wall	5.7+	Bill Schneider, Kevin MudRat MacKenzie, John Pikus
2016 Aug 6	Climb After Slime	Marcy-Panther Den	5.8	Alan Wechsler, Kevin MudRat MacKenzie
2016 Aug 6	You Moss be Kidding Me!	Marcy-Panther Den	5.7	Alan Wechsler, Kevin MudRat MacKenzie
2016 Aug 27	Revelations	Marcy-East Face	5.8+	Kevin MudRat MacKenzie, Nolan Huther, Loren Swears
2016 Sept 17	Psalm 23	Haystack-V Wall	5.7	Kevin MudRat MacKenzie, John Pikus, Jaryn DeShane
2016 Sept 17	Windjammer	Haystack-V Wall	5.7	John Pikus, Kevin MudRat MacKenzie, Jaryn DeShane
2017 Jan 14	Kitty Cake	Haystack-North End	WI2	Doug Ferguson, Kevin MudRat MacKenzie, Walker Wolf Bockley
2017 Jan 27	Needle in a Haystack	Haystack-North End Tiers	WI3	Doug Ferguson, Walker Wolf Bockley
2017 Feb 18	Chimæra	Marcy-Feline Wall	WI3-	Matt Dobbs, Kevin MudRat MacKenzie, Jace Mullen
2017 Mar 10	Ride the Lightning	Haystack-Ramp Wall	WI5-	Alan Wechsler, Kevin MudRat MacKenzie
2017 Mar 10	Skip the Lightning	Haystack-Ramp Wall	WI3+	Alan Wechsler, Kevin MudRat MacKenzie
2017 June 3	Slacker Cracker	Marcy-Chimney Wall	5.9	Adam Crofoot, Kevin MudRat MacKenzie, Jaryn DeShane
2017 June 15	All Ryled Up (V1 Marcy's Great Chimney)	Marcy-Chimney Wall	5.7	Jaryn DeShane, Kevin MudRat MacKenzie
2017 Aug 27	Anorthofright	Marcy-East Face	5.9-	Steven St. Pierre, Kevin MudRat MacKenzie
2017 Sept 16	Panther's Pinnacle	Marcy-Chimney Wall	5.9	Kevin MudRat MacKenzie, Steven St. Pierre
2018 Feb 1	Spiritus Draconis	Marcy-Chimney Wall area	WI4+	Kevin MudRat MacKenzie, Jaryn DeShane
2018 Feb 17	Charybdis	Marcy-Huge Scoop	WI4	Kevin MudRat Mackenzie, Laura Duncan, Brent Elliott
2018 Feb 17	Scylla	Marcy-Huge Scoop	WI4	Brent Elliott, Kevin MudRat MacKenzie
2018 Mar 24	John 3:16	Haystack-V Wall	WI4	Kevin MudRat MacKenzie, Loren Swears
2018 Mar 24	PG-13	Haystack-V Wall	WI4	Kevin MudRat MacKenzie, Loren Swears
2018 June 9	Paws Off	Haystack-No Man's Land	5.8	Kevin MudRat MacKenzie, Steven St. Pierre
2018 June 16	Moonraker Runout	Marcy-Agharta Wall	5.8+	Kevin MudRat MacKenzie, Ken Hebb
2018 June 17	Castle Column	Marcy-Agharta Wall	5.8+	Kevin MudRat MacKenzie, Ken Hebb
2019 Jan 5	Apex Predator	Marcy-Chimney Wall area	WI4-5	Aaron Courain, Kevin MudRat MacKenzie, Alan Wechsler
2019 June 8	The Lioness Rampant (Top Rope)	Haystack-Ramp Wall	5.11d	Allison Rooney, Kevin MudRat MacKenzie
2019 June 28	Cracks of My Tears	Marcy-Feline Wall	5.10a	Kevin MudRat MacKenzie, Loren Swears

The Chronicles of Panther Gorge:
Trip Reports from August 9, 2009 – February 17, 2018

The primary features of Panther Gorge.

General Approach for Context

The following text is not a guide but is provided for context while reading the narratives.

Our standard approach of 7.8 miles starts at the Garden Trailhead in Keene Valley and follows the Phelps Trail to the Marcy-Haystack col. The route passes by Johns Brook Lodge, Bushnell Falls, and Slant Rock. I've been told that it may be easier from the Adirondak Loj via the Van Hoevenberg Trail (then down the Phelps Trail to the col) if you're a ski mountaineer. A round-trip entails 16-19 miles with 4,000'+ of vertical gain including bushwhacking and climbing. The exact mileage depends on the location of the specific cliff. The duration of our day-trips varies between 11.75 and 22 hours with a mean of roughly 16.5 hours. Weather, trail and internal conditions, as well as route location and difficulty, are the primary variables. See the reference plates for additional context regarding the routes and cliffs.

The *Panther Den* is the first wall on Marcy, roughly .2 miles south of the Phelps Trail on the right side (west) of the drainage stream. A 300' long glade along the cliff's base leads down to the forest where roughly 250' of bushwhacking leads to a buttress before the *Feline Wall*. A steep, mildly concave slab with a gully to its right characterizes this wall. Bushwhacking another 300' leads to the *Agharta Wall* marked by an obvious cliff with several roofs below a large slab. A small drainage stream after a buttress (about 125' downhill) leads up to the *Huge Scoop* – the last of Marcy's north-end climbing walls. This is characterized by an obvious rectangular scoop with a gully (*Twin Fracture Gully*) to its left. A series of smaller cliffs, gullies, and slides including the *Overhang Slide* and *Chimney Wall* sit between the *Huge Scoop* and Marcy's *East Face* one-quarter mile to the SSW.

The Haystack side hosts three free-standing pillars that are located on the left side (east) of the drainage stream roughly 525' south of the Phelps Trail. A series of other cliffs is located between the spires and the *Ramp Wall* 350' to the south. This cliff was named for its obvious left-rising ramp. The largest slab in Haystack's northern array lies south of the *Ramp Wall*, and roughly 600'-700' beyond this sits the *V Wall*. In between the slab and the *V Wall* lies *No Man's Land*. Getting to either cliff requires careful navigation. There is nearly vertical bushwhacking and several areas where one can get boxed in by smaller ledges. In summary, there is no easy access to Haystack's most remote cliffs. The following aerial shows a rough lay of the land in Panther Gorge. There are no obvious trails in the Gorge, so I always carry a GPS, map, and compass.

The approach from Keene Valley.

Learning the Terrain:
In the Beginning, There was Grand Central Slide

With: Mark Lowell on 2009 August 9

The beginning is an exciting stage especially when it is not obvious – when a person doesn't recognize it as a beginning until years later. In this case, climbing Haystack for the first time in 2004 was one of the final challenges in my quest to become an Adirondack Forty-Sixer, someone who has hiked the 46 High Peaks of New York. I finished the original quest, but the view of Marcy's *East Face* and the magnificent white scar that arced around its northern edge like a giant closing parenthesis marked a hidden fork in my path. It planted a tiny seed that manifested itself half a decade later. At that point, I'd never climbed an exposed slide or imagined that people did such crazy things. In 2004, the flank of Marcy was merely part of a beautiful panorama, so I took several photos that eventually served as a guide for several trips.

Grand Central Slide (likely named by members of Ski to Die, Adirondack backcountry ski pioneers) was known to skiers well before our ascent, but it was unknown terrain in my eyes. I had no technical climbing experience in 2009, so my impression from the photos was that it was impossible to attain the slide's bottom which started atop a cliff. Pictures from several different perspectives, each with the sun at varying angles suggested there might be sections where I could bushwhack up, albeit precariously. Four possibilities came to mind: a sizeable crack adjacent to the *East Face* (actually a gully of loose stone), a steep vegetated slope near the face, the actual crevasse (a waterfall) or ledges immediately to the north of the falls.

I suggested the scramble to an adventurous bushwhacker named Mark Lowell who hesitantly agreed after I promised that I wouldn't lead either of us into a predicament beyond our skill level.

Grand Central Slide

I was on a multi-day slide climbing trip that began on August 7 when I incorporated Marcy's *Grand Central Slide* as the last leg. I bushwhacked Gothics via the *True North Slide* before following an algae-covered slide down the Gothics/Armstrong's col to the Orebed Trail where I camped at Orebed Lean-to. I awoke the next morning feeling ill and removed the most ambitious segments from my itinerary. My primary target was Saddlebacks' *Back in the Saddle* slide (before Tropical Storm Irene made it more accessible) and a trek to the southern end of Panther Gorge. I decided to take the "easiest" path to Panther Gorge which was over Mts. Basin and Haystack. Since I felt under the weather, I took the opportunity to smell the roses and napped on Haystack's windless summit under a blue sky. The break provided another opportunity to study Marcy's *East Face* and *Grand Central Slide*. The scar looked dry and appealing.

When the sun dipped toward Mt. Skylight, I descended Haystack's southern trail to the Gorge to set up camp at a designated site near Marcy Brook – a bivouac sack covered by a sil-nylon tarp served as my shelter. Darkness settled in the valley as I waited for Mark who planned to hike in from Elk Lake. The lean-to was full, so I pondered how he would find me in the wee hours of the morning. I then remembered that my headlamp had a strobe setting. It flashed while I slept until Mark woke me at 2:45 a.m. The alarm roused us at 6:50 a.m. Shortly after, I saw a patch of retreating blue sky as the sun lit Skylight

Marcy Brook.

and Marcy for the first and last time of the day. The forecast called for rain in the afternoon.

After breakfast and the usual early morning rituals, we stuffed our packs with the day's necessities and stashed the unnecessary items in Panther Gorge Lean-to. I silently ran the "what-ifs" of our adventure through my mind. I think I speak for both of us when I say we were excited, yet apprehensive. I estimated our rock hop to the slide base would take about an hour. A friend named Craig warned in a recent trip report – our only beta – to bear right at a fork with a tributary leading west to the *Old Slide* on Marcy's southern aspect. We encountered the tributary twenty minutes into the bushwhack. The right fork looked gloomy which dampened our spirits.

Small cascades led to mild beaver activity where the grade eased and the brook diminished in size and volume. The woods looked inviting and loosely woven at several points. We took these opportunities to walk along the edge. Marcy's *East Face* appeared and disappeared through the trees as we walked nearer – what a dramatic sight! Eventually, I saw the top of our target. We then used line-of-sight navigation until we encountered a two-foot wide dry gully which led to our first steps on the lowest slabs of *Grand Central*'s drainage stream. Climbing room-sized stacked boulders presented an energy-siphoning challenge. I could feel my excitement rise in spite of the dropping cloud ceiling. As we reached the base of the cliff, we felt a cold mist. It was 9:20 a.m., and we were perched at roughly 3,870' in elevation. I thought, *So much for pictures with any depth of field or sense of scale.*

We looked up in awe at the ragged leaning gash in the cliff with a cascade to its right – *Panther Gorge Falls* according to E.R. Wallace. My hopes of climbing it withered when I saw water dripping from moss, areas of less than suitable handholds, and loose rocks. Our second choice was via ledges to the north; I looked up and felt uneasy. Even so, we explored them – Mark volunteered me to lead. The initial 20' was steep with plenty of holds. After that, the choices seemed too precarious and wet for soloing. We'd have to rely on the meager security of grass and moss. I thought that I could climb up, but not down if the upper tier proved unclimbable. I finally succumbed to the thought, *Don't die before you see the real slide!*

Our next move was to descend south and re-cross the drainage below the boulders. We then bushwhacked up to the slope near the *East Face*. We looked at the aforementioned gully and moved on. It seemed similar to a section of Colden's Trap Dike, but I knew not what was at the top and the mist wasn't getting any lighter. It would have to wait for another trip.

The final and most realistic option consisted of climbing up the steep terrain between the *East Face* and the slide. The area was different before 2011 when a rock-fall stripped some of the trees from the slope. We stumbled our way up ever higher in the three-foot-tall grass. At 10:20 a.m. we found slab that offered enough handholds to begin the scramble up to the slide. The bushwhacking was precipitous – going up ledges overgrown with cedar trees and moss. A faint deer path (complete with scat) led through some of the undergrowth until, after 20 minutes, we climbed high enough to access the cliff top. A quick push north led to a void in the trees – the tell-tale sign of a slide.

Our first duty after several hoots of excitement was to relax and re-nourish. I took out my camera as Mark cracked open a bottle of bubbles – yes, bubbles – to celebrate. This was apparently a long-standing personal tradition. I quipped that he was using it to measure wind velocity. Photos from Haystack hinted that the first half of the slide was mainly slab and textured enough to scramble without feeling too exposed. The top portion looked loose and sandy. I estimated that it was roughly 40 degrees with an occasional steeper segment. The surface underfoot was rough and water-carved. Various steps, dikes, and faults offered easy climbing up limitless options. Moss only intermittently spotted the slab. Above our position, the slide looked like sets of steep rounded bumps. Below, the water flowed diagonally across the slide in a gully. Spring melt must be amazing to behold as the water cascades over the cliff to the talus below.

Looking north from the slide.

While the ground underfoot was intriguing, views of Haystack were disappointing and restricted to the lower slopes. The cloud ceiling continued to fall but it wasn't yet raining. Even wet, the slide offered enough traction. I'd long since learned how to climb on damp rock. After some time, conversation, and food we packed and began the ascent. So much to see and so little time – it was late in the morning, and I knew the bushwhack to the summit would be a grueling time-sink. We hoped to finish before harsher weather rolled in. Mist was ok, rain would be annoying, but lightning would make the situation dangerous.

The slab continued up a similar grade with comparable features until one-third of the way to the top where it steepened. A small dike crossed the swath and offered an accessible route to the next section. At its top (about 4,000' in elevation), we reached the clouds and lost all views. The higher we climbed, the eerier the scenery became until it felt like we were hiking through a Tolkien-like realm. We took photos of each other in the gloom. An ethereal glow surrounded Mark in one photograph, and I looked ghost-like in another – obscured by the fog while standing under a spooky dead tree.

Higher, the slide eased in grade as the white stone became more acutely stepped and strewn with rubble. Overgrown with birch trees, it narrowed before turning at a large boulder at 4,300' in elevation. This elevation marked our ascent from a shallow valley toward Marcy's eastern ridgetop. Here it became steeper and ever narrower. It was loose underfoot, so we walked side by side to avoid playing "friction climber bowling."

Finally, the slide ended in a gulley of slab and boulders at 4,500' in elevation. Above was a tangle of moss and contorted trees. There was no herd-path though the trees allowed our shoulders through with some squirming. Only a couple of small ledges impeded progress. The ever-increasing mist and wind obscured our vision to the point that only a

Left: *Ascending into the clouds, Photo by Mark Lowell.*

Above: *Mark Lowell climbing easy slab.*

compass provided reliable navigation. After twenty tiring minutes, a decrease in grade signaled that we'd reached the top of the ridge where we needed to turn toward the summit. The growth was typical for an eastern aspect High Peak summit ridge – dense evergreens. Another hour of pushing led to intermittent blueberry bush-covered erratics and occasional outcrops of stone. Stiff cripplebrush eventually became the dominant tree cover before the summit crown. I know this sounds crazy, but I thoroughly enjoyed the two hour push through the dwarfed trees. I'm not sure what that says about my sanity, but our continual bantering helped time pass quickly. Never before had I heard anyone refer to krummholz as "crotch-floss" – Mark did. This was a real adventure!

Three summit stewards were hunkered down out of the wind when we reached the summit at 1:30 p.m. We'd set a subjectively lofty goal and succeeded though in the beginning we'd accepted failure as a realistic outcome. I felt like this was a breakthrough climb; it dissolved a psychological barrier. There was no rest for the weary, however. Strong winds furiously whipped the clouds across the High Peak. We began to feel chilled, so we started walking south to Four Corners. Paradoxically, both of us had to remove our mist covered glasses to see. The blowing fog made wearing them impossible. Of course, we couldn't see far without them either. We must have looked quite humorous – decrepit men trying not to fall while slowly scanning for the yellow paint blazes that led to the shelter of the treeline.

It was 3:30 p.m. when we closed the loop at Panther Gorge Lean-to. There was no time to dally – we had to repack, eat and begin the long walk to Elk Lake. The rain fell more steadily during the trek, and we didn't escape the fog until reaching the trailhead, some nine miles and four hours later. Time seemed to pass slowly; we yearned to be free of the heavy packs and wet clothing. Regardless, this seemed like a fitting end to a 22-mile hike for Mark and a three-day trek over roughly 25 miles for me. We reached the trailhead at 8:15 p.m. and, to my surprise, found my wife and parents waiting near the car with smiles and food! Thus ended our first trip into Panther Gorge.

Two Marcy Slides and a Skylight Bushwhack

With: Greg Kadlecik on 2012 May 12
Areas: Marcy *Grand Central Slide*, *East Face*, and Skylight
Duration / Mileage / Vertical Gain: 5:00 a.m. – 10:45 p.m. / 21 mi. / 6,650'

Where to begin – This trip combined three different objectives. I wanted to explore the slide track along the southern edge of Marcy's *East Face*, an objective since climbing *Grand Central* three years earlier. I assumed it was too steep to climb based on its perspective from afar, but reality proved otherwise. Skylight's eastern drainage seemed compelling; did it end in a featured cul de sac? I wanted to bushwhack from the trail at the Marcy/Haystack col into Panther Gorge – the few tales I'd heard made it seem mysterious. Little did I know this would be the first of dozens of descents from the north pass.

On the Trail

Greg and I met at the Garden Trailhead and began walking at 5:00 a.m. – chatting and waking up under an ever lightening sky. It was in the low 30's – chilly, but comfortable with a forecast that called for highs in the low 70's. The sky grew bluer as we discussed the possibilities for the day. I brought up the Marcy slide as an option if we felt ambitious. My habit is to shoot for the moon and settle for less if needed.

The first trial began at Slant Rock when ice and rotten snow covered portions of the trail. We didn't bring traction devices, so each step in our trail runners was a delicate dance on a snow spine that deepened as we gained elevation. A few post holes and thousands of carefully placed steps later, we arrived at the Marcy/Haystack col at 8:30 a.m. We were ahead of schedule.

The elevation fell away as we trekked south-southwest into subjectively new territory. The drainage harbored several feet of unconsolidated snow, so we stayed to the west side seeking the path of least resistance. It was moderately loose, so I could easily get my shoulders through the trees. The intimate view of Haystack's western flank (aka Horse Hill) was intriguing. The craggy terrain looked like a shadowed maze of chutes, slides and unique contours from Marcy's summit. Up close the large talus and other features took on an entirely new light. They made me feel insignificant as we descended deeper into the maw. I pondered a future exploration of the area even though we were currently in the midst of an exciting trek – subconscious foreshadowing perhaps?

Marcy's northern walls were overwhelming – massive cliffs loomed in the soft morning sun. I didn't know they had names but would learn them over the coming years. *Wow*, was all I could think. The first cliff that I now know as the *Panther Den* didn't yet have the long grasses that are waist high at the end of summer. Last year's growth was brown and slippery. The view was inspiring with vertical walls at our fingertips and the glacial valley falling away in the background. Under the canopy, we wound around tree trunks, over some light blowdown and dropped down several ledges in the stacked talus draped with moss – "hanging lakes" as Verplanck Colvin described the vegetation. I was in awe of the area. Greg and I bantered back and forth like kids on Christmas morning. I later noted (after learning the cliff names) that we'd descended toward the valley floor from the *Feline Wall*. This descent led into dense talus. Farther along we came to *Grand Central Slide* and visited the magnificent waterfall.

Under the East Face, Up the Margin Slide, and Down the Old Slide

We descended *Grand Central*'s drainage until coming to an acceptable ramp on which to re-enter the woods on our journey south. A new rockfall from the top right-hand side of Marcy's *East Face* left a scar in the forest 200' wide and well over 100' in length. It effectively stripped the grassy meadow that I'd climbed in 2009. Beyond and directly under the face was an open expanse of ground that served as our route south. It was dramatic, beautiful and peaceful. Dead grasses were so slippery that it was reminiscent of winter butt-sliding. Marcy's dark cliffs above, Haystack across the valley, beaver ponds glistening in the mid-morning sun, and soft ground underfoot – what more could one ask?

My reservations about the southern slide track, what we soon named the *Margin Slide*, became less of a concern as we approached the base at 10:30 a.m. I believed it to be roughly 40 degrees with some steeper sections and a band of ledges (the crux) about 250' higher. I asked Greg if he was agreeable to the climb and there was no hesitation in his answer; we were committed.

I changed into rock climbing shoes and took out a length of nylon webbing for emergencies. The anorthosite of the "new" slide was cleaner than the old mossy face just a few feet north. Various ledges and cracks led up the slide, while the *East Face* held more exposed pitches. We first had to get up the first few feet of our line; this was a challenge. There was just enough water and moss near the bottom to make it precarious. We tested one area then another until we won the war, my rock shoes made it easier than Greg's boots.

The subsequent hundred feet entailed climbing on steep clean rock riddled with small ledges and cracks. More than one line looked appealing though we stayed close to the main face. Two hundred and fifty feet higher, however, we found ourselves near the side of a vertical wall that traversed north across the top of the face.

Left: View down the Margin Slide.
Right: Greg Kadlecik standing below the upper cliff band with Marcy's East Face in the background.

The sun had climbed high enough to be quite warm, but a stiff breeze kept us comfortable. The beaver ponds looked inviting from afar, and Greg talked of paddling or at least lounging on a kayak on their surface. Haystack looked like an anorthositic monster still in torpor. Its cliffs met Marcy's at the north pass from which we began the bushwhack. The broken ledges close at hand humbled us. I felt like I was deep in the wilderness.

Above was a vertical ledge roughly 15' high that decreased in height as it curved down onto our slide track. It transitioned from a solid wall to broken ledges. I had no desire to climb anything vertical when I was 250' above the base without a rope. I found a fourth class weakness. Part of the face had cracked, and a few small steps led up to a rail of grass on which I could traverse to higher ledges. Greg explored a couple of other options before following.

We then climbed to the second crux of sorts, a nearly vertical climb – 10' up a small series of steps. I jammed my hand into a secure location and, short of my hand detaching from my arm, felt confident as I moved upward where I gripped the cracks and climbed onto the last section of the slide. The pitch slightly decreased as we ascended to an elevation even with the top of the *East Face* slab (about 4,000' in elevation). Several shoulder height overlaps and small runs of friction slab led to low-angle rock. Greg followed confidently, and we walked up the remaining 100' of the slide to absorb the panorama and discuss our upcoming strategy. The time stood at 11:15 a.m., our day had only just begun.

We left the top of the slide on a heading of 240 degrees (true north as opposed to magnetic north) after a 15-minute break to rehydrate and eat. I wanted to avoid a fir wave that was directly below our position. Less than 10 minutes later, we walked onto another slide – the eastern-most pencil-thin track of the *Old Slide* on Marcy's southern face. It was roughly 35 degrees in slope and old as evidenced by heavy moss and algae growth. A steady stream of water flowed from far above. We were only part way up, but I cared not about the top. This was just a route down.

Enough open rock was exposed to make our descent safe. We moved slowly and carefully watched our footing when we encountered one of the many cascades or ledges. The slope declined as we neared the base and then emerged on the primary drainage stream of the *Old Slide* near an overlook I visited years prior. A 15-minute bushwhack led to the "Elk Lake to Marcy Trail" and Panther Gorge Lean-to. It was time to bushwhack up Mt. Skylight.

Skylight Bushwhack with Eastern Rubble Slides

Skylight's eastern aspect has a dominant tributary that leads to various old-exposure slabs/ledges and a couple of insignificant slides that sit in a bowl of sorts. Above, the terrain steepens with technical slab and ledges surrounded by firs and cedars that act as sentinels. Then comes the krummholz, my lovely krummholz. As the crow flies, the distance from Marcy Brook to Skylight's summit is roughly one mile, but navigating through this terrain seldom leads in a straight line.

We followed the trail south from the lean-to until it turned eastward, then trekked over to Marcy Brook. Neither of us had an altimeter or GPS, so we navigated by line-of-sight and compass…the perfect day for it. We intersected the brook farther south than I'd planned which placed the bowl to the northwest. We compensated by following Marcy Brook up a couple of hundred feet until we found an open view. A stream flowing from the west appeared to be the approximate size of our target drainage so up we went.

Greg scrambling up an unnamed slide on Skylight.

This side of Skylight is dense, very dense, so we rock-hopped as long as possible. Large nodes of opalescent labradorite were especially plentiful and shined green and blue in the bright sun. We climbed boulder upon boulder until, an hour later, we reached a mild bend with a small sandy slide on the right-hand side. I compared it to a picture and verified our position. A quick trek southwest led to the largest of the target slide tracks, a minor run 600' long and about 30' wide. It was primarily rubble so climbing the unconsolidated debris robbed us of energy with each step. The real work began at the top – a strenuous ascent out of the bowl through downward growing tree branches.

We took a break on top of a small wet cliff and enjoyed the views of the eastern peaks while lenticular clouds built over Haystack and Dix. Bad weather was closing in. Farther along we fought through the cripplebrush with every step. It was dense enough that we needed to stop every hundred feet or so to keep track of each other and check the compass. A scant few boulders and some exposed slab appeared as we neared the top of Skylight nearly four hours after leaving Marcy Brook.

The bowl was less dramatic than I'd imagined though the ascent was beautiful the entire way. In the end, I believe our escapades on the Marcy slides overshadowed the adventure of Skylight. The Gorge is that intriguing. We'd been driving hard for 12 hours as we descended from the summit to Four Corners on a spine of ice and rotten snow. Our exit was at hand though we still had to climb Marcy. It was 6:15 p.m. when we reached the summit rock under strong winds driven by a weather front. Roughly nine miles of hiking remained until we were back at the Garden.

A deep snow spine covered the trail between treeline and the Haystack trail intersection – tenuous walking. We closed the loop at 7 p.m. though Greg and I wouldn't reach the trailhead for another four hours. Snow and ice complicated our descent to Slant Rock where we took a much-needed break in the company of a three-toed woodpecker. These quiet moments with wildlife after an ambitious outing are incredibly special. The bird seemed as intrigued with us – two bedraggled hikers – as we were with it. All good things must come to an end, but the journey to explore had just begun.

The Great DeRanged Traverse

Adapted from my article in the 2015 September/October issue of *Adirondac*.

With: Greg Kadlecik on 2012 June 24

Area: Marcy *Grand Central Slide*, Haystack Bushwhack remainder of Great Range

Duration / Mileage / Vertical Gain: 4:00 a.m. – 11:45 p.m. / 26 mi. / 9,100'

The Great Range Traverse – Rooster Comb, Hedgehog, Lower Wolfjaw, Upper Wolfjaw, Armstrong, Gothics, Saddleback, Basin, Haystack, and Marcy – has an enduring history as one of the best, if not most difficult, day hikes in the High Peaks. It consists of a seemingly endless series of rugged ups and downs between mountains and accumulates more than 9,000 vertical feet of elevation gain.

The traverse has long inspired hikers – Herbert L. Malcolm used it as a component of a 24 hour hike in 1932. The range has lost none of its luster in modern times. Fast forward to May of 2005: *Backpacker* magazine included it as one of America's hardest day hikes. The hiking community continues to keep it fresh by creating various derivations. The possibilities are endless, whether measured against speed, linkages to other mountains, or during different seasons. It was in this vein during spring of 2012 that an idea materialized during an email exchange with Greg Kadlecik. He too has a masochistic affinity toward ludicrous bushwhacks combined with lengthy hikes. Our exchange went something like this:

MudRat: "Hey, I've got an idea – what do you think about bushwhacking down Marcy's eastern flank, crossing Panther Gorge and then bushwhacking Haystack via a serpentine drainage on its western side?"

Greg: "Great! Let's do it; I was looking at that drainage."

A couple of days later we upped the ante to make the day more difficult (and thus more fun) while remaining within our perceived personal limits.

MudRat: "You know that idea about scooting through Panther Gorge?"

Greg: "Yup...really looking forward to that."

MudRat: "Well, what do you think about combining it with a full Great Range Traverse...a Great *DeRanged* Traverse?"

Greg without hesitation: "Great! I'm in! I've never done a Great Range Traverse before!"

Neither of us had bushwhacked Haystack via its noticeably cliff-riddled western aspect. The serpentine drainage seemed like the path of least resistance. The bushwhack floated to the top as the primary goal of the day. We agreed to reassess our resolve once we reached Haystack's summit. Navigating off-trail and pushing through dense forest is more strenuous than using a maintained trail. Were we up to the task of completing over 20 miles with over 9,000' of elevation gain, including a complicated bushwhack? Our final itinerary contained just the right amount of uncertainty and adventure to suit our desires, though we each likely shared the passing thought, *Oh my, to WHAT did we just commit?*

Mt. Marcy and Panther Gorge

We began walking under a cloudless sky with temperatures in the 50's at 4:45 a.m.

– ideal conditions. Time passed quickly as our excitement built. We arrived on Mt. Marcy's summit at 8:30. Completing the first of many goals lifted our spirits. We needed the psychological boost before disappearing into what we thought might be an arduous scoot through the Gorge. We weren't naïve; we hadn't hiked in weeks and had never crossed the Gorge in this fashion. The outcome was uncertain which was half the fun of it – our Great DeRanged Traverse could end on Mt. Haystack.

We began the descent a couple of hundred feet north of the summit via a depression between Marcy's ridges-carefully avoiding the delicate high-elevation flora. Thick trees with stone outcrops decorated the immediate landscape. Haystack, merely a silhouette since the sun was still low in the sky, loomed threateningly across a seemingly impenetrable sea of green split by the vast void of the chasm.

Looking toward Haystack from Marcy.

Gravity aided in our descent as did loosely knit trees. They weren't as dense as I envisioned. Hidden ledges and sod-holes offered intermittent challenges as the Cloudsplitter's ridges grew taller on each side.

A small mossy drainage stream led to a jumble of blowdown preceding the rubble-strewn bend in *Grand Central Slide*. To our surprise, it had taken only 50 minutes of bushwhacking to reach this point.

Hungry blackflies dampened our elation. They seemed to be attracted to rather than repelled by DEET. Lower down; weathered stone, dikes and rippling ridges in the stone created a subjectively safe descent. A meager trickle of water enhanced the colors under the bright sun. We stood in awe of the magnificent view of Panther Gorge and its variegated carpet of green from the top of the overlook at the cliff-top/slide bottom. The western face of Haystack sat beyond. Its scarred flank still looked intimidating, but we were committed to the task.

The new rockfall on the face confused the descent; the route wasn't how I remembered it. We stayed relatively close to an overhanging cliff to our south and descended via a series of precarious ledges. One hundred feet to the south was the ramp that I used in 2009. We descended the ledges carefully and used far too much energy; energy we'd need to climb the subsequent nine mountains. Below, at the base of *Panther Gorge Falls*, we refilled our hydration bladders and mentally prepared to take on Haystack.

Bushwhacking Haystack

Edge of the world – the top of Panther Gorge Falls.

The walk through Panther Gorge was idyllic on a blanket of sphagnum with Marcy Brook gurgling gently in the background. It was the calm before the bushwhacking storm. A few minutes' walk led to a drainage that flowed from our target heading. The stream seemed to cut through the steepest terrain and it wasn't long until we found ourselves mired in blowdown overgrown with small firs. The up-close views of sheer cliffs on either side were humbling – I never thought I'd be climbing them in the future. Deep shadows seemed to etch the stone revealing every crack, overhang, and corner. I appreciated the natural lines of the anorthosite.

No worthwhile bushwhack is complete without an error or two, however. We navigated using map and compass as well as the slide on Marcy to derive our position. Rugged terrain can easily redirect one from their desired heading. It was impossible to make line-of-sight adjustments, so we did our best to guess our location. Thus we circumvented a small cliff slightly askew of our intended heading. The minor adjustment led us north of the target drainage. We reassessed our position 400' in elevation above the floor of the Gorge. Terrain markers like *Grand Central Slide* seemed too far to the south; we needed to readjust. Thrashing up Haystack's side was challenging and redirecting was easier said than executed. In hindsight, this portion of the outing helped orient me for future climbs up the aforementioned cliffs.

Persistence paid off, and our change in course led directly to the top third of what can only be described as an overgrown drainage with a few insignificant patches of mossy rock. It was not the narrow track of clean stone that we had envisioned though I'm sure it was lovely in days long past.

The bushwhacking became more arduous in the krummholz above the drainage; our only respites were the scattered knobs of rock that formed a broken yet direct line to the summit. Each formation was a unique work of art sculpted by the hand of God. Some were rounded while others had sharp edges with angular overhangs. One, in particular, looked much like a giant interlocking puzzle. Along each was a narrow corridor through which we could squeeze. Others were easy to scramble up and provided unobstructed views of our route to Haystack's summit.

The winds blowing from Marcy seemed to whisper, "You've almost made it!"

The time was 1:30 p.m. when the words on the wind became truth, and we topped out on Haystack. The 1.4 mile bushwhack had taken 4.5 hours with 1,450' of vertical gain. I told Greg, whose legs were bleeding because he wore shorts (oops!), that the west side was easier than Haystack's eastern *Johannsen Face*. It had taken almost nine hours to reach the summit. Should we commit to climbing the other eight mountains of the Great Range?

We didn't feel the need to reassess or talk of failure, we just looked at each other and simultaneously said, "Here we go!" Within that phrase was the inherent context that we were going to complete this project. "Here we go!" implied that we felt well enough to continue safely.

At the day's end, we knew the Panther Gorge diversion had cost us precious energy. Greg was experiencing knee pain, and I was working through stomach cramps. Our bodies ached, but our tenacity remained intact as we finished the day in a steady rain which seemed typical of many of our hikes. I find humor in many things so when I got turned around less than a quarter mile from the car and started back uphill, I could only chuckle. We'd successfully bushwhacked through the Gorge and around cliffs some 10 hours earlier, but got lost near a frog pond adjacent to the road. I blamed it on the 19 hours of hiking. It was 11:45 p.m. when we reached the Rooster Comb trailhead; it felt like the Promised Land.

Greg walking through Haystack's thick krummholz.

Circumnavigating Marcy's East Face: A Day with a Forest Ranger

With: Scott van Laer on 2013 August 24
Area: Marcy *East Face*, Unnamed Slide, *Grand Central Slide*
Duration / Mileage / Vertical Gain: 5:30 a.m. – 10:30 p.m. / 18+ mi. / 6,400'

Route: Garden Trailhead to Interior Outpost & Johns Brook Lodge > Marcy/Haystack col > Bushwhack south to Grand Central Slide, traverse base of East Face, climb Margin Slide. > Bushwhack north across the top to a small unnamed slide and descend. > Descend Grand Central Slide and bushwhack north out of Panther Gorge and back to the Garden.

    I learned much during this outing with Forest Ranger Scott van Laer. Sharing the trail with him deepened my insight and increased my respect for those in his profession. His ethics and breadth of knowledge were broad. Scott had overnighted at the DEC Interior Outpost; I left the Garden to hike to the cabin at 5:30 a.m. – the parking lot filled soon after. Temperatures hovered just below 60 degrees as dawn approached. The walk up the South Side Trail faded quickly from memory in my pre-awake stupor. What thoughts I mustered fell to what awaited atop the *East Face* and what might have changed since last spring.

    I was awake and vibrating with excitement by the time I reached the outpost. It wasn't long before we were walking to the Marcy/Haystack col. Upon arrival, Little Haystack was still blanketed by a massive shadow, the minutiae of its cliffs seemed flat; we'd see them fully lit on the way out. I found the first sod-hole after the *Panther Den* (this is a bushwhacking theme). Some characteristics of the terrain were different from my last visit – there was more blowdown, and some of the drainage streams were wider. *Grand Central Slide*'s drainage also had more blowdown across it, something that kept me from recognizing it at first. The changes in nature are intriguing; the cycle of destruction and rebirth, unending.

Left: Scott on the East Face. **Top Right:** New trees grow amidst the storm damage in the center of the Gorge. **Bottom Right:** Scaling the ledges of the Margin Slide.

Along the Bottom and up the Face

Greg Kadlecik and I had traversed below the base shortly after the snow melted when the vegetation was dead and brown. Scott and I waded through tall ferns, a beautiful green carpet below the magnificent face of Marcy. One-half hour later, we came to the *Margin Slide*. We opted for a different line than Greg and I previously took, one that was more exposed on the East Face proper. We friction climbed up the slab and along a ramp. It wasn't long before the magnitude of the day began to sink in. I felt like I was home again.

Scott thought that the face had similar features to *Chapel Pond Slab* and I voiced my agreement. About 200' up and south, I traversed over to the rougher and cleaner rock along the *Margin*. In and of itself this was a bit sketchy and required perfect placement of the feet and hands between bits of brittle moss. Scott continued up the slab along an island of grass and balsams in search of a different line. Seeing a ranger high on the *East Face* with the cliffs in the background was a dramatic sight.

I looked at his position and the slab above – steeper with heavy moss growth. I then set up a belay from a tree as he retreated to rougher stone and tied in. Perhaps it wasn't necessary, but the Gorge is no place to tempt fate. By the time he reached my position, an audience had gathered high above on Haystack. We must have appeared as tiny dots on the brown-gray face. The rest of the climb was exposed, but with a completely different feel – up through the crux of the *Margin Slide* and on to low-angle slab.

Bushwhacking to Grand Central Slide

We took a short break at the top of the slide to re-nourish, study the topo map and feed the blackflies. Earlier in the week, I marked potential problem areas on a photo. My goal was to bushwhack between the slab and a series of small ledges upslope. I wanted to find a decent overlook, but some things are easier said than done. We embarked on a heading of 29 degrees true north. The forest was dense. Truck-sized pieces of Marcy's overgrown upper ledges had shifted over time to create crevices – fracture caves 15' deep. It was a place of potential danger and exceptional beauty. Some will, in future days, tumble down the face and add to the talus field.

The author in a talus cave at the top of the East Face. Photo by Scott van Laer.

A half hour from the slide top, we approached an opening in the canopy along a wall of anorthosite. One of two things would happen. We'd either have to retrace our path and go around the small cliff or perform an exposed traverse across the top of the white strip of the *East Face* – the area of the recent rock-fall. I caught my breath while Scott ventured forward and reported that it was okay to cross and of moderate angle. The caveat was that a slip would send a person tumbling down 400' of ever-steepening slab and over the cliff above the debris field where our circumnavigation began. The granular stone offered ample traction with an inspiring view. A steady breeze kept the blackflies – late season nuisances – at bay.

We fought the urge to recline for a more prolonged rest. Such was the beauty of our isolated perch. With time marching on, however, we continued and redirected our heading to 326 degrees true north to intersect the top of two small slides between our position and the top of *Grand Central*. A direct hit at the top would minimize the bushwhack.

The forest loosened as we rounded the ridge and reached our target. Given its location, the slide would hardly be worth exploring as a stand-alone goal, but it was an interesting bonus some 200' long. It was more a series of exposed ledges than friction slab so descending was tricky, but paid off in time savings.

Closing the Circuit

We intersected *Grand Central* just below the rubble zone at an intersection with a mossy stream – about the same elevation that Greg and I entered during the Great DeRanged Traverse. The blocky stone of the watercourse created a natural path of descent though we wore rock climbing shoes to be safe. We were starting to feel the exertion of the day, and I was hungry. Even the blackflies were beginning to look appealing as flying bits of protein!

Scott approaches Grand Central Slide.

We rested on the cliff top and absorbed our final expansive view of the Gorge from the west. The next portion was one of the trickiest of the day. The ledges to the north (those Greg and I used during 2012) were wet and steep, so we sought a more straightforward route and closed the loop at 4:30 p.m.

Scott looked fresh; I felt less ambitious. We'd scoped Marcy's cliffs immediately north of the slide runout during our descent from the north pass and saw open glades along their bases—areas we'd use in the future. I came up with the idea to try and get close to them to save energy during the next 600' of elevation gain. My strategy turned treacherous when I led us into an expansive talus field, an area of man-eating holes amongst truck-sized boulders stacked atop each other and overgrown with vegetation. The talus maze slowed our progress, and I missed the glades. With 10-20 foot deep holes and crevices scattered about, we had to be careful. Caves and passages underneath the blocks were fascinating, however. It was another hidden gem (likely part of Mt. Marcy Cavern), and another reason to return and explore. Once free of the boulders, we found familiar terrain and began to trek north where I lost our exact line of descent. The terrain's slope pulled me close to the central drainage stream – another area littered with stacked boulders. I'm adept at learning the hard way.

Our conversations continued once on the trail, and I got a chance to witness his interactions with hikers as he checked on their preparedness. It was evident that he loves his job. It was also apparent that he enforces the rules fairly. The outing expanded my knowledge of the Gorge, but more importantly, gave me a glimpse into the life of a ranger. The conversations with Scott made a strong impression and increased my respect for both him and those in the profession. It was the beginning of a friendship and the day was a blessing in every sense of the word.

Marcy's East Face

With: Anthony Seidita (lead) on 2013 September 5-6
Area: Marcy *East Face*
Route: *Ranger on the Rock* (5.6)
Reference Plate 5

The *East Face* of Marcy is the crown jewel of the Panther Gorge technical slides. The face is one-quarter mile wide and laid out as follows: The *Margin Slide* along the southern edge is followed by friction slab that leads to a sizeable arrowhead-shaped flake (pitch 2 of *Revelations*). This marks the beginning of a huge bulge that gets steeper until it meets a vegetated gully that vertically splits the face. The northern side hosts a series of broken cliffs (home of *Anorthofright*) below slab with several tree islands.

Each visit to the Gorge added another piece to a giant unassembled puzzle. The more I learned, the more I was drawn to explore. I studied nuances of the slab and possible belay points as preparation for this trip, but my technical climbing experience was limited, so I only had a vague idea of what to expect during the climb. This trip marked a turning point in the evolution of the Panther Gorge journey and my attitude toward climbing. It was my first backcountry technical climb and first multi-pitch route after years of scrambling and soloing (climbing without a rope). It unnerved me and made me question my motives. I'd compartmentalized my fear of heights after years of slide climbing, but the old demons came out of hiding on the *East Face*. I even grappled with a passing thought that perhaps I was too old to learn, that I should have started this when I was 20, not in my mid 40's.

Anthony and I planned a weekend with an ambitious agenda. Day one was reserved for Panther Gorge and the next day for top-roping Basin's Amphitheatre. Slant Rock seemed like a perfect jump-off point for both. Thursday, September 5th found us beginning from Keene Valley at 8:00 p.m. A 65-pound pack made progress slow, but before I realized it, hours had passed, and it was nearly midnight. The Slant Rock Lean-to was full, so Anthony erected a tent at one of the nearby sites along Johns Brook, and we settled in at 1:00 a.m. for a few hours of sleep.

A restless night did nothing to help my ambition as I begrudgingly rolled out of my sleeping bag at 6:30 a.m. We began the ascent up the steep trail to the col after a hearty breakfast – the beginning of what would become a 16 hour day. Though I can usually retrace my steps, I fell off of my previous bushwhacking route into the Gorge which placed us close to the central drainage stream – a repetitive theme in the early trips before we dialed in the approach during 2014. Huge holes slowed our descent. It took over an hour to reach the bottom of the Gorge where a new band of blowdown slowed us again. We arrived low along the drainage of *Grand Central Slide*, but we were free of the talus maze.

We had traversed across the base of the *East Face* and were ready to climb by noon. We began after a silent prayer. None-the-less, butterflies in my stomach frantically flapped from a mixture of excitement and a rising feeling of caution as we started a committed climb up a route based on a few pictures and semi-educated guesses. I scanned the giant brown-gray slab in awe. The cliff at the top loomed intimidatingly.

Our line began on a beautiful brown and white water line; the rock was grippy with small divots in its surface. Intermittent flakes provided comfortable hand and footholds

Anthony soloing pitch one of the new route.

until a large bulge forced me to traverse left toward a grassy corner that offered a relaxed stance. I regained my composure as Anthony explored a more exposed area before he ran into crumbly lichen. He then traversed to my position as I photographed him against the backdrop of the northern cliffs.

Chunks of feldspar offered bomb-proof footholds as the slope grew steeper and our exposure increased. Anthony climbed over the corner and soloed upward. We were, by now, committed – no backing down without creating an anchor and rappelling. A nagging inner dialog changed from a distant drone to an imperative shout, and I vocalized my desire to begin a protected climb. Anthony agreed as he reached a small ramp where he could build an anchor. Such was the first half hour of our climb with the western flank with Haystack as a silent witness.

Our next target was a prominent tree island with a large dead birch 100' to our right. The quality of the protection to the green oasis was unknown; we were now exploring in every sense of the word. Anthony led as I belayed. A solid overlap of anorthosite held a cam (a type of removable protection used in rock climbing), but the options for additional protection were limited. The first roped pitch went well, and I followed as he belayed from the tree island. We were about 200' north of the *Margin Slide*. Distant photos taken from Haystack hinted at the details of the next pitch. There was a possible line between our stance and a large corner with balsam trees. The butterflies in my stomach started fluttering again as we studied the daunting traverse to that position. A large bulge in the face increased the open-air below us. Above was a dicey wet section overgrown with moss. Small areas of rock showed through, but it looked less than optimal.

Anthony crossed and walked up a small ramp to a nearly level terrace about 40' from the tree island. He cleaned mud out of a small overlap and placed a cam to protect himself. I felt my stress build as I watched – my inexperience didn't interfere, but it intensified subtle thoughts that I might otherwise have ignored. He spent an hour searching for alternate areas to ascend. The face adjacent to the aforementioned corner was too mossy; he tried climbing a few steps up before backing off as a bit of dirt tumbled down the cliff. He eventually settled on cleaner yet less protected pitch of slab below a 10-foot wall. He

Marcy's shadow on Haystack.

placed a 2" cam deep in a crack at the wall's base and set his mind to the next task.

I began to feel out of body as I watched him try to scale a nearly vertical wall; groping for a hold on the upper slab. Slip! He caught himself, down-climbed and traversed left over the pocketed stone with bits of moss thrown in to spice it up.

Once protected amongst a sturdy stand of birch, he yelled, "On belay!" It was my turn.

I was accustomed to soloing and, when possible, I try and keep natural protection below. This route seemed counter-intuitive and intimidating without such protection. I compartmentalized an internal scream for help and replaced it with the knowledge that he was belaying me. He'd climbed with style – so could I! With the comforting feeling of a taut rope at my waist alleviating the fear of falling, I realized that the surface had many features – edges, crystals, and subtle "slopers." I was always able to maintain three points of contact even if one was only a tiny shard of feldspar. The traverse from the wall to his stance was psychologically easier, but physically more difficult with the moss. The knot in my stomach eased once I was seated in the trees. I enjoyed the views of the sparkling beaver ponds and Haystack with its occasional summit visitor.

Anthony had previously mentioned that the last pitch looked easiest. He was correct. We were situated roughly 75' below the cliff band at the top of the slab and decided to solo the remainder. I scrambled up while Anthony coiled the rope. With the route behind us, I relaxed and contemplated the experience thus far. I was only sure of one thing; that it felt good to be at the top on a narrow shelf of grass with trees at hand! I'd learned much about myself in a few short hours.

We'd been at the game for three hours, and there were more uncertainties ahead; concerns that flitted about in my mind during the climb. How would we get down? We still didn't know if a rappel down the fracture was feasible. If that failed, was there a weakness up through the cliffs into the krummholz so we could bushwhack to *Grand Central Slide*?

We walked north and found a gully. Beyond was more slab and trees. I studied my photos and poked around the area to see if this was our target route of descent. I expected something more dramatic, but we were in the correct area – 550' from the base with evening closing in. The slab was completely shadowed, and the temperature was getting chilly.

We were using a single rope, so rappels were only 100' long. Anthony continued to lead and found suitable anchor trees. Our first rappel took us down a small ledge and through the trees. The next was down a section of slab. Thereafter, photography (yes, I'm always taking pictures) became more difficult. My focus was on staying safe and checking that I was properly protected before leaning back on the rope. A vertical chute 80' long and 10' wide was the most interesting section. After that, we rappelled south across the slab in an attempt to minimize the walk to our packs. Two more full length rappels down moss-dotted stone placed us at the bottom. *Ranger on the Rock* was up, but our outing was only partly over, and the lean-to was far away.

Exiting the Gorge

Two weeks prior, I'd bushwhacked out of the Gorge via the north end. Anthony and I had no desire to execute a night exit through the talus fields. The remaining choice was south. I set my mind on how to avoid the beaver ponds as well as blowdown fields between the face and Marcy Brook. I took a last look up at the darkening face and breathed a sigh of resignation as we readied ourselves for a punishing exit.

We bushwhacked down the runout from the *Margin Slide*, an area filling in with small balsams and several regions of crosshatched deadfall. The terrain leveled as we reached its bottom and skirted the ponds along their southern edge. A distant opening through the trees gave us a glimpse of their beauty. The forest loosened on approach to Marcy Brook. Twilight embraced the valley as we walked along the babbling brook and passed the confluence with the *Old Slide*'s drainage stream. Small flumes and cascades occasionally interrupted the tedious rock-hop to the trail. The last remnants of light faded

Anthony navigating a blowdown field to the west of the beaver ponds.

One of the deep pools of Marcy Brook.

as we replenished our water supply near Panther Gorge Lean-to at 7:30 p.m. – perfect timing! We'd been in the Gorge roughly 11 hours and still had to climb the steep path up approximately 1,700 vertical feet to Haystack's summit and then over Little Haystack. Little did we know that our adventure was far from complete.

A Windy Mt. Haystack and the Milky Way

The character of the trail up to the Haystack junction resembled how I felt…eroded and dirty. Even so, the mileage and time passed quickly with conversation as a distraction. Anthony suggested that I take a climbing course to become more familiar with knots and rope management. A good idea, but I was silently processing whether I EVER wanted to try another technical climb. I enjoyed the challenge, but I had a hard time compartmentalizing my fear of heights on this scale.

The next section of trail is one of the steepest in the Adirondacks. We hiked for what seemed like an eternity in the dark when strong gusty winds hinted that we were nearing tree line. Still sheltered, we changed into heavier layers, extinguished our headlamps and ate while reveling at the inky darkness of the moonless night. Lights from Elk Lake, Plattsburgh, Burlington and a host of other communities were all that broke the blackness. I settled back and closed my eyes to relax before opening them to a magnificent overhead sight – the Milky Way. I let my mind drift and pondered my place in the universe. If Mt. Haystack made me feel small, the galaxy made me feel virtually non-existent.

Once moving, our first steps above tree-line were both eye-openers and garment removers. Anthony nearly lost his hat as my hood flapped violently against my head. Stronger gusts swept up from the Gorge like a giant hand checking our balance. Our rhythm became one of "step, balance, look for a paint blaze – repeat." I loved it! The full-body workout (as if the previous exertions weren't enough) continued for 300 more vertical feet until we found a sheltered nook on the summit proper. The wind got stronger as we descended the ridge. The first couple of gusts knocked me several yards to the side until I used my trekking pole to brace myself. Haystack is hardly a knife-edge ridge, but it felt precariously narrow as it dropped off into the black abyss.

The protective trees between Haystack and Little Haystack offered a short respite from the wind. Little Haystack, the last major hurdle, was even windier. Tired, but exhilarated, we began the trek down to Slant Rock at 11:30 p.m. By the time we reached camp, my blood sugar was low. Anthony was kind enough to cook dinner as we talked about the day (and I recovered). The memories seemed surreal as I drifted off into a sound sleep. Daybreak found us stiff, but enthused, as we prepared to visit Mt. Basin's Amphitheater. That, however, is another story.

Haystack's Conjoined Slides: Day 3 of 3 in Panther Gorge

With: Anthony Seidita on 2014 June 1
Area: Haystack Southern End
Route: *Haycrack* (5.3)
Lead Climber: MudRat
Duration: During 3 days of camping
Reference Plate 9

Looking toward the Agharta Wall.

Anthony enjoying late spring snow.

Anthony Seidita and I created an itinerary dedicated to exploring as much of Panther Gorge as possible in three days. We hoped to focus on climbing, but the weather sometimes determines the objectives. The approach trek to Slant Rock took care of Thursday night. The terrain seemed wet, but we awoke Friday to pleasant weather though storms were predicted later in the day. A quick ascent to the Haystack/Marcy col soon found us bushwhacking three-quarters of a mile into the Gorge. It's always "fun" balancing on blowdown and jumping holes between blocks of talus with 65-pound packs, but that's what we signed up for.

By 9:30 a.m. our camp in the north end (just below the legal elevation limit for "at large" campsites) and a couple of hundred feet from the drainage of *Grand*

Central Slide was set up. It was one of the few dry flat areas nestled between a large boulder and blowdown fields. The first two days found us exploring the northwest talus field with its small caves, portions of the northwest cliffs, beaver ponds, and upper Marcy Brook. We formed a basic mental map of the area, one that would help in future years. We attempted to put up (add) another route on Marcy's *East Face* but got chased off by a thunderstorm that deposited ¼" of hail around the tent.

Our third full day, June 1st, involved the most climbing. Bluebird skies ruled, and parts of the area began to dry out. Our camp placed us about 30 minutes from a series of slides that decorate Haystack's western flank near the southern end of the Gorge. The two closest to the beaver ponds, the *Conjoined Slides*, were steep and captured our interest during a walk through the area the day before. I'd studied them from afar in 2009, but assumed they were too steep to safely climb – wise given my experience at the time. The slides shared a common release point at a birch-filled section of rubble above an obvious headwall.

Their debris fields lie at 3,550' in elevation (the top is about 4,000'). Thus, they're short yet worthy climbs at around 500-600 ground feet in length. Each contains some low fifth-class pitches in addition to scrambling, so they're serious climbs as slides go. Both have unique features so, taken as a pair, they offer a full day of diverse climbing. The icing on the cake lies in their spectacular location – eye level with Marcy's *East Face*.

Various cliffs and slides on Marcy.

Haycrack on the Northern Slide

We found the slides by following Marcy Brook past the southernmost beaver pond and walking east up a two-foot wide rill. The stream led slightly north of the slides, so we left it on a heading of 90 degrees true north. It was only about 300' to their base. Tight pliable balsams made for a scratchy 10-minute bushwhack before we stepped into a grove in full pollination – an instant allergy attack! Spring was just beginning in the Gorge.

Leaves were barely beyond budding and insects were just emerging, including a moth near our camp that crawled out from behind a root to dry its new wings.

Above the rubbly debris field sat a staggered series of large ledges. The first was about 20' high, so we bushwhacked to its left before climbing six or seven terraces via trap dike-like chutes, small slabs and grassy ramps with a few exposed moves. This capped the first segment of the slide (about 80') and led to a flat terrace below the technical portion – a magnificent face split by a handcrack from its base to an overhanging wall.

We brought a 60m rope, cams, and nuts. Anthony noted that we had enough gear to climb Half Dome – better safe than sorry. My initial strategy was to follow the crack 80' to a large overlap, traverse left to a corner, then friction climb for 20' to a crevasse. This seemed like the perfect finish with a good belay station. Portions of the slide were still seeping with water and glistened in the sun. It was also coated in slippery red algae. Thus we opted for a variation.

I friction climbed from the side to a right-leaning overlap and followed it up 10' to the handcrack. The rock quality was excellent with divots (similar to most of Colden's slides). Once in the crack, I felt completely safe with unlimited options for hand and foot jams. Sharp andesine feldspar crystals also gave the adjacent face sufficient traction. It was a fun climb along a slightly serpentine line that crested a bulge after about 60'. The slope decreased near a foot high overlap 80' from the bottom. Though its entire 150' length could be climbed in one pitch, I set up an anchor at the overlap and belayed Anthony for practice. He then led the remainder of the route by following the crack up to the wall and traversing right on a low-angle albeit wet slab. A final down-climb over a 6' high wall and across easy rock led to the woods. We named the route *Haycrack* and rated it 5.3 – "fun five" climbing. I was satisfied since it was my first backcountry lead.

A short bushwhack led to the top of the adjacent slide. We then doubled back to the original slide once we were above the overhanging headwall. There were ledges, small stepped chutes and the top of the slide proper. *Haycrack* was hidden below which presented a wonderful feeling of exposure and offered us an expansive view of Marcy's eastern aspect.

Southern Slide

We explored the adjacent track rather untraditionally. First, we rappelled down the top half before crossing through the trees to collect our packs near the start of *Haycrack*. We then traversed along a 30' wall to the base of the southern slide and soloed up to our exit point from the two rappels.

A couple of note-worthy incidents happened during the rappel including a scream from Anthony – "Rock!"

I'd rappelled first and was, thankfully, tucked out of the way when the small boulder zipped by and crashed into the trees below. We also flushed a dark-eyed junco from her mid-slide nest in a tuft of grass and peat moss. Four small mottled eggs were protected in a pocket of grass – the bird was happy when we left and quickly resumed her nesting duties.

Description from bottom up: The southern slide track began with a couple of small terraces below a dramatic lower face. A handcrack sat to the right while a tempting left-leaning ramp/corner was positioned to its north. The dihedral had a fingercrack which made it a fun climb up to a short section of friction slab. The steep initial pitches made the remaining portions feel very exposed. A low fifth class fingercrack then led 50' up to a markedly different area of the slide where blocky terraces with abundant features – cracks, ramps, small ledges and coarse anorthosite – led to the most exposed portion

Anthony rappelling down the southern slide.

a few hundred feet up. The slide then transitioned into a face/friction climb on a 45+ degree slope. Differential weathering provided bomber holds for both feet and hands in many areas. A wall below smaller terraces and an overgrown rubble field then led to the confluence with the northern slide.

Part of the beauty of camping in the Gorge is that one doesn't need to rush the exit. We followed the drainage back to Marcy Brook and sat near the gurgling watercourse. It was only 4:00 p.m. A small pool below a cascade reflected the forest with Marcy's *East Face* in the background. The warm sun and lack of blackflies lulled us into relaxing for an hour before walking back to camp. The following day was supposed to mark our exit from the Gorge, but we decided to pack and make a late day escape to Slant Rock Lean-to at 6:45 p.m.

Bushwhacking out of the Gorge with full packs and without the exit completely "dialed in" was indescribably frustrating. The minefield of haphazardly stacked talus, hidden holes, and blowdown from recent Derechos and the Big Blow of 1950 challenged our mettle. A few less than graceful acrobatic moves, crawling and grumbling finally placed us at the glade below the *Panther Den* where we fell to the ground for a brief respite before the final bushwhack. A mile later found us at Slant Rock Lean-to cooking dinner to the calls of thrushes, warblers, and vireos. The sounds of the night were broken by the roar of the wind over Point Balk – a perfect ending to another trip.

All Things Holy on Haystack

With: Adam Crofoot (lead) on 2014 July 12
Area: Haystack's *V Wall*
Route: *All Things Holy* (5.7)
Duration / Mileage: 5:00 a.m. – 6:30 p.m. / 19 mi.
Reference Plate 8

Adam Crofoot leading pitch one.

The trip to Panther Gorge with Anthony originally included an exploration of a cliff below Little Haystack. I referred to it as the *V Wall* on account of its shape and position between a gully and a trap dike that meet at its bottom forming a blunt tip. Its bumpy appearance made it seem like moderate climbing from afar. Anthony and I didn't get to explore it, but it remained on my mental to-do list. When Adam Crofoot, a hard-climbing local, emailed after we met at a high-angle rope rescue training session, we set plans in motion to climb the wall.

We descended along the Marcy walls, and I asked his opinion as the bumpy cliff came into view across the valley. He was interested, so we took the path of most resistance across the talus at roughly 3,700' in elevation. Once on the other side, we explored a string of intriguing cliffs en route to our quarry. We bushwhacked up the Haystack massif to a large featureless wall and threaded our way up and south. A forested ramp above smaller ledges led to the base of a shield of anorthosite. After that, we hugged the cliffs and scrambled up ever-steepening terrain through cedar, small mountain ash and a few balsams – 4th class bushwhacking at its best! Haystack guards itself well on all sides.

The canopy below the cliff opened to a grassy corridor as the ground leveled underfoot. We continued to work our way south scanning for viable lines. Our diversion was well worth the energy even if just for the view of Marcy and her northern cliffs – an opportunity to shoot beta photos for future use. The stone above our position was slightly off-vertical in many areas despite its appearance from afar. Its many crack systems were appealing

Left: View to the south.

Top Right: Adam on pitch two.

Bottom Right: A rare perspective of Marcy's ridge.

but short compared to our hopeful line of approximately 500'. I hoped the quality of our prospective line was worth the effort. Questions in mind revolved around whether it would be solid or chossy (loose or crumbly) and dangerous. Either was possible.

I realized how much there still was to explore as we walked along. Take climbing out of the equation, and it's a photographer's dreamscape; balanced blocks and slices of the cliff perched at peculiar angles, steep gullies, unique geometric lines and wide multi-colored slabs. As we approached a dominant gully forming the left-hand border of the *V Wall*, we found ourselves on an increasingly vertical yet tree-covered slope. Once we realized that we weren't setting ourselves up to walk off anything too precarious, we dropped down a smaller gully and contoured over to the base of our target.

Looking up revealed a weathered face with bulges, deep cracks, and blocks; easy technical climbing from my perspective. I knew another gully bordered it to the south but was surprised to find a trap dike a couple of hundred feet high. It looked similar, yet smaller, than its big brother on Mt. Colden. The angular dike had a cascade running from a sea of dense evergreens at its top. From inside the dike, the side of the *V Wall* rose vertically with several viable climbing options, one of which would become the first pitch of our route. I thought of starting at the bottom of the V, but Adam had a better idea that would add a harder and more exciting start. Of three good choices including a fingercrack and large chute; the lowest was an obvious left-rising handcrack.

Adam organized the gear as I shot photographs. It didn't take long before he was ready to climb. Once on lead, he quickly scaled the wall. I pondered the arena in which we were climbing as I belayed – the dike fell away into the woods below. The vertical wall with Adam high up the crack (and ready to disappear around a corner) framed Marcy's

East Face and *Grand Central Slide*. As usual, I felt humbled by the area and thrilled with our project. I followed and cleaned the pitch; four or five cams over 90'. The edges of the crack were not smooth. Instead, they were weathered and had acute angles which offered a host of holds. It was a clean climb other than a few loose pieces of stone in the crack itself. Small edges on the face were copious enough to make the footwork intuitive. The end of the crack led into a narrow left rising gully. Adam belayed from a small platform just below a grass island – roughly 1/4 of the way up the wall.

The line of the second pitch seemed evident though nearly anywhere would have worked. Cracks and pitted anorthosite were the themes. Adam traversed about 30' across to a right-rising crack and followed it for 100' to a small corner and another crack. This led to the top of the *V Wall* and into a vegetated slide runout. A technical slide constituted the third pitch. He chose an appealing line, aiming for the more difficult areas to make it interesting – the same tactic he used below. The slide was steep with a crux move about 50' up from the base. A couple of bulges led to a more vertical step with a thin crack set just out of my reach. Beyond, the face decreased in slope and got mossy at the top. The upper segment had a thicker crack and bomber holds. I crossed a wet V-shaped gully at the top and climbed a 10' vertical wall where Adam had built an anchor in a horizontal crack.

Above was the fourth and final pitch. It started after a short, dense bushwhack through tamarack, balsam, and cedar. He eyed another rising handcrack running up to the top of the 40' wall. Attaining the crack was the crux of the pitch, perhaps the route. I watched as he disappeared into the greenery; the trees swayed to and fro while he tried various options. Though low, a nearly vertical section covered by thick wet moss complicated the first moves. Only a shallow crack and few nubs of stone aided in traction. Thereafter, the climb was straight-forward up two parallel cracks. A large tamarack tree at their top made an ideal belay station.

We'd earned a break and relaxed in blueberry bushes surrounded by a sea of krummholz. In sum, the route was 505' long over four pitches. We only had to bushwhack up to the Range Trail – about 250' of elevation gain over 800 ground feet with some intermittent ledges and knobs of stone thrown into the mix. The first cliff, around 50' tall, was fun, but I'd already changed into sneakers. I bailed partway up after skidding off a hold. Adam continued up, and we met at the top of the pitch. Continuing, we navigated toward the col between Horse Hill and Little Haystack.

Taking a break during the exit bushwhack.

I huffed and puffed once on the trail and quipped that Adam's heart rate was barely elevated – he's a bulldog at bushwhacking and climbing. The day was young, so we decided to hike to Haystack's summit which we reached at 3:30 p.m. At the day's end, 6:30 p.m., we'd logged 19 miles over 13.5 hours. I knew future trips would not be so kind – this outing seemed almost too perfect. Exceeding our time estimate was a pleasant surprise.

South on Marcy and Climbing the Gorge's Largest Free-Standing Pillar

With: Adam Crofoot (lead) on 2014 August 16
Area: Marcy *Agharta Wall* & Haystack *North End* Pillars
Routes: *Wreck of the Lichen Fitzgerald* (5.8+) & *For Whom the Lichen Tolls* (5.9)
Duration / Mileage: 4:45 a.m. – 9:30 p.m. / 16.75 mi.
Reference Plates 1, 6

Left: *Adam below the Agharta buttress.* **Right:** *Adam leading the flake on pitch two.*

Significant explorations and sleep are uncertain bed partners. I awoke at 1:30 a.m. on the morning of this outing and finally gave up on sleeping a few hours later – pre-trip jitters and a restless mind. I was resigned to a long hard day by the time I reached Adam's house. Allison Rooney dropped us off at the Garden Trailhead, and we were setting a solid pace by 4:45 a.m. The primary concern in my hazy mind revolved around the wetness of the stone. Had the wind dried it from the recent rain? We were taking a chance during this trip, a possibility that our efforts would be for naught. The dew point was equal to the temperature – sticky conditions that don't allow the rock to dry quickly. Nonetheless, we believed it was worth the gamble.

We had our hearts set on putting up a couple of new routes on one or both sides of the Gorge. They were lofty goals, but I often enjoy that even if I have to settle for less in the end. Our focus was on Mt. Marcy's *Agharta Wall* and a free-standing pillar in the mouth of the Gorge. The pinnacle was a secondary goal, something to do if time allowed.

We crested the Marcy/Haystack col at 7:40 a.m. which placed us below the *Agharta Wall* in a field of soaking wet ferns an hour later. While the small cascades draining from the wall around our hopeful line were beautiful, they dashed any thoughts of climbing the intimidating footwall. I grumbled. There was another relatively dry high-quality line a few hundred feet south, however. Foul weather was approaching, but we'd have a chance to accomplish our goal if it held off long enough.

Left: Kevin traversing to a crack on pitch one. Photo by Adam Crofoot.

Above: View from the first belay.

Wreck of the Lichen Fitzgerald (5.8+)

The *Agharta Wall* lies slightly north of a huge rectangular depression, a dramatic feature that bears testimony to gravity's partnership with weathering. The missing stone makes up the talus that Anthony Seidita and I crawled through earlier in the summer. Adam and I noted a line up a buttress on the right side of this feature. We hoped that a series of flakes and cracks would lead to the upper wall. I looked up our potential line and realized that this was going to be my most challenging climb to date. I reminded myself of all the reasons that I thought this was a good idea while thoughts of self-preservation rebutted each reason.

The morning mist, wind, and temperatures slightly above 50 degrees created exciting climbing conditions. Small lenticular clouds hovered over Elk Lake like UFOs while clouds blew over Marcy and obscured her summit. We were in for a backcountry adventure with all the bells and whistles. There was no discussion on who would lead – I was still learning.

Adam began the route by face climbing up to a series of three corners/cracks/ramps along the northern edge of the scoop. He climbed on double ropes. This was the first time I'd used doubles, so I suppose this constituted "on the job" training. Nine miles from the trailhead is the perfect place to learn. No? The two ropes are clipped through the protection in such a way as to avoid rope drag. His climbing was meticulous, so I watched with the eyes of a student. He'd inspect an area, place a cam, remove it, brush a little dirt out of a crack, study it and, if necessary, find a better location to protect himself. Meanwhile, I belayed and learned the nuances of managing two ropes.

He traversed north from the edge toward a vertical crack below a small roof about 75' up the wall. The crack led to a diagonal traverse to an off-width crack (one that's bigger than your fist yet smaller than your body). Two birches grew from the cracks near a couple of loose spikes of stone. Beyond, he placed protection in the bottom of the off-width crack. He then traversed to the edge of a ginormous flake (forming the crack) and shimmied up its vertical knife edge to the first belay station on a 6" ledge.

It had taken two hours to climb roughly 150'. This was the money pitch, though I didn't appreciate it at the time. My internal dialog drifted to and fro, chipping away at my confidence – how would I do this? I was about to find out.

I cleaned the protection as I worked my way up each of the ramps. A deep crack was at the base of the third corner which overlooked the scoop to the south. The rugged beauty of the water streaked depression was magnificent. I took a breath and traversed to a crack where I could jam my hands and secure my position. Traversing across the 75-degree face on tiny holds was the most challenging section of the pitch, one that made me appreciate Adam's climbing skills. He made it look effortless while I likely looked like a scared spider.

Much of the time it took Adam to lead the first pitch was consumed by route finding near the aforementioned spikes. Once up the vertical crack and past the roof, I realized why he'd taken such care. The slope increased, the blocks felt loose, and the small trees made traversing awkward at best. Though loose, the blocks were large enough to remain in place so long as the climber was careful. I felt more secure once positioned on the edge of the flake. I locked a leg behind it and took a breath to regain my composure. I began to appreciate the experience. There's no comparable feeling to straddling a half inch knife-edge 100' above the forest floor. I noticed that the edge got wider above my position; it was the border of a house-sized buttress. The large piece of anorthosite on which I sat was detached, only gravity held it in place – at least for the immediate future. The crack was over 30' deep, its bottom covered in pebbles.

I moved over to Adam's position on the small ledge and belayed him as he ascended the second pitch. I wasn't yet used to such airy belays, but doing something is the best way to learn and desensitize oneself. Adam climbed out of sight while following an obvious line via the left-rising crack. The rope disappeared quickly, so the climbing was obviously easier. I broke down the anchor and followed after paying out 170' of rope. A fascinating network of hand and fist-sized cracks, each delineating another large piece of stone that would someday fall into the Gorge was above the off-width crack. The angle was lower – steep slab climbing – so I felt more in my element. I relaxed and looked up; the rope gently arced to the right and vanished behind a tree-island. I found Adam anchored underneath a left-arching bulge adjacent to the dark stone at the top of the *Huge Scoop*. He started pitch three by climbing up the bulge and onto weathered low-angle slab.

I glanced around and noticed that the weather was deteriorating, not that it mattered since the last pitch was already wet. We "enjoyed" a light drizzle as the clouds socked in. Combined with wind and temperature, I felt chilly while belaying. Adam angled slightly left toward a large chimney in the ledges. The chimney seemed appealing from below, but the entire area was soaked. He studied the features then tapped to check for exfoliating rock before traversing right. A small wet wall constituted the final challenge. Once above, he belayed me from the krummholz.

The time stood at 3:30 p.m. when we finished putting up *Wreck of the Lichen Fitzgerald* – a tribute to the Edmund Fitzgerald in combination with a lichen-based theme that would recur shortly. I took the time to shoot video and asked for his thoughts.

He began, "Well, we've got 400' of rope wrapped around every twig, and it's raining..."

Three rappels and an hour later found us back at our packs. The weather was holding steady, but we gave up the thought of trying to add another big line – there was, however, that appealing pillar at the mouth of the Gorge! We began the day with ambition, and it hadn't waned.

For Whom the Lichen Tolls (5.9)

After an hour of steep fern climbing, bushwhacking and talus hopping, we crossed the drainage to the pillar on the Haystack side. The free-standing spike of crack-riddled anorthosite is one of three in a group mentioned by Old Mountain Phelps in S.R Stoddard's classic, *The Adirondacks Illustrated.*

Clouds over Marcy wept a light drizzle and seemed to hint, *I'll make you work for this!*

Meanwhile, Adam studied the aspects and found the best way to reach an obvious fingercrack that he'd spotted from across the valley – the optimal line to the top. I was warm from the bushwhack and didn't don a jacket or gloves as I belayed. I make this point because it was part of my undoing when I followed the route. Temperatures in the 50's and wet stone created the perfect setup for cold hands. Adam climbed the slightly overhanging southern face on abundant holds

Adam approaching the crux of For Whom the Lichen Tolls.

to a ledge on the southwestern corner. Moving from the corner to begin the crack climb looked difficult. With solid protection in place, he climbed to a horizontal seam and followed the crack slightly right and to the top.

I began in fine form on the overhanging bottom corner. Once on the ledge, I realized that the crack wasn't merely vertical, but slightly overhanging. Foregoing the use of gloves and a jacket while belaying caught up with me – I was chilled and rushed the moves with numb fingers. After several tries, my "fine form" turned into an amusing freak show as I slipped from the crack while grumbling under my breath that I didn't climb it cleanly. Adam heckled me from his perch on the table-sized crown. I stayed the course and found the last 10' comparatively easy. I was curious about what the top of the pillar looked like and found it crisscrossed by deep cracks with piles of rubble.

We looked south. The view was superb, but the weather was getting oppressive. It was time to retreat with two climbs under our belts. I rappelled first. The last 25' found me swaying to and fro next to the overhanging section. Hanging free enunciated the difficulty of the pitch. At the time, this was "above my pay grade." I knew, however, that I'd get stronger over the coming years.

The Phelps Trail fell under our feet at 6:30 p.m. though we "only" had to walk another 10 miles back to his house, a piece of cake [insert sarcasm]. I often say that all proper adventures begin and end in the dark. This was turning into such a trip.

The satisfaction associated with concluding a successful day in less than ideal conditions defied words. It solidified my belief that the Adirondack backcountry still hosts unexplored terrain. In a world of interconnectivity, days like this reiterate that the heart of adventure still beats strongly. There's much to see around the next corner. Add good friends to the mix and the journey is all the more worthwhile.

A Climbing Trilogy: CrazyDog's Halo, Watery Grave, and Panther's Fang

With: Adam Crofoot (lead) on 2014 September 27
Area: Marcy *Agharta Wall* & *Panther Den*
Routes: *CrazyDog's Halo* (5.8), *Watery Grave* (5.10a Top Rope) & *Panther's Fang* (5.8+, FA 1965)
Duration: 5:15 a.m. – 9:15 p.m.
Reference Plates 1, 2

Adam and I couldn't resist one more visit to Panther Gorge before colder weather tightened its grip on the highlands. The days were getting shorter which meant a longer time trekking with the soft glow of a headlamp. As much as I enjoy hiking in the dark, it sometimes makes mustering ambition difficult. It wasn't until the sun rose over Basin's ridge, about five miles in, that I became more alert.

The bushwhack into the Gorge was dry, a delightful contrast to the conditions we experienced in August. By 9:15 a.m. we were staring at the *Agharta Wall*. We continued down and descended to a drainage stream then followed it up to the *Wreck of the Lichen Fitzgerald*. Blackflies swarmed as I donned my harness and helmet – yes, they still haunt the area in September. We set the packs on a ledge below the dominant left-facing corners that border the right side of this portion of the wall – *Wreck* was about 40' to our left. I said a prayer for a safe climb, checked that the packs were out of the way of any rocks we might dislodge and the excitement began.

Adam belaying the author up the amazing cracks on pitch one of CrazyDog's Halo.

Left: Checking our location using a beta photograph.

Above: Spectacular autumn colors abound in the Gorge. Photo by Adam Crofoot.

The first pitch of the new line was the most difficult – the trend for this area is a low crux with moderately angled slab in the center and a small cliff band at the top. The anorthosite was dry with dominant splitter cracks and corners. An appealing crack about halfway up led to a chimney that barely accommodated my body. Thereafter, we stepped left onto the 75-degree face using ½ inch edges to traverse south. Adam set up an anchor in a horizontal crack, and we relaxed. Leaning back from the anchor, we could scan the autumnal glow of the canopy, predominantly yellow from the birches. A light haze softened the southern view.

I led the second pitch and followed a fingercrack up the slab. The pitch was similar to slide climbing only steeper. Weathered divots in the surface and chunks of feldspar made the climbing delightful. The crack petered out partway up, so I traversed to an overlap below a large tree island that made a perfect belay station. The view north across the *Agharta Wall* slab and the previously established *Cloudsplitter/Toma's Wall* routes were both awe-inspiring and intimidating. The wide slab of the wall abruptly ended atop a series of roofs.

Another bushy island led to steeper face-climbing below a chunky cliff band. The other named routes ended through opposing corners to our right (the same as the *Agharta* ice route) so we aimed for a crack roughly 50' to the left to keep our line independent. The broken features of the cliff looked intriguing but ready to tumble at any moment. Would they in reality? It is doubtful. Nevertheless, Adam spent time studying one large block at the bottom of the cliff – ensuring it would not shift under pressure. The block seemed to be one of several chockstones holding up the interlocking wall. Tons of downward pressure also kept it stable.

Adam then climbed to a ledge, traversed to another corner and belayed me from cracks at the top of the face. I realized why he took such care when I saw the block up close. It was detached from the ledge and resonated when tapped. The cliff was a small talus cave

Interlocking stones at the top of the Agharta Wall.

system, though not large enough to fit a person. *CrazyDog's Halo* was complete. It was my turn to pick a name, so I chose one close to my heart and named it after my wife, Deb (aka CrazyDog). She worked in neuroradiologic research for over 25 years. The Halo was her first and favorite research project. She also deserves a halo for supporting my antics over the years.

We waded through the krummholz to the rappel webbing at the top of the *Wreck of the Lichen Fitzgerald*. We used this to rappel down the "old" route. By this time the sun was baking us – it was high in the 80's – a marked contrast to our last trip.

Watery Grave

Adam proposed an idea after we'd descended to the belay station of the Wreck route; to top rope a new route on the face in between the *Wreck* and *CrazyDog* lines. The Edmund Fitzgerald rests in a watery grave on the bottom of Lake Superior, so the proximity to the *Wreck* lent itself well to *Watery Grave* as a route name.

Adam rappelled, and I belayed him from the small ledge on the near vertical wall. I was still getting used to hanging from such stances – trusting my life with a few nuts set in a crack. Working the double ropes kept me blissfully distracted. The new line climbed small edges on a steep face and broke through a one-foot roof below a fingercrack. Above that, he followed the crack and traversed across the face, climbed a larger crack and met up with the *Wreck* line.

I then rappelled and gave it a try. He rated it at 5.10a – harder than I could climb at the time, but it was worth a shot. All was well until about 35' up on the crux where I fell. I wasn't surprised. I merely re-climbed and, after slipping a second time, called it good. I wanted to save my energy, and I didn't think the outcome would be any different. Feeling the thin flake of stone comprising the crux bend under my fingertips was a memory I won't soon forget. It was time to bushwhack north and climb a final route.

The Panther's Fang

We hugged the cliffs as we walked and dropped our gear in the grass partway up the *Panther Den* at an obvious crack in the vertical face – the *Panther's Fang*. This was the first named route in the Gorge (circa 1965 by Craig Patterson and Ronald Dubay). Adam described it as a classic, and it didn't disappoint! The route followed the crack but used the edges on the adjacent face. It ended after 110' at an old piton in a crack above a ledge. It felt like a hard 5.8 from my perspective; the crux was slightly overhanging. It was beyond my leading ability at the time, but the future is an empty canvas, and I vowed to come back and lead it someday after finishing other projects on the docket. Our energy was still high when we exited the Gorge at 5:00 p.m. Dinner at Slant Rock with the impromptu company of Ranger Scott van Laer capped the adventure in style.

A Winter Bushwhack: Attempting Marcy's Chimney

With: Adam Crofoot on 2014 December 27
Duration / Mileage: 13.5 hrs. / 19 mi.
Reference Plates 4, 10

A day out in the backcountry is all about enjoying the scenery and, during this trip, the challenge of exploring the Gorge during a different season – my first winter bushwhack in the area. A firm snowpack created a relatively relaxed approach by winter standards. We hoped to find a good ice line to climb. *Agharta*, added in 1999, was the only documented route.

My pace was slower than usual. Trail conditions were covered in what Adam referred to as "VFRG" (various forms of refrozen garbage). Johns Brook was flowing at normal levels though it was unfrozen. Ascending the trail was tedious thereafter – something akin walking on snow while avoiding water running in some areas. Postholes from both bare booters and hikers wearing snowshoes hinted at the warm weather present the day before. The constant energy drain from breaking through the thin crust over the next several miles

Left: *Adam below the crux in Marcy's chimney.*

Above: *A free-standing pinnacle on the Chimney Wall.*

eroded my ambition. Even my pack felt unusually heavy. I was nearly spent by the time we reached the pass at 10:30 a.m., almost five hours after leaving the Garden. That was a record time for me – on the slow side of the scale.

I broke trail for a few minutes before Adam had to take the lead. I was definitely off my game. The spectacular natural artwork of winter distracted me. Icicles and frozen gullies bedecked Haystack's cliffs and ledges. A strong wind blew low hanging clouds from south to north intermittently obscuring the views and diffusing the soft morning sunlight. Lower down on Marcy; we found the *Agharta* ice route in fragile condition. The first pitch was covered with a thin sheet of delaminated ice with water running underneath – dangerous for climbing. Any hopes that it might be climbable evaporated especially when I later heard a resounding, "Crack!" A piece of ice had broken off a nearby cliff.

Adam continued south through the woods and across several gullies. I came to a sudden stop and plopped in the snow as my blood-sugar levels dropped. A quick snack revived me. I gave the thumbs up, and it wasn't long before we were climbing up a small slide with a large roof. I recognized it as the spot where Anthony Seidita and I spent an hour lounging during a camping trip. Huge ice formations covered the upper walls, a significant change from summer conditions. Neither of us realized it at the time, but a few months later we'd "put up" our first ice route, *Pi Day*, in this location on the *Overhang Slide*.

We explored the surrounding area and found a few possible ice lines that weren't in any condition to climb. This area is characterized by smaller single pitch cliffs, one with a needle of stone balanced high above the ground. We named this the *Chimney Wall* in 2017 – on account of the wide chimney that splits it down the northeast aspect. The chimney was our target for this trip and it appeared that there was a thin ice line to climb. Adam racked enough gear for an outright assault: pitons, rock gear, spectre ice pitons, and ice screws.

He quickly climbed the first 20', jamming cams in the walls every now and again. He broke through a slight overhang to a stance near a more significant overhang (a narrow chimney during the summer). The ice thinned and was brittle. He spent the next hour and a half searching for protection and a way to break through the obvious crux. Climbing partway up the left side led to what looked like good ice until he kicked it with the front-points of the crampon. It shattered and funneled down the chimney; I dodged the chunks as he cursed. He backed off and studied it before committing to a climb up a thin veneer of ice on the wall. I paid out ten then twenty feet of rope while watching him climb with only the tips of the tools and front-points embedded in the ice. He reached the top of the section only to find a snow-slope with no ice. He could climb no farther and was unable to place any gear – a scary predicament.

I sensed his tension, and a note of panic sounded deep in my mind. Forget the climb, I was worried about his safety. Unbeknownst to me, water was running down his sleeves as he contemplated the best way to retreat without protection. Time seemed to slow as he delicately descended the vertical wall with only the smallest tips of metal saving him from an injurious fall. He finally reached a safe stance, and I lowered him from two chocks and an ice piton. He changed into dry clothing once on the ground. We managed uneasy smiles. Well, this was certainly an adventure!

Our thoughts focused on the exit; climbing ambitions were at an end. We were situated in a semi-technical gully that breaches Marcy's smaller cliffs. Adam had scouted this during the summer and knew it led out. It was time for a 700-foot ascent up to the Van Hoevenberg Trail. We climbed to the gully's top where we soloed some low-angle ice under a curtain of frozen daggers before walking into the woods. It was time to don

Looking at Haystack's V Wall from the Overhang Slide.

the snowshoes. The forest was surprisingly loose compared to my expectations and what I'd experienced on other areas of Marcy's eastern slope...a nice change! Our bushwhack to the Van Hoevenberg Trail through knee-deep snow took slightly more than an hour. We intersected it above the Phelps Trail intersection and noted the location for future excursions.

The 8.4 mile exit took another four hours. All the while, I felt the weight of the pack and lack of energy – was I feeling my age? I later weighed the pack at 55 pounds. The ice tools, crampons, snowshoes, micro-spikes, ice screws, rope, extra layers, water, food, and emergency gear added up! Carrying such heavy weight for 19 miles over 14 hours had broken my endurance. I turned to more constructive thoughts and considered how to minimize non-crucial gear for future trips. In the end, we'd gathered valuable beta and enjoyed a winter adventure. Sometimes the mountain does not want to be climbed according to our vision.

3.1415

With: Adam Crofoot (lead) & Anthony Seidita on 2015 March 14
Area: Marcy *Overhang Slide* (*East Face* and *Huge Scoop*)
Route: *Pi Day* (WI3+)
Duration / Mileage / Vertical Gain: 5:00 a.m. – 5:30 p.m. / 14.75 mi. / 4,400 ft.
Reference Plate 10

The cold winter of 2015 seemed to last forever. Perhaps it was the weather, or maybe just the pressures of life made it feel long. In any case, long-awaited plans came to life as a sub-zero spell finally broke. Our thoughts centered on putting up a new ice climbing route. We watched the forecast as March 14th approached. It called for temperatures in the 30's with a possibility of rain at our target elevation. Waiting for a better weather window would push the limits of ice season in the Gorge.

I nearly threw the alarm clock across the room when it sounded at 3:55 a.m. I spent the night tossing and turning as I subconsciously pondered the uncertainties of the venture – would the snowpack be supportive, could we dial in our new approach, would the annoying ache above my left knee subside, would the rain be a problem, would the ice be safe…? We'd diligently prepared; the rest was in the hands of God.

I met Anthony and Adam at the Adirondak Loj (yay Melville Dewey). We divided the gear to distribute weight but in the end our packs each weighed 45 pounds between two ropes, ice screws, rock climbing gear, axes and the usual winter necessities including three types of traction: microspikes, snowshoes, and crampons. We began walking at 5:00 a.m. on rock hard trails which expedited our approach.

Fast forward to our bushwhack at 8:30 a.m. We left the Van Hoevenberg Trail high on Mt. Marcy after hiking almost seven miles. If we navigated correctly, we'd thread our way

Above: Anthony below the ice of Pi Day.

Right: Adam and the author in the snowfield below the slide. Photo by Anthony Seidita.

through the cliffs and into the Gorge via the gully along the *Chimney Wall*. I can't stress how dangerous this approach can be if you aren't intimately familiar with the nuances of the cliffs. It's not the place to embark on a blind bushwhack – the last thing one wants is to descend 700' (especially in unconsolidated snow) only to find themselves atop a precipice 400' above the floor of the Gorge. See the search and rescue section for examples.

I took the first step off-trail and broke through a light crust to my shin, happy to avoid most of the spruce traps. The terrain steepened as we descended from the ridge and into one of the several moderate gullies. Each leads to a different area atop one of the technical climbing walls. Even high on the ridge, there were obstacles such as smaller ledges draped in ice. Adam eventually took point as Anthony and I regularly checked the heading. We soon found our jump-off into the Gorge – the top of the gully. It seemed like a ridiculously steep drop by bushwhacking standards. Armed with crampons and a single ice tool, we didn't feel that ropes were necessary. Unsupportive sugar snow under a surface of crust created a tedious and precarious descent.

I need to digress for a moment since this relates to the ice route described below. Pi (π) is the ratio of a circle's circumference to its diameter and is approximated at 3.141592653. A single snapshot of time found us struggling down the gully on 3/14/15 at 9:26:53 a.m. I'm done channeling my inner geek – back to the outing.

We passed along a northeastern facing wall that got ever taller as we entered the heart of the Gorge. The chimney of the wall, the same one we tried several months earlier, still didn't hold enough ice, so we continued downward. Walking was easier on the avalanche debris at the bottom. It was akin to walking on blocks of concrete, a stark contrast after the unconsolidated descent down the gully. We changed direction after climbing around a buttress and broke north to what we named the *Overhang Slide*. This is a relatively short slide with two large overhangs, one at the bottom and one near the top. I thought back to when Anthony and I enjoyed lunch on it during June of 2014. It is a place that offers particularly magnificent views.

We descended to a glade below the lower overhang and stared up at the wall of ice near the top, an enticing climb. Adam and I were intrigued by it several months earlier, but it was much fatter now. We agreed to go no farther – this would be our day's target. I relaxed and scanned the Gorge. From this low, the view north was partially occluded by trees, but Haystack loomed majestically across the way as small wispy clouds drifted across its summit. The beaver ponds to the south contrasted like pearls against the dark forest. I thought of the many people over the years who have gotten lost on Mt. Marcy and wandered into the Gorge only to need rescue or, in the worst case, recovery. This is both a beautiful and unforgiving area.

Adam was the strongest and most efficient climber of the party. He began the route with a short vertical climb leading to the low-angle slab and quickly disappeared from view. Pieces of crust slid over the edge and passed by us into the glade. A couple of hundred feet higher, he set up a belay from a tree near the upper overhang. Anthony and I climbed the snow/ice at the same time, each on our respective rope. I was accustomed to soloing slides, so using a rope on the low-angle section felt counter-intuitive.

We surveyed the scene from a stance below the overhang. I motioned toward the premium line (likely WI5).

Adam retorted, "Your lead!"

The ice was bearded – white colored and obviously rotting. There were, however, several other options that were easier to protect and safer to climb. The cloud ceiling was lowering, and Haystack had disappeared. The cliffs to the north, however, were still in view. The *Agharta* ice route was in shambles. Only its top near the cliff-band was intact. The middle section of ice was free of winter's frozen hands, the slabs wet with runoff.

The weather continued to close in as we progressed. Fog blew up past Adam as he methodically climbed the left-hand side of the icy wall. Chipping through the rotten surface to place the screws into more solid ice was tedious, but necessary. He followed an appealing line incorporating short vertical sections and a couple of small ice ramps. He finished the line at the top left-hand corner of the wall and found some secure trees from which to belay. The entire Gorge was, by now, socked in and the light sleet had transitioned to rain. Thank God for protective layers. We continued to climb; first me, then Anthony.

Once at the top, I listened to the wind and the sound of ice falling as Anthony chipped his way up – the combination of sounds, sights and overall feel of the day made it serene. A quick rappel brought us

Adam leading Pi Day. Photo by Anthony Seidita.

down to our packs and our precious stash of food. Our route, *Pi Day*, was completed by 1:30 p.m., but the day was far from over. We contemplated our exit and knew it would be grueling.

By the time we reached the bottom of the gully again, I was thankful for the avalanche debris. It offered a stable base on which to walk. The following 300' of vertical ascent over 450 ground feet can only be described as heinous. Adam was in the lead, but unseen like some phantom in the fog that cast an occasional piece of crust down the gully and onto my helmet. Anthony brought up the rear, but only after reorganizing a few items in his pack. I climbed and looked back every few steps. He seemingly dematerialized in the mist. Adam used snowshoes, Anthony and I used crampons. I'm not sure which was better, but the ordeal seemed endless as we thrashed our way up the gully on all fours. Yup, this is what we call fun, but nothing worthy is easy!

The following 700' of elevation gain involved no navigational skills, just retracing our steps and overcoming the occasional ledge of unsupportive snow. It's amazing how much energy one can expend climbing a mere six feet. Cresting Marcy's ridge into the winds with low visibility was cause for celebration – we were back on the Van Hoevenberg Trail. Experiencing such conditions exemplified why some unprepared hikers easily get turned around. We reached the Phelps Trail intersection at 3:30 p.m. and changed gear. Adam switched to skis which made his descent fun and relaxing in comparison to our "slowshoes." I cared not. We'd added a new climb, had a stellar time and enjoyed the day. We arrived back at Adirondak Loj at 5:30 p.m. after 12.5 hours of adventuring (a short duration for a climbing trip in the Gorge). I had a new respect for Panther Gorge during winter, a respect that roused my appetite for additional excursions.

Racing the Storm: Misty Climbing on Haystack and a Flash Flood

With: Adam Crofoot (lead) and Allison Rooney (lead) on 2015 May 30 (during a May 29 – June 1 camping trip)
Area: Haystack *Ramp Wall* & *North End*
Routes: *All Battered Boyfriends* (5.7), *Less than Zero* (5.5) & *Eye For an Eye* (5.8)
Adapted from "The Wild Side" in *Adirondack Outdoors* magazine, Spring 2016
Reference Plate 6

Each spring I anticipate the end of mud season and tromping through rotten snow. I'm usually giddy by the time June arrives. Adam and Allison Rooney, his girlfriend and hard-climber, were ready as well. We set a mutually agreeable weekend aside, but the forecast looked unsettled as the time approached. It seemed that a brief window on Saturday, May 30, 2015, would be the optimal time. Adam and I had had good luck putting up routes in between poor weather windows – even if it meant getting a little wet at the day's end. This trip seemed like an equally fair bet.

We trekked seven miles from the Garden Trailhead in Keene Valley to Slant Rock Lean-to on May 29, 2015. Our previous backcountry climbs were single day outings, but we decided to camp to better time our ascent with the window of fair weather. So, at 4:45 a.m. the following morning, we readied our gear and with sleepy resolve trekked up to the Haystack/Marcy col. It wasn't far into the bushwhack when I heard Adam yell an explicative. Allison's shoulder had snagged a branch. It slapped Adam in the eye

Left: *Adam and Allison in a corridor behind the Ramp Wall.*

Above: *Allison leading For Whom the Lichen Tolls. Photo by Adam Crofoot.*

and punctured his eyelid. He was resolved to press on with blurry vision and a red eye after assessing the extent of the injury.

We exited the trees to find that the Gorge was socked in. Low hanging clouds blew in from the south, the winds shifting the damp trees to and fro. It felt ominous yet inspirational. There was no time to waste with storms settling in mere hours later. We sought dry stone on Haystack rather than descending deep into the Gorge. Adam and I had spotted a wall with an obvious left-rising ramp – the *Ramp Wall* – the previous year. Several cracks and interesting possibilities existed on the front. Walking across the talus from one side to the other was easier said than done, however, and climbing mossy ledges covered in krummholz with heavy packs was tiring.

Allison climbing into the fog on the Ramp Wall.

The cliffs of Haystack often hold surprises when one explores them up close. The *Ramp Wall* is, in reality, a large fin of anorthosite connected on the north end, but separated from massif by a 15-foot wide corridor. We explored it thoroughly before committing to a route. A steep ramp of chossy stone allowed us to access the top of the wall via the corridor. I turned around and looked south out of the slot. It seemed like we were inside of a great tomb. Breaks in the fog allowed intermittent views of the Gorge.

We walked around to the front after satiating our curiosity. Allison decided to lead the first route by starting slightly uphill from the lower right-hand corner of the ramp. The face had horizontal cracks requiring several cool moves. Everything looks easier from below and, as is often the case, the route was more challenging than it seemed. Forty feet higher, she entered a wide slot between opposing corners and disappeared onto the ramp where she scrambled a few feet downhill. After that, she climbed a right-rising crack and belayed me to her position. Adam followed. While managing the rope, Allison inadvertently punched me in a region that's best left unpublished (there's a point to revealing this detail).

Adam swapped leads and took the route up a blocky corner. He held his position while placing gear by stemming (ascending by pressing one's feet on opposing faces). Following another crack, he found the top and belayed from a huge boulder. We followed and found Adam anchored to a large block calmly scanning the cloudscape. There was no view, but we'd put up our first route of the day, *All Battered Boyfriends* (5.7). Lest anyone take offense at the name, it was derived from the flailing limb that pierced Adam's eyelid and the light punch I received.

Our next route was located 50' uphill on the same wall. The line began along a grungy left facing corner below the upper end of the ramp. An appealing lightning bolt shaped fingercrack drew Adam's attention. He chose to lead even with a red eye that wouldn't stop tearing. Loose blocks and a closer inspection of the crack changed the direction of his ascent. The crack was shallow and filled with moss, but the adjacent face offered an easy climb up to a small ledge.

The final few moves followed a wet corner with several cracks to an annoying cornice of moss (the last pitch of 2017's *Skip the Lightning* ice route). I remember throwing my leg high to hook my heel on an algae-covered ledge, wet from seepage—ah, backcountry climbing! Adam set up an anchor and lowered from the stronger trees higher on the hill. The route became *Less Than Zero* (5.5). It deserved less than zero quality stars, but it was still a fun route. One can't be picky when most of the stone is wet.

Adam's eye worsened as the day wore on. He was done leading, and I wasn't in the right headspace to jump on the "sharp end." That left Allison.

The clouds had lifted, and we studied a cliff about 100' north of a small grungy drainage. Allison was up for one more lead. This would become the gem of our three new routes. An appealing wall of flaking yet attached stone with various cracks on its southern wall dictated the line. She climbed up to a fistcrack in a square block to a right facing corner. Small loose-looking blocks led ever upward past two small pillars. I belayed and watched her disappear before climbing a deep vertical crack roughly 80' above. The final crack was the most thrilling part of the pitch and worth the effort. I climbed next, then Adam. She named it, *Eye for an Eye* (5.8), in reference to Adam's injury.

The line was adjacent to a drainage stream that cascaded over a small cliff. Areas that are wet and unappealing during the rock climbing season often indicate that they hold ice during the winter. Nolan Huther and I returned to this location during the following February where I led the new route, *Fly By* (WI3).

The sun finally came out and revealed a spectacular view of the walls on Mt. Marcy and the underlying valley. This is what climbing in Panther Gorge is all about; new routes, rough terrain exuding a profound sense of wilderness and interpersonal camaraderie—not to mention a certain amount of blood, sweat, and pain. We bushwhacked north into the mouth of the Gorge and re-climbed our pillar route, *For Whom the Lichen Tolls* (5.9), likely one of the best pitches on Mount Haystack. Allison led then Adam and I climbed while thunderheads coalesced and boomed their warnings from afar. The wind became stronger, droplets of rain dotted my sunglasses, and the temperature began to drop. It was time to retreat. Neither of us wanted to bushwhack out in a downpour with lightning dancing across the sky.

We trekked out of the Gorge while avoiding a few deep pockets of snow – I couldn't resist lobbing a snowball at Allison while Adam laughed then commented that it would amuse him if we timed our arrival at the lean-to with the arrival of the impending rain. Adam's comment was prophetic. The deluge arrived on our heels at 6:00 p.m.

Flash Flooding

One might think that the climbing was the crux of the day, yes? No. A strong storm moved through the region shortly after the rain commenced. Trees bent, and lightning flashed

Flash flooding at Johns Brook.

as the rain blew sideways. We enjoyed nature's show of power in comfort and safety while eating a hot dinner. The storm raged on long after we'd eaten, but we were focused on discussing and documenting the new climbing routes before we forgot the details. Two gentlemen from Canada were also overnighting in the lean-to and chimed into the discussion.

Dusk approached as the rain briefly relented. Richard, a trail runner coming off the Great Range suddenly appeared. He was wearing a hydration pack and dressed in spandex shorts, a short-sleeved shirt, and a thin rain poncho. He was soaked through after getting trapped above tree-line during the height of the storm. He announced that Johns Brook was too high to cross and asked for suggestions on where to ford it. The usual level of the brook is only ankle deep at the crossing. Distracted as we were, we didn't immediately process the implications of his words. We imagined that the water might be slightly higher than normal, but didn't visualize it flowing dangerously. We grew curious and walked down from the lean-to. The changes were hard to believe.

Small springs between the lean-to and the Phelps Trail below were overflowing. Johns Brook had risen nearly four feet and turned into an impassable torrent. The continuation of the Phelps Trail on the other side of the brook was unrecognizable; water cascaded down the stone stairs. Richard was shivering, and temperatures were forecast to plummet into the 30's though they were 80 during the day. We loaned him clothing and suggested that he spend the night in the shelter.

Richard recounted part of his experience, *"Waterfalls formed on Little Haystack, pouring on my head. I ran over it while lightning was still blasting. I ran for dear life."* Fast forward to his descent, *"The trails were filled with water up to my knees. I was still at 4,000 feet! As if all the rocks weren't treacherous enough by themselves, they were hidden under a stream of freezing water."* The rainfall had mixed with melting snow.

Meanwhile, there was a tragedy unfolding in Feldspar Brook which had also risen to dangerous levels. Feldspar Brook is located a few miles to the southwest of the lean-to as the crow flies. A 34-year old woman from Montreal, Quebec had been hiking Skylight and Gray with a companion. She fell off a log and was swept downstream. Sadly, her body was located early the following afternoon (Sunday).

Back at Slant Rock, storms passed over throughout the evening. Claps of thunder intermittently shook us from a light sleep. We occasionally checked on Richard to see if he was ok. After a sleepless night, he awoke and surveyed the brook. It had receded to a safe level, so he thanked us and made his exit. We lazed around in our bags until late morning, dreading the wet slog out. Moderate rains eventually diminished to a light drizzle when we began the seven-mile trek back to the trailhead. Johns Brook was thigh deep when we crossed, and the Phelps Trail was running with cold water for over a mile.

We needed to ford Johns Brook again near Bushnell Falls where the width and volume were greater than at Slant Rock. The thought weighed on my mind during the walk. Would it be possible? In the end, the waist-deep water was strong but manageable for experienced hikers. We unbuckled our packs in case we slipped and spotted each other during the process.

I arrived home excited about our adventure, but soon read about the Feldspar Brook tragedy. It unnerved me. We were able to enjoy the storm while another person fought for her life – so very sad. The Adirondacks are a place of unparalleled beauty and full of opportunities for adventure, but the backcountry can be deadly. Many of us in the hiking community share stories about difficult trips we've endured. As such, we also feel a common bond and mourn such calamities.

Climbing Like a Cat on a Wet Tin Roof

With: Bill Schneider (lead) on 2015 June 14
Area: Marcy *Panther Den*
Route: *Cat on a Wet Tin Roof* (5.8)
Duration: 5:00 a.m. – 9:45 p.m.
Reference Plates 1, 2, 3

It had only been two weeks since the last visit, but my body felt up to another beating/adventure. I'd heard stories about a climber named Bill Schneider – good stories from Adam about a veteran of the Gorge from a decade prior. This marked my first of many climbs with him as we pursued a common interest – exploring the unexplored. Our target was the, then unnamed, *Huge Scoop*. Close-up observation shows that it was likely formed as pieces fell away over eons or were peeled by the glaciers. This square depression offers roughly 200' of steep technical slab (with about as much width) surrounded by vertical walls at its top and to the climber's right. A smaller vertical wall with parallel cracks lies to the left. A chossy gully delineates the left-hand side from the smaller southern crags. This gully would soon be named *Twin Fracture Gully* and is home to the 2018 ice routes, *Scylla* and *Charybdis*.

Features of the lower Panther Den area.

Exploring

We met at the Rooster Comb Trailhead at 4:45 a.m. Bill is a fan of alpine starts, and this may have been slightly later than he wanted. Morning for me, however, arrived all too quickly when my alarm sounded at 3:55 a.m. On approach to the Southside Trail (which saves elevation compared to the Northside Trail), we heard Johns Brook roaring and decided to take the Northside rather than risk a dicey crossing and tanking the trip .5 mile from the trailhead. The trail was muddy and wet, yet our feet remained amazingly dry – a notable event in the Adirondacks.

Once in the Gorge, we pondered the condition of the available climbs as we walked along the walls. We weren't pleased. Heavy rains had saturated the area, and we were soaked from bushwhacking. The faces of stone wept beautiful but disheartening cascades.

The previous day's warm sun hadn't dried the rock enough so finding a safe route was challenging. It's disappointing to expend so much energy on approach only to have nature thwart the climb. This frustration is familiar to anyone who has spent significant time in the mountains – all can't be perfect each time.

None-the-less we continued south to the *Huge Scoop* where we studied the possibilities. Our hearts felt heavy. As we feared, most of the obvious lines were as wet as the other walls. I'd hoped that the main drainage areas were on either side of the depression, but several came down the primary cracks in its headwall. Regardless, we opted to explore. Bill climbed the slab (about 5.7) to a corner along the right side. Beta photographs suggested obvious weaknesses in the face. Some of these were deceptively difficult. Bill worked his way up, sometimes on wet slab – his disdain for damp rock was obvious. I was equally disheartened with the climbing prospects.

On a positive note, the area was magnificent to photograph – natural artistry as I often say. The jagged edges of the broken headwall contrasted with the straight lines of the adjacent corners and various cracks. Simply being there and climbing the slab was thrilling. Bill climbed partway up two options on the right-hand wall, but the cracks were all wet, and prudence won in the end. We retreated with a vow (and a bit of grumbling) to return in a few weeks. The day was young, so we packed our gear and sought options to the north. I knew of an alternative line that looked more promising. We marched back up through the gnarled forest to the *Panther Den*.

It was 1:30 p.m. when we readied ourselves for a second climb. The line was on the lowest vertical corner of the *Panther Den* where a faint herdpath descends into the woods. Blocky ledges led up to a vertical wall. This is where we sought a new route and what would eventually become the ice route *By Tooth and Claw* – also Bill's lead.

Cat on a Wet Tin Roof

Bill offered me the lead. I geared up and looked at the choices: blocky terrain slightly to the south (not very challenging), a 15-foot vertical face with no protection or a mossy set of blocks below a small gully. I chose the vertical face (about 5.7). Though unprotected, it looked like it had a few edges that could be connected. I climbed about seven feet up and probed with my hand. My fingers hit a patch of sand and slipped. I felt off-balance so, rather than risk falling, I turned and jumped back down to our grassy ramp – however awkwardly. I studied it further and tried again, this time finding firm foot and hand placements. Once on the ledge, I placed a cam in a vertical handcrack and climbed more confidently. It was on.

The next 135' of climbing was up cracks and pitted rock along the corner of the wall. There was a gully to my right, but that didn't look challenging enough. I eventually crested a large terrace and set up an anchor to belay Bill. Once he reached my position, we scanned the wall. It was 25' high with several defined cracks. One looked more enticing than the rest and led up to an overhang which, upon closer study, was a towering free-standing spire. I climbed about halfway up and, after placing a few pieces of gear, couldn't progress. The crack wasn't entirely clean and, combined with the wetness, was more than I was able to lead. It would have been easier if dry.

Bill opted to give it a turn. Decades of experience paid dividends, and he completed the climb. In the end, climbing the crack wasn't as straight-forward as it appeared. The gear placement was awkward. Above, he followed the corner formed by the spire and found a second 20' tall vertical wall. The wall and spire formed a chimney that would end the route in style. There was little gear that could be placed near the chimney, but it was a secure climb.

He set up an anchor in the krummholz, and I followed. I took time to admire the spire and chimney. Looking through it from the top, showed a slice of the green forest below. I love finding hidden recesses and unique perspectives while climbing. The surprises are seemingly limitless.

We decided to walk off the top via the forest rather than rappel. The decision subjected us to a horrendous experience, especially in rock climbing shoes. The krummholz was among the thickest I've seen. I led the way with rope still attached (it was easier than coiling it in a tangle of sharp limbs). We trekked north and eventually located more loosely knit forest. Once free from the "forest of 1,000 daggers," we walked back down the grassy slope to our packs for a quick snack. *Cat on a Wet Tin Roof* was up. Visualize, if you will, how a cat slipping on wet tin might appear. The mental image is a close approximation of how I looked while attempting the wet crack below the spire. When all else fails, find humor in the situation!

It was nearly 6:00 p.m. when we bushwhacked out of the Gorge. Hordes of hungry midges drove us from Johns Brook Lodge like children being chased by bears. They are the worst of the Adirondack pests. Midges (punkies or no-see-ums) make one's skin feels like it is on fire. We arrived back at the Garden trailhead after 16 hours and 50 minutes of backcountry excitement. We were tired but still had enough energy to plan another trip to complete our unfinished route – we'd make sure it was dry. *The Pride* would become a reality two months later.

To climb in the Adirondacks is to make do with what nature doles out.

Top: Bill at the top of a free-standing pinnacle on the Panther Den.

Bottom: Looking down a chimney formed by the pinnacle.

Sometimes conditions are perfect; these are the rare occasions when the mountains are friendly. Other times, one assesses, presses on, and accepts the results of the decision. There are still other ventures during which one retreats entirely with hopes of exploring another day. This trip was a combination of the latter two. I found this to be a trying day even by Panther Gorge standards; the fruit of our labor was well-earned.

Rumours of War on Marcy

With: Hunter Lombardi (lead) on 2015 July 11
Area: Marcy *Huge Scoop*
Route: *Rumours of War* (5.9)
Duration: 5:00 a.m. – 9:15 p.m.
Reference Plate 1

Looking up the *Huge Scoop*.

I was studying the photos and dreaming of warmer days during the winter of 2015 when a close-up of a rectangular scoop at the southern end of the Marcy cliffs caught my eye. Its cracks begged to be climbed. The scoop is a 200′ tall slab capped with an intermittently vertical and overhanging cliff riddled with parallel cracks. Most of the cracks run an additional 200′ up through various small roofs, chimneys, and overhangs. I was resigned to avoid the right-hand corner – it was reserved for a future trip with Bill Schneider. The next appealing option was the most obvious line – a large central crack that dissects the cliff, a plumb line from the bottom of the slab to the forest above. It had potential to be a stellar route.

I'm tenacious once something's drawn my attention, so I waited for drier weather and planned another trip. The *Huge Scoop*, our name for the area, is farther from the Marcy/Haystack col than other area rock climbs (as of this trip) except those on the *East Face*. It's a solid hour's bushwhack from the Marcy/Haystack col. I explained these logistics to friend and climber, Hunter Lombardi, who signed up for the adventure.

We crested the north pass of the Gorge at 8:45 a.m. and began bushwhacking. As we exited the dense forest onto a grassy slope at the base of the *Panther Den*, I heard Hunter exhale with awe. It was his first visit to this remote location.

He turned and said, "This IS the promised land!"

I retorted. "There's no place quite like it, just wait until you see what lies to the south." I turned and walked down the glade with a smile. I love introducing friends to inspiring locations.

We arrived at the base of the *Huge Scoop* at 10:00 a.m. A swarm of hungry blackflies came soon after – someone apparently rang the dinner bell, and we were on the menu. Each wall of the scoop is riddled with fractures shooting in various directions. It is a dizzying arena with the slab running at a slope surpassing 45 degrees along a vertical wall on the right. I studied the cracks. The nine mile walk would be for naught if they were too wet to climb – it had rained heavily though not for several days. The running water Bill and I found during June had decreased to minor seepage, but the cracks were still moist. We discussed climbing an adjacent line and opted to make a decision once at the base of the headwall. I led the first pitch up 180' of technical slab placing protection only occasionally before setting up an anchor at the top below the headwall.

A light wind kept the blackflies at bay as I looked at the nearby cracks and found that the center offered the driest option. Perhaps the day wasn't lost. I belayed Hunter to my position while soaking in the scenery. The blocky overhangs and split anorthosite made me feel insignificant. Evidence of nature's raw power surrounded us. The sound of one of the blocks falling from the cliff and splintering the forest below must be unimaginable.

First ascents can be tricky, and I feared the line might appear deceptively easy. I'd studied every nuance of the crack over the last year, but two dimensional photographs only reveal so much information. I'm often surprised in disconcerting ways. After an internal debate, I slapped pride to the side and conceded the lead to Hunter. The Gorge is a dangerous place to test one's skills only to find them lacking. I knew he was the stronger climber. Hunter assessed our proposed line from below the wall and felt confident that he could lead it. This would be our second pitch and the crux.

Hunter described the experience in its entirety:

We weren't sure what we were getting ourselves into which is, perhaps, what drew me in the most. The Gorge climbs are, for the most part, terra incognita and we are the first ones to explore this high in the scoop. There are few places nearby that offer that type of mystery. I guess that's what I love about the Adirondacks - it's always an adventure. Pitches two and three were just as exciting and enjoyable as the slab climb. They were easy to protect, in fact, they ate gear except for the last 25' of pitch two. The moves were fluid for the entire length – 405' – yet required diverse climbing techniques. The route was a combination of hand, finger and off-width cracks as well as slab and chimneys.

Hunter below pitch three.

I always find it amazing that a single route can hold unique experiences for each climber depending on one's experience level. Most of the moves allowed for intuitive climbing, but some felt quite awkward. These thoughts cemented my confidence in the decision to relinquish the lead to Hunter.

A small grassy island 75' above the first pitch served nicely as a belay ledge. A vertical crack with a few cams anchored us securely as we discussed options for the third pitch. Weathered slab led to a rising ramp that led into a chimney with a handcrack in the back. Again, it was wet in the back, but it was easier than below. I felt the sharp feldspar crystals dig into my arm as I jammed it in to secure myself so I could look at the scenery. The cliff fell away along a distinct buttress that Adam Crofoot and I climbed twice last year – *Wreck of the Lichen Fitzgerald* and *CrazyDog's Halo*. My position offered a new perspective of other potential routes in the Scoop and on the side of the *Agharta* buttress.

Once above the crack and on low-angle slab, it was easy to climb to the end of the route. We used a single rope so our rappels were limited to 100' feet at a time. We angled south to a small tree island adjacent to a large gully – another feature I felt compelled to explore. For the second rappel, we again found trees strong enough to support our weight and descended the vertical wall of the gully. *Twin Fracture Gully*, as I labeled it, was roughly 25' wide. Two distinct fractures joined at a confluence about 100' below the top. Large overhangs capped each. Hunter coiled the rope and wore it backpack-style as we descended the chossy gully. Further along, we reached a large boulder that blocked the way. It was time for a few dicey unprotected moves on the algae-covered stone!

We were back at the base of the slab with the blackflies 10 minutes later at 4:30 p.m. The route had taken six hours to put up. It was harder than we'd anticipated and I looked like I'd scrapped with a catamount. All that remained was the exit though we attended to one final detail before leaving. The route begged for a name with dark overtones – *Rumours of War* seemed appropriate. The Book of Revelation speaks of "wars and rumors of wars." Even a secular interpretation holds meaning; if you want to climb this route, you will battle to get to the base and climb hard to succeed. The trip in its entirety was 19 miles. Do it in a day to make it a war.

Inspiring cracks in the Huge Scoop.

The Kitten's Got Claws, and so does Marcy

With: Justin Thalheimer on 2015 August 1 (split leads)
Area: Marcy *Feline Wall*
Route: *Kitten's Got Claws* (5.7+)
Duration: 5:10 a.m. – 8:40 p.m.
Reference Plate 1

Justin leading as the route steepens near the top of the wall.

I didn't want to delve far into the Gorge during this outing, so the *Feline Wall* seemed like an appropriate choice. The wall has steep consistent slab with a plethora of cracks and room for a new route. I was curious if the cracks were as deep as they looked from below. Edges on the face also looked appealing, and since slab climbing is my specialty, it seemed like the perfect fit.

My partner was Justin Thalheimer. We hadn't yet climbed together, but had chatted online and briefly met at the 2015 Winter 46er dinner. Like Hunter during July's trip, this was Justin's first time in the Gorge. He too gasped in awe when he broke through the trees and saw the view from the *Panther Den*. I smiled. Such reactions always inspire me. I pointed out the various named routes as we descended and arrived at the *Feline Wall* at 10 a.m. I contemplated other potential lines as we passed, but had a particular idea in mind for this trip.

View down the Feline Wall with the Panther Den buttress on the left.

The *Feline Wall* is a long technical slab that steepens halfway up. The best cracks are above the lower half. It has a broken buttress to its north (this would become *Promised Land* during September) and a set of staggered roof systems to the immediate south. The feel is different than any other cliff in the area. It's narrow which promotes an intimate feeling in my opinion. It also offers stellar views of what we've been calling the *Panther's Shield*, a blank slab on Mt. Haystack – another dream line.

The bottom of the slab was mossy, so we started climbing from a grassy ledge about 15' from the glade. I decided to lead the unprotected crux pitch at the bottom – I was developing a habit, however unintentional. The first protection was 20' above the ledge. A fall below the first piece of protection guaranteed a tumble down 35' of 70-degree slab. I wouldn't die, but it wouldn't be pleasant. I set the thought aside and studied the face. Holds weren't evident, and only small protruding crystals were available to climb. I eyed an overlap high above and took a tentative first step onto an eight-inch protrusion. I crimped a nub (grabbed a hold only large enough to be grasped with the tips of the fingers) with my right hand and felt secure. Repeating the maneuver several more times placed me at the point of no retreat – and that's when the fight against the weather began.

I was 25' above the base when it began to drizzle. I audibly groaned. I didn't want to contend with slippery stone before I had a piece of protection in place. I needed to get to the overlap. The slab required study to find the right holds in the right places. It probably wasn't long, but it seemed like an eternity before I buried my fingers under the overlap, placed a cam and relaxed. A small pod in the face took another critical piece of protection, and the game was on. The spitting rain abated, but for how long? The clouds still looked threatening.

The author resting after the climb. Photo by Justin Thalheimer.

I traversed left on small edges to minor cracks and placed a shoddy piece of protection that held long enough for me to rest. I could hang from the protection, but it wouldn't hold a fall. More face climbing led to a couple of deep fingercracks that formed an "A" where they met at the top. The right-hand crack widened to a handcrack that ate the cams. They were deep as I'd hoped. One hundred and ten feet above, I set up an anchor near a corner and stood on small ledges where I belayed Justin to my position while watching rain clouds build over Elk Lake.

I suggested that Justin take the second pitch so we could both partake in leading. The top looked reasonably straightforward up a visible crack along the left-hand side of the face. This line would keep it independent of *The Cat's Meow* that followed the center of the face (FA by Bill Schneider, Adam Crofoot & Nic Gladd, 2003).

Though it was August and I was originally concerned about the heat, I felt chilly and put on a rain jacket as Justin climbed. One can never predict the weather. Rain occluded a nearby ridge before passing by – a near miss. Another cloud coalesced over Allen Mountain to the south. I felt the wind change and watched the clouds move quickly overhead. A few more drops fell as the storm over Allen blew eastward. I later found out that Upper Jay and Wilmington endured heavier showers.

Justin climbed the blocky crack to a corner and short chimney-like area before stepping right onto the face. He was heading toward a gully located at the top left. A clap of thunder from an anvil cloud on the other side of Haystack got our hearts pumping.

Justin said, "That isn't good..." His voice trailed off like the distant echo of the thunder.

The skies soon cleared and we climbed to the top. The final few feet led out of the gully and onto the face before entering a vertical cedar womb. This comical bushwhack led to a stout pine tree from which we rappelled. Managing the rope amongst a tangle of trees in a three foot wide corridor was absurd. Two rappels of 100' each along the left-hand side led to an area down which we could scramble back to our packs. It had taken about four hours to put up the route. I photographed an adjacent face to the south. Two enticing cracks drew my attention. They'd make excellent, if not runout pitches for a future route. Plan, plan, plan.

The outing included an engaging mix of conversations. We're both Christian and each feel a closeness to God in the deep wilderness – the more remote, the better. We toyed with a spiritual name for the route but settled on *Kitten's Got Claws* to remain consistent with the feline theme of the wall. The name seemed to fit since it looks easy from below, but has a few surprises – get out your claws. This summer was shaping up well; this trip was yet another beautiful day in God's country responding to the persistent call of the panther.

Hunting with the Pride

With: Bill Schneider (lead) & Adam Crofoot (lead) on 2015 August 30
Area: Marcy *Huge Scoop*
Route: *The Pride* (5.9-)
Duration: 5:15 a.m. – 8:15 p.m.
Reference Plate 1

Two weeks before on 2015 August 16 with Bill Schneider

If you do something long enough, you inevitably run into a kink. Bill Schneider and I set aside two days to camp and develop routes. Hit and miss thunderstorms on Friday evening, the night before, soaked the region. We hoped that warm temperatures, light winds, and the sun would dry enough rock to make the trip worthwhile. We'd rolled the dice and come out on top before. The camping/climbing packs weighed in at 55-60 pounds each: about normal. We grumbled but found our pace on the approach. We reached Slant Rock at 8:30 a.m. A few hundred vertical feet below the Haystack junction we smelled smoke, a scent that became more pungent with every step. Our first thought was that someone had built an illegal fire in the center of the trail. Our hackles rose. Instead, we found a ranger, two first responders and a woman packaged in a sleeping bag with a broken leg. She'd spent the night awaiting rescue. We watched the evacuation from above. The thumping sound of the helicopter dulled as we crested the north pass and plunged into the wet forest.

As always I was thrilled to be back "home" when we broke out of the trees along the *Panther Den*. We descended the glade and prepared to ascend an unclimbed corner; Bill scooted quickly up the bottom but encountered wet cracks about 50' up. The water forced a retreat. We hunted for dry stone lower in the Gorge and found an inferior low-angle line dry near its base, but the main walls and best lines were flowing with small rivulets. Our options were dismal and the sun hadn't shined as brightly as we'd hoped. High humidity would make camping unpleasant, and we doubted that conditions would change for the following day. Sometimes the best thing to do is cut one's losses. We cut ours and walked back to the trailhead after 13 hours.

The sting of "defeat" was palpable; the strain on our bodies from carrying such weight up the rocky trail didn't help. We decided that a three-day window of clear weather would be prudent in the future (though I don't always listen to my advice). Another day in the Gorge, another adventure even if it wasn't the one we envisioned! There's a lesson inherent to every trip. Sometimes the lesson is frustrating and humbling – it's all part of the experience. Such days keep one from taking climbing or oneself too seriously.

August 30

Though I'd only met Bill recently, we put our time together to good use with three trips into the Gorge over a month and a half. We were on a quest to finish what we started in June when the corner of the *Huge Scoop* was too wet. The proposed line seemed like a grudge match with Mt. Marcy. We're tenacious (or stupid) enough to continue until we either succeed or get too old to try! "Good things come to those who wait" is an overused

Left: Bill leading pitch two.

Above: Various features in the Huge Scoop.

but often appropriate phrase. When a clear weather window preceded August 30th, we decided to finish the project with Adam Crofoot in the mix. I prayed that the route would be a success. In the end, the experience surpassed expectations. Adam commented, "It would be a classic road-side climb."

The approach had, by now, become nearly second nature. Pace, breaks, food, etc. were dialed in. Our usual routine places a brief break immediately after Hogback Brook, a longer one at Slant Rock and a final respite to replenish the water supply at a spring near the Haystack Trail junction. Our next stop was the climb.

We arrived at the *Huge Scoop* at 9:30 a.m. I breathed a loud sigh of relief when I saw that the upper corner/roof system was dry. We unpacked, flaked the ropes, sorted gear and readied a small climbing pack with necessities for the ascent. Adam was leading the slab along the corner 30 minutes later which gave us ample time to accomplish the goal if all went well.

While I was belaying, a pebble zipped by with a "whirrrr." Even small projectiles travel fast enough to do damage. It wasn't long before Adam had climbed the first pitch (5.7) and set up an anchor in the top right-hand corner. We followed, and Bill began studying

Adam climbs the handcrack of pitch two.

the next pitch; the crux was his to lead. The obvious line followed a crack up a multi-tiered roof system then traversed right to a deep splitter crack formed when a house-sized piece of anorthosite shifted a few inches.

He moved left across the slab to a crack below a precariously cantilevered stone. The intimidating block was four feet long with space between it and the cliff. It projected over the underlying slab, and common sense screamed, "Do not touch!" Bill dubbed it the *Dong of Death*, a name that spawned a string of jokes for the following nine hours. Bill traversed back to the corner after brushing past the tip of the anorthositic "dong." Lichen made traversing the slab difficult.

He was soon systematically navigating the first tier of the roof; his movements made the pitch look easy as he buried gear deep in the crack of the corner. I watched with a slight bit of apprehension. I noticed two trains of thought passing through my mind. My fear of heights briefly escaped from its holding pen, something that occurs every now and again. I was also in "student mode" – watching and committing to memory how he placed the gear and worked the ropes. The double ropes were placed nearly parallel to one another and positioned in such a way that eliminated rope drag. He continued past the final tier and explored up and left (slightly above the roof). He found that the best line did, indeed, lead to the aforementioned splitter crack. The traverse was the crux of the line. There was little to grab, and only small holds underfoot. Once at the crack, he climbed another 15' to its top where he built an anchor and belayed. I climbed next.

I brushed the *Dong* with my shoulder en route to the corner. Even that made me uneasy. The cliff was comprised of six distinct tiers fractured both horizontally and vertically (such as the *Rumours of War* route 50' to the left). It looked like a portion of the cliff might collapse if the *Dong* was released though that's likely just my perception. Once at the corner, I realized the quality of the route was excellent. The cracks were deep, and the horizontals on the adjacent wall made foot placement intuitive. Bill had placed cams deep in a wide crack that swallowed my arm up to my shoulder. My fear of falling evaporated. A few more moves set me beyond the lip of the roof where I held myself in place by a secure finger lock in a smaller crack. I felt apprehensive as I looked at the crux.

Traversing right toward the next crack meant leaving the security of the area to which I was clinging – it was only about seven feet to the next good hold (my wingspan is six feet from fingertip to fingertip). Only small (crimpy) holds aided the traverse. I moved out and shoved my arm up to my wrist in the splitter crack…just as my foot slipped. I was on belay, so I wasn't going to fall, but my body swung slightly past the crack in which my arm was jammed. I felt my radius and ulna flex and knew that they were close to breaking. My arm went numb to the shoulder – another alarming sensation given our location. It was several seconds before feeling returned. I ascended the vertical crack; sharp crystals within scraped and dug into my skin. The feeling reinforced my feeling of security.

I heard Bill say, "Look up here!"

My gaze was answered with the shutter click from his camera. I'm usually the one uttering such words to partners perched in unnerving positions. The crack transitioned to a "horizontal" at its top which created bomb-proof handholds. I climbed up and clipped into the anchor. Bill had followed an exhilarating line. Adam broke through the roof like a master. It didn't take him long to reach our position. I was free to hang over the side with the camera while Bill belayed – the perfect setup that also gave us a chance to chat about our respective reasons for visiting such a remote area.

Bill reached out, touched the adjacent wall and looked back at me. "Nobody's *ever* touched this before, nobody."

My smile matched his. "That's definitely part of the allure," I said. "No feeling compares."

I then realized that Panther Gorge had forged a unique brotherhood over time. Only a handful of people feel inclined to subject themselves to a day this long for a route that may or may not "go."

Adam led the third pitch, first traversing out to the left along a fingercrack. The protection ran out, so he worked back to the anchor and put the route up a small corner that led up to the dimpled slab near *Wreck of the Lichen Fitzgerald* – more moonrock (a nickname for the weathered anorthosite). He kept the routes independent of one another by aiming for the right-hand of two opposing corners. He climbed another short corner after 120' and belayed near a steep run of slab with…wait for it…more cracks.

Pitch four followed the cracks in the wall up to the forest where we bushwhacked through a sea of krummholz to the belay station atop the *Wreck* line. The day seemed to flow smoothly compared to some outings in the past. There was no rain, no threatening clouds, no biting flies – it was perfect. We were smart enough to carry 2 liters of water with us, so we didn't dehydrate by underestimating the route or water supply. All that remained was the rappel. We followed the 2014 line of descent.

After 5.5 hours, we were back at our packs basking in a moment that can only be defined as a feeling of pure fulfillment and friendship in a remote, peaceful setting. We discussed adding a shorter route but wanted to finish before 9 p.m. Adam and I had to work the next day, and it was nearly 4:00 p.m. Additional ambitions would have to wait.

With the approach, exit and bushwhack on the Marcy side dialed in, the route and sometimes weather were the primary wildcards at this point. Seepage on the walls and the exact line determine how long a day will take or if it will even "go" at all. The long moderate multi-pitch routes average between 4-6 hours each, but they are worth the effort. The memories will last a lifetime and, God willing, the routes will endure far longer.

Finding the Promised Land

With: Dan Plumley on 2015 September 19
Area: Marcy *Panther Den* Buttress
Route: *Promised Land* (5.8)
Duration: 5:30 a.m. – 12:30 a.m.
Reference Plates 1, 2

Three, two, one..., "beep, beep, beep." It was an act of sheer will that removed me from the bed when the alarm sounded. After a summer of early morning weekend starts, getting up in the dark was wearing thin. Decreasing daylight and the wear and tear on my body, especially my knees, from so many trips with a heavy pack did nothing to boost my ambition. It was time to make one last rock climbing trip into the Gorge. Dan Plumley of Adirondack Wild accompanied me.

I've learned much over the years about pushing my limits. I experienced several internal warning signs as I readied myself, so I knew to err on the side of caution during this foray. I'd be leading most of the climb, so I targeted an easy route on a buttress adjacent to the *Feline Wall*. It looked like comfortable slab climbing to a huge boulder halfway to the cliff top.

A 4:30 a.m. start put us at the Marcy/Haystack col at 11:00 a.m. Twenty minutes later, I broke through the krummholz near the *Panther Den* and waited for Dan as the wind whipped up the valley. Gusts were forecast to be strong, but I'd be happy so long as the associated rain held off until after the climb. As I've mentioned, I find it satisfying to listen to each person's exclamation when they behold the view for the first time. I was well ahead of Dan and waited on a rock at the top of the glade. A thrashing sound signaled his approach.

I was already wearing a smirk when I heard, "Holy crap!" which echoed off the crags of Haystack – precisely what I expected.

We descended and re-entered the woods a few hundred feet lower. Ten minutes later we reached the lowest portion of slab before the *Feline Wall*. The wall hosts three routes: *Kitten's Got Claws*, *The Cat's Meow* and *The Bushy Pussy*. We would begin our route on the buttress to the north; it overlooked the trio of routes. The hour hand passed noon by the time we were ready to climb. Sunset was at 7:00 p.m., so we had sufficient time if all went smoothly.

I quieted my mind before selecting a starting point below a rising ramp that led to steep face climbing. Small edges and nubs then connected to a horizontal crack 50' above the glade. It was steeper than I'd envisioned, but there were also more cracks than I initially thought, so it struck a comfortable balance. I "welded" the chocks into the cracks, tugging on each piece hard to set them, and climbed while absorbing the views. A glance to the south spotlighted the *East Face* – always an inspiring sight.

Continuing, I followed more finger and handcracks. They petered out 10' below a band of cedar and grass – the crux of pitch one. My legs began to tremble from exertion as I held myself in place, my big toes lodged in the crack, to study my options. Only my fingertips holding nubs of feldspar and the friction of the climbing shoes would enable

Above: Sheer walls surround the crux of the route.

Left: The author leading pitch three. Photo by Dan Plumley.

me to get to the bench of vegetation. It was time to either go for it or slip. *Trust the shoes and the gear below*, ran through my mind.

It worked out fine though I showered Dan with dirt and more than a few dead branches as I gained a stance. Easy crack climbing led to a spacious terrace below a roof formed by the aforementioned house-sized boulder; I set up an anchor and belayed Dan. The first pitch of 160' was complete. I scanned the panorama and relaxed. The view below showed a unique perspective of the *Feline Wall*. I grew curious as to what was above the boulder but wanted a mental break from leading. Dan worked his way up and commented on my gear placement—the chocks were firmly placed which made extracting them strenuous from awkward positions. Dan took the next short pitch up a large crack. He then walked up a ramp until he could climb over the lip of the roof. Low-angle slab led to a room-sized boulder. Beyond was dramatic terrain, more-so than I'd dreamed. What rugged beauty! Meanwhile, the wind increased and whipped our clothing about – weather was moving in.

An inspiring traverse begins pitch three. Photo by Dan Plumley.

I led pitch three. A traverse on a vertical wall in between our position and a steep run of slab was the first challenge. I walked over to the wall and found a deep handcrack below a small ceiling – an easy traverse. There were ample places to put my feet and lock my hands, so I relaxed and 'played' around as Dan belayed and photographed. The slab was positioned between two opposing walls. A wet gully that turned vertical ran up the left side (home of the 2016 ice route *Sorry, Kevin*). The combination created a visually stunning arena in which to climb, and was thus my favorite pitch of the route. I put on my geology cap for a moment and realized that it was a gully, not a trap dike as I originally believed.

I considered my options once on the slab. Climbing the gully would result in placing gear in loose stone. It was also less technical and led to wet ledges. The face with its many small edges and cracks seemed like the most appealing choice. I ascended to a narrow edge 15' up and placed a cam. I was above a mossy area along the bottom of the right-hand corner and needed to traverse to place protection. Getting there was easier thought than done. The details are a bit fuzzy, but I made a few moves and was soon standing in a large hole in the dihedral. I jammed a cam in a crack and worked back toward the center of the face then up to two parallel handcracks above a loose block. Loose blocks are an ever-present danger in the Gorge. The cliffs have not been cleared of debris as they are in the more popular areas.

I continued up to a section of low-angle slab which led to a vertical wall with several cracks and a short chimney below a ceiling. I studied the options along with the clouds and wind. I felt a drop of rain – the first of many – and hurried my pace. Once up the chimney, I climbed to a second chimney where I ran out of obvious moves. All progress halted for a short time. It looked straight-forward from below, but it was overgrown with wet moss. My remaining option was an exposed traverse and face climb next to the top of the gully. There were several difficult areas on the route, but this was my psychological if not the physical crux as any fall would not be clean.

I finally climbed into cedars growing on the nearly vertical face. My somewhat zig-zag path up the slab without extending the slings enough from some of the pieces created considerable rope-drag, so I felt like I was climbing with weights on my back. For those that aren't familiar with climbing, each piece of protection/carabiner into which the rope is clipped creates friction. The more angles, the more friction. This was a battle in and of itself! The subsequent bushwhack up to two stout trees on the opposite side of the moss-covered gully was comical and resting was a relief.

The weather continued to deteriorate as Dan climbed in a steady drizzle driven by strong winds. I heard grunting and hooting about 30 minutes later as he approached. He was sitting next to me at 4:30 p.m. – *Promised Land* was up!

We still had to rappel down the gully. I was curious to study the vertical chute from inside its walls. It was intermittently blocked with large and small stones. I abseiled over the first terrace and, once clear, hung free. I slowly spun under the roof. The section below was similar. The terrain after the 100' rappel felt similar to Colden's Trap Dike. A fourth class descent of 150' brought us to a final short rappel. I found myself dangling in front of a 30' deep cave created when large stones blocked the gully and formed a roof – another intriguing feature. This is why I love to explore.

Heavier rain threatened as we reached our packs at 6:00 p.m. The clouds engulfed Haystack. The welcoming Gorge suddenly felt ominous – I find it interesting how inclement weather and encroaching darkness can change one's perception. I knew we were in for quite a ride when the wind changed direction a second time while we rested near the *Panther Den* – and me without my raincoat. We pushed through the krummholz as the clouds furiously whipped heavy rain up the Gorge. Dan looked like a spectre in the dark forest as we crested the col and emerged on to the Phelps Trail which was flowing with water. The slippery stone slowed our descent. My pace was a little faster than Dan's so I waited at regular intervals and turned my headlamp off to enjoy the darkness. His headlamp looked like a distant firefly, a bouncing point of light illuminated the rain and, eventually, his form as he drew closer. The rain tapered off and the winds calmed as we reached Slant Rock. I thought, *Perhaps it will be dry for the remainder of the walk*. Did it? No.

We arrived at Johns Brook Lodge at 10:30 p.m. where the winds regained intensity. We again "enjoyed" something slightly shy of a downpour until reaching the trailhead. My fleece was soaked and heavy, but warm. I quipped that the rain would stop upon our arrival at the Garden. Yes, God has a sense of humor because the rain abruptly ceased as we signed out. Dripping, but thrilled from a day of climbing, we walked through the fog to the car and closed another chapter.

Tour de Gorge:
Exploring Marcy and Haystack with a Night Exit over Marcy

With: Adam Crofoot & Allison Rooney on 2015 November 21

Duration: 5:10 a.m. – 11:10 p.m.

Mileage / Bushwhack Mileage / Elevation Gain:

Approx. 20.75 mi. / 20.75 mi. with 1.7 mi. of bushwhacking / 6,000'

There are trips when a solid plan gets even firmer with the input of friends. The original itinerary was simple; to relax and explore. I hoped to reconnoiter the smaller cliffs south of Marcy's multi-pitch walls and bushwhack through the talus fields. I also planned to skulk around the crags on Mt. Haystack before exiting via the north end. Adam suggested that we bushwhack out the south end to the Elk Lake to Marcy Trail and climb Marcy before returning to the trailhead. It sounded like a grand idea, and it was easy to reorganize the original plan to suit our collective goals. The final plan involved bushwhacking along the Haystack cliffs, then crossing to Marcy and skirting the base of the cliffs to the *East Face*. We'd exit via the beaver ponds about halfway down and follow Marcy Brook south. Good things rarely come easily; great things sometimes ache afterward – in that context, we had a great day.

My family realized that my itineraries were often flexible and moderate changes were normal. My father (one of the people to which I send trip itineraries before each outing) enjoyed following the markers generated by my SPOT tracker. It wouldn't take him long to contextualize any changes to the original plan.

Adam atop a huge boulder on Haystack with the Panther Den in the foreground and Marcy's East Face in the background.

Left: A talus cave under two boulders.

Above: Panther Gorge Falls covered in thin ice.

The forest was still shaking off the night as we passed Johns Brook Lodge. I admit that I was thrilled to be spending a day toting a light load compared to the usual climbing pack. I was also relieved to have a relatively easy agenda without a climb in the mix. Rocks on the path beyond Slant Rock were covered with a veneer of ice. The entrance to the Gorge was underfoot at 9:00 a.m. We entered the balsams and held close to the broken crags of Haystack. Finding boulders fallen during ages past is typical, but a few tower above the treetops. We spied one from the base of a cliff and navigated toward its triangular peak. I stayed behind to take photos as Adam stood on its top. The Gorge dropped away behind him. The presence of a human seemed insignificant compared to the nearly 200 acres of cliff-surrounded forest.

We then fought through the dwarf forest, across stream beds, and up ledges to the *Ramp Wall* where thin ice covered portions of its base. Rough stone was transformed into a smooth rippled surface. Parts of the wall are prone to being wet which makes rock climbing challenging but bodes well for ice climbing. We then followed a drainage stream full of deep talus caves down to the next obvious boulder. When viewed from Marcy, this house-sized stone is the most dominant boulder in the area. I'd been curious about its details for years. A crack running up an overhang on its west side would make a great boulder problem – bonus points to anyone tenacious enough to carry a pad in! We descended along its north side, and Adam disappeared around a corner under the overhang. What a marvelous area. The boulder was perched against a slightly smaller one. Together they formed a cave with rubble strewn about the entrance. I pulled the camera out, set it to video and followed Allison as we muttered comments back and forth. The markings, colors, and chockstones in the ceiling created a visually intriguing area. Rubble and bottlenecked sticks in chokepoints hinted that it must have significant water flowing through it during spring and after storms.

Allison explored a smaller passage that abruptly ended, but there was an exit to the left. Gerald D. Murray's 1934 foray into Panther Gorge (detailed in the history chapter) partially inspired this trip via the Haystack side. The boulder cave reminded me of his description, "The heavy walls leaned over me, as a malignant blind threat of crushing death or lonely starved imprisonment, if I should stir a fundamental bit of the structure. A light lacking, the low black chamber behind kept its mystery. I clambered out of the cave."[1] We exited the eastern side of the tunnel, climbed some fourth class stone to the top of the boulder and surveyed the scene.

This is what exploring is all about, I thought.

Across the way, the *Panther Den* and *Agharta Wall* had delicate smears of early season ice. The *Agharta* ice climbing route was thin as were several unclimbed lines to its north. I took photos and made mental notes for use during the winter months.

The next stop on our tour was along an obvious section of steep nearly featureless slab – what we've dubbed the *Shield Wall*. The woods north of the *Shield* were steep and covered in a semi-loosely knit forest of cedar trees and balsam. Allison was in the lead when I heard her yell. We rushed over and found her in obvious pain spouting a few choice words into the forest; a branch had stabbed deep into her ear and caused a pulsing sound—the sound of pain. We looked for blood, worried that it had perforated her eardrum. She wasn't bleeding, whew! She's as tough as nails and wanted to continue rather than exit.

It is easy to get "cliffed-out" on this area of Haystack, so we set off on separate yet adjacent tracks in hopes of finding the most straightforward way down. Allison stayed low, I angled across the center, and Adam took the high road. I found a way down the ledges, tripped and instantly found myself hanging upside down by my ankles...chuckling like an idiot. I freed myself and dropped to soft ground before walking over to the base of a steep slab near the *Shield*. The forest below had been cleared sometime in the last 10 years (at a guess). It was obvious what had happened. A refrigerator-sized boulder fell from above, hopped the slab (leaving no scrape marks) and landed in the woods. It was sitting in the center of a small crater. The impact had scattered smaller stones and broken trees in the surrounding area. It is interesting to stumble upon such evidence of nature's power – the cycle of destruction and rebirth.

It was nearly 11:30 a.m. by this time. Rather than continue along Haystack, we felt it best to cross over to Marcy's *Chimney Wall* to study the smaller cliffs located to the south of the *Huge Scoop*. Crossing the Gorge in this area meant navigating the talus fields with their many caves and stone sculptures, each unique from the next. Most memorable was a 30' plate of stone trapped between larger monoliths, one forming a huge roof. It would make the perfect storm shelter though I doubt I'd ever find its location again.

The streams flowing down Mt. Marcy were icy and slippery with verglas (thin ice) as we ascended toward a slide south of the *Huge Scoop*. Frozen waterfalls and small cascades decorated the landscape. There are many small cataracts tucked under the protective canopy of trees. A blocky cliff and small glade sat at the top of the stream. We then bushwhacked for a few minutes to the south which led to a slide topped with an overhang – aptly named the *Overhang Slide*, home of the *Pi Day* ice route. The route was just beginning to form. It would soon be 10' thick. We walked up a gully and explored cliffs with splitter cracks, overhangs and other features that stoked our curiosity. This was all the justification we needed to return with climbing gear.

Continuing south, I heard the rush of water as we neared the ledges preceding *Grand*

Early season ice lines on the Agharta and Feline Walls.

Central Slide. Allison arrived first and yelled – she was in awe of the waterfall. The cliff on the left is about 100' high and overhangs above a cleft that splits the ledges. The adjacent face was covered in cauliflower ice formations with water running underneath. Every so often a small piece would bounce down and whiz past. I always find this area difficult to leave – such is its beauty, but we still had much ground to cover. To continue south, one must descend the slide drainage roughly 100 vertical feet and skirt around a buttress. This leads to the bottom of a rockfall that cleared the woods at the bottom right of Marcy's *East Face*. We climbed the rubble and worked our way along the grassy glade below the great face. Ice smears had begun to form here as well as on the walls of Haystack.

Bushwhacking is easy along Marcy's face as long as one takes care to listen for any ice that may be sliding down – after all, there's a clear border between the stone and forest for a reason. It can fall at any time especially on sunbaked aspects. Walking along the base can be perilous. Two friends followed a similar hiking track a week after this trip; one was hit by a small piece of ice that fell from *Pi Day*. It knocked him down and gave him a concussion along with a multi-colored bruise. It could have been much worse had the piece been larger.

We relaxed near two deer beds below the southern edge of the *East Face* – the *Margin Slide*. Depressions in the grass were a dead giveaway, but it's not surprising considering I've also seen bear scat in this area.

I shot more video as Allison quipped, "We should call this *Tour de Gorge*." Agreed!

The time was approaching 3:00 p.m.; we needed to battle the forest once again. The tour wasn't over. We still wanted to explore the beaver ponds before exiting to the Elk Lake to Marcy Trail. We have yet to find an easy route from the *East Face* to the beaver ponds, so we struck east toward the northernmost pond. The bushwhacking theme was tight balsams growing on talus. We balanced on deadfall and crossed a few substantial blowdown fields – just a few of many including a ring of deadfall on the Haystack side.

We found a surprise at the ponds. The northernmost pond was full whereas it was

Thin ice forming on Marcy. This forms the Apex Predator ice route (FA 2019).

nearly dry from a hole in the dam two years earlier. Gnawed trees, wood chips, and well-used beaver slides decorated the edges. Several hundred feet south we found a larger pond. It was empty with a thin sheet of ice around its edge. It crackled as we walked, the sun set behind Mt. Skylight.

We continued to bushwhack south through blowdown fields and dense balsams interspersed with a few more loosely knit areas. Signs of humanity make their way into even the most remote Adirondack nooks. Allison found a deflated balloon with the word "Frozen" on it. She tucked it in her pack – Panther Gorge cleanup crew. It didn't surprise me since Anthony Seidita found a "Happy Birthday" balloon to the north a few years prior. Farther along, we crossed a small stream that drained the *Old Slide* on the south flank of Marcy. We were soon paralleling Marcy Brook and spent 30 minutes walking along its bank; Adam to its west and Allison and I to the east. He found the way of least resistance. She and I used a strategy of brute force tinged with a bit of tenacity though we eventually took Adam's example and crossed over where we enjoyed the relative freedom of an intermittent herd path. Two hundred feet farther led to the trail where we took a break before ascending to Four Corners between Mounts Marcy and Skylight. The ascent drained my energy since I'd mismanaged my food, but a short break, sugar, and GORP alleviated the issue.

The consolidated snow along the side of the trail aided us as we approached the height of land. Dusk had overtaken the forest, so it was difficult to differentiate verglas from rock. We changed to microspikes as a weather front moved through – more perfect timing and a recurrent theme of adventuring in Panther Gorge. The calm day turned windy and cold, so the real excitement began when we broke Marcy's tree-line. It was long-since dark. Wind gusts added spice to the outing and made footing difficult in dull microspikes on bare rock. These moments make me feel alive! We reached Marcy's summit at 5:45 p.m. Only 9.5 miles stood between our position and the trailhead. The other side of Marcy was thick with névé and bullet-proof ice. A careful descent led back to the verglas covered trail where poor footing slowed our pace and increased our grumbling. The exit was slow and deliberate, but uneventful. We needed snow to fill in the trails, but dreaming didn't help our reality. One foot in front of the other for hours on end was the only way out. After a full 18 hours at 11:10 p.m., we arrived at the trailhead. It was a relaxing random scoot (bushwhack) with the crux on Marcy's summit rather than a cliff.

A Blustery Winter Ascent by Tooth and Claw

With: Bill Schneider (lead) & Devin Farkas on 2016 January 30
Area: Marcy *Panther Den*
Route: *By Tooth and Claw* (WI4)
Duration: 5:20 a.m. – 9:05 p.m.
Reference Plates 1, 3

Left: *Devin walking down the glade below the Panther Den.*

Above: *Snowy cliffs on Marcy.*

Keene Valley should have been firmly in the grip of winter; it was January after all. Instead, the temperatures were unseasonably warm, and the snowpack was moderate. Less snow equals easier bushwhacking, so I pondered how much ice had formed in the Gorge where temperatures were cooler. Thus far it had been a spectacular year for backcountry ice climbing. Sadly, conditions were terrible for the skiers. Bill Schneider and Devin Farkas, assistant director of the Outdoor Program at St. Lawrence University, were enthusiastic about adding a new line on Marcy, so we commenced planning and set a date. It's a blessing to have friends that like to suffer! A variety of photographs taken during the *Tour de Gorge* trip showed locations where the ice might be "in" (able to be climbed).

Temperatures hovered near 15 degrees at 5:00 a.m. as we sorted gear; they were forecast to rise to the mid-thirties in the valley – perfect. We hoped to have a firm crust on which to bushwhack from the trail to the climbing walls. We stepped off the trail at 10:00 a.m. and I sank to my knees in the snow even while wearing snowshoes.

I muttered, "So much for easy," and broke trail to the *Panther Den* while dodging snow bombs unleashed from the balsams.

Bill and Devin emerged soon after I crawled out of the final coniferous barrier. This trip marked Devin's first visit to the "promised land" – God's country. His expression hinted that he wasn't disappointed.

A large right facing corner that's usually wet during the summer held some ice though it was thinner than I expected. Mt. Haystack hosted ice flows on nearly every cliff. I thought that linking them would make an interesting route for the future. We descended to the southern end of the first glade where continuous tiers of ice led up to the vertical crux of *Cat on a Wet Tin Roof*. Enticing as it appeared, we wanted to explore more in-depth and find the longest line.

Bill broke trail to the *Feline Wall* where Devin took over the lead. A smear of partially delaminated ice touched down. Marcy's dark anorthosite had absorbed enough heat to make this potential line appear unsafe. It was safer a few months earlier. A nearby gully held enticing possibilities, however. I took photos and sent them to a friend, Matt Dobbs, who would climb it a month later with Charlie Beard and Jesse Colangelo-Lillis. They named the route *Sorry, Kevin*.

We climbed up the left side of the *Feline Wall*. I needed a rest, so Bill and Devin continued down to the *Agharta Wall* where the *Agharta* ice route was fat. They spotted no viable options for a new independent line, so we re-ascended to the ice tiers at the *Panther Den*. This is what hunting ice is about; exploration, trial, and error. We'd spent seven hours thus far, so moving deeper than *Agharta* felt ill-advised. The days were longer than in December, but it was past noon and we needed to make a choice if we wanted to exit by dark.

We did the typical dance of changing into climbing gear; a fun exercise in cold temperatures. I stomped around to get feeling back in my extremities while belaying Bill on lead. The first strikes of Bill's tools shattered the brittle ice. He tried several options before down-climbing and restarting on a thick adjacent run of water ice. We hoped that the recent rains in the valley and temperature inversions meant running water at elevation. This would have produced better conditions, but it had snowed where the lines on Marcy sit.

Devin enjoying the first pitch.

Bill leading the chimney on the second pitch.

Moderate winds swirled the snow north up the pass as Bill climbed out of sight. My toes numbed as I considered the characteristics of the route – would this hold consistent ice to its top or would it be broken by terraces of snow? The Gorge is a roll of the dice in any season so I hoped that this would be a good choice. An hour later, he set up an anchor, took up the slack, and put Devin and I on belay. I started climbing via a short vertical pitch before entering a narrow gully preceding a tier of thick white and yellow ice. I loved what I saw! Tier upon icy tier led to a large right facing corner. Another vertical section led to the belay station 150' up from the base. Any concerns about the quality of the line evaporated. It was interesting and offered a stunning view of Haystack's crags. In contrast to the routes on the southern/ southeastern slabs that are prone to baking, this area was protected from the sun by a nearby buttress. (Based on the second ascent in 2017, this is a reliable route.)

The warm valley temperatures didn't equate to warm temperatures on Marcy during our trip. The ambient temperature hovered around 20 degrees. Strong winds accompanied our ascent, so the wind-chill adjusted temperature was roughly 0 degrees. My feet warmed from climbing, but they became numb for a third time at the belay – a constant battle for me that I accept as part of the game. Ice climbing is not always comfortable.

Devin followed, and we regrouped on the spacious terrace. He then belayed which freed me to photograph the scenery across the chasm and the action at hand. Looking down the offset tiers was inspiring. Shades of white, brown and green led to the forest. Thousands of trees poking through the snow looked like bristles on a giant brush.

Bill scaled an ice-filled chimney (a mossy dripping mess in the summer) situated in a corner on the left side of the terrace. This was the money-pitch, but the ice was even more brittle than below which forced Bill to strike delicately to keep it from shattering. Nonethe-less, small plates occasionally broke off and bounced past our feet. Bill's meticulous technique hinted at his years of experience. I watched and learned.

The weather seemed to be changing. Strong winds became gustier. Nearby ledges that were covered with snow upon our arrival were blown clear before Bill topped out. The small shards of ice set free by his tools took flight to the south while miniature tornadoes of snow swirled along the wall. It was impossible to hear any voice except Devin's who was standing only a few feet away. Without vocal communication, three tugs on the rope signaled that it was time for me to climb. Given the temperatures and wind, I was happy to be on the move.

A series of awkward moves in the chimney led to another terrace where I could rest and look around. The large free-standing pinnacle of stone that forms the chimney pitch of *Cat on a Wet Tin Roof* sat to the right. I felt exposed as I committed to climbing a thinly-iced corner. As a follower, I wouldn't fall more than a few feet, but I wanted to climb it cleanly. The short wall led to a final committing move – a step up and left to lower angle ice below a left facing corner. Another 20' led into the krummholz and a talus cave that we nicknamed *Bill's Man-Cave*. He'd found a protected nook about 30' into an icy tunnel and was belaying from a pinch-point between two pieces of stone. The 250' *By Tooth and Claw* route was up. It had a completely different feel from *Pi Day* to the south.

Two rappels placed us back at the base at 4:30 p.m. Our escape from the Gorge fell in sync with a setting sun and ever-increasing winds that lashed the north pass. The efforts of trail-breaking hours earlier paid dividends; our footprints had consolidated into supportive pads. Thus the trip back to the Phelps Trail seemed more relaxed than in the summer when roots and talus are underfoot.

Some people may think that the overall effort of visiting the Gorge is too high a price for 250' of ice climbing. I believe it is a small price to pay for such indelible memories. These trips are not about the climb in and of itself, but the overall experience and uncertainties of a true adventure. It is a bonding experience with both the natural world and one's friends. Perhaps it is just my affinity for the area, but the memories forged during these outings seem to become more vivid over time. If the pattern continues, my later years will be filled with unforgettable remembrances.

One of the large boulders on Haystack in the north end. There's a small cave under this one.

Mt. Haystack's First Ice Routes: Orson's Tower and Fly By

With: Nolan Huther on 2016 March 5
Area: Haystack *North End*
Routes: *Orson's Tower* (WI3+) & *Fly By* (WI3)
Duration: 5:30 a.m. – 8:00 p.m.
Reference Plate 11

I rallied for a last big winter trip, heeding the call of the mountains after nearly a month of fighting the flu. The ice on Mt. Haystack captured my attention during the last trip. Photos of two short yet appealing lines fueled my urge to climb before an inevitable meltdown that would accompany the warmer weather and rain forecast for mid-March. No technical ice routes had been documented on Mt. Haystack, so it seemed like an opportune time during a winter suited for ice climbing at elevation.

A last-minute message to Nolan Huther, a student at Clarkson University in Potsdam, New York, secured a partner. I sent the message on Friday afternoon…for a trip the next day. Not everyone can cancel plans, finish homework, pack, secure extra gear, and mentally prepare for a long day with only three hours' notice. We'd never climbed together, but I knew from discussions that he was up to the outing.

The first couple miles' walk from the Garden was a dance on frozen mud and ice. It felt as appealing as it sounds. The subsequent few miles changed to an inch of snow over ice – bony conditions that were only slightly less tedious than the frozen mud. We finally reached semi-wintery terrain on approach to Slant Rock. It all changed at the Marcy/Haystack col when we stepped off-trail. Snowshoes kept us on top of a partially-supportive crust some of the time, but we fell into spruce traps as well. It was nice to find snow somewhere this season even if it wasn't very deep. We were trekking on only three feet of snow; some winters in the past boasted well over 10' of snow in similar terrain.

This trip marked Nolan's first time in Panther Gorge and his first backcountry ice climb; he reveled in the adventure. Only later when he authored an online article would I find out just how much he appreciated the outing. He broke trail to help me conserve energy for leading the climbs. Our first target was 500' south of the trail on the Haystack side. It was conveniently located 50' north of the free-standing pillars. We walked directly to its base in less than one half hour and were preparing to climb by 11:00 a.m.

The ice flow was 90' tall and split in the center by a narrow buttress of rock. The left-hand flow offered the most appealing line along another wall of rock to its left (a nice bonus if one brings a few pieces of rock gear). I started climbing and placed screws in bulletproof ice. Razor sharp edges did little to ease their entry. The route was likely "fat" and hard since it was protected from the sun by a buttress to the south. Awkward moves on account of the cedar made climbing the vertical pitch challenging, thought-provoking, and fun.

I rested on a terrace above the crux. A 15' curtain of hollow ice was centered at the route's top while several consecutive bulges sat to the left. I chose the latter option where the ice looked more solid. At the top of the bulges, I buried the pick of my left-hand axe and bounce-tested it. It held fast. I then swung the other tool. Time suddenly slowed as

Top: The author rappelling down Orson's Tower. Photo by Nolan Huther.

Left: Nolan rappelling down Fly By.

Above: The free-standing pillars.

the left-hand tool tore free. *The leader NEVER falls* echoed in my thoughts. The pick was only embedded in ice covering semi-consolidated snow.

    My body twisted from the force while the tip of the right-hand pick caught on the paper-thin bark of a sapling. The tree saved me from a fall that would have found me on a ledge some 15' below. I'd placed a screw, so I'd have gone no farther, but I would certainly have sustained injuries. In addition to the obvious perils of falling from a cliff, ice climbers risk being impaled by the tools, crampons, and ice screws if they take a lead fall.

I gathered my wits and took the route up a final bulge and into the krummholz where I set up an anchor and belayed Nolan. I scanned the scenery and felt the rope pull tight; he must have slipped getting one of the screws out – likely the one I had so much trouble placing. All the while, I scanned the cliff across the way. The view of Marcy's *Panther Den* was spectacular. Broken columns of stone were riddled with unclimbed smears of ice birthed from thick ice flows at the top. Nolan was soon next to me reveling in the feeling of climbing the first new route of the day.

The near-fall on the way up made me question the wisdom of attempting a second route – internal head-games are sometimes difficult to overcome though I wanted to "jump back on the horse." I didn't want fear to take root. I told Nolan that I might not be up to leading another line, but that we should rappel and bushwhack south to explore the options since we were near another gully.

I suddenly heard someone yelling and thought, *What the…?* A lightbulb turned on as I recognized the voice of Doug Ferguson of Mountain Skills Climbing Guides. He'd started a trip at 3:00 a.m. and had already climbed Gothics' North Face, Saddleback, Basin and was en route to Marcy. We chatted for a few minutes before he spotted us on the cliff. I tried coaxing him into the Gorge to lead a route, but he had different plans in mind. Nolan snickered at the absurdity of the encounter as we conversed across the void of Panther Gorge.

I felt relief and satisfaction once I'd rappelled to the base. *Orson's Tower* (WI3+) was done. A short bushwhack led to the aforementioned pillars (towers) – the inspiration for the ice route name. Orson Schofield Phelps described these "shafts" in S.R Stoddard's *The Adirondacks Illustrated* (see Phelps). The pillars were partly coated in delaminating ice. It was thin enough that I spotted a potential rock climbing route on its southern side; something for the upcoming summer perhaps. We bushwhacked south to a piece of talus that offered a view of both the Gorge and our potential second route. I silently considered the options, still shaking off the negative self-talk. A few minutes later, we arrived at its base – a wet chossy gully during summer. Today it was an inspiring 10' thick wall of nearly vertical yellow and blue ice. I studied it and regained my confidence; the ice was considerably softer which would make climbing easier.

Nolan put me on belay, and I started climbing. The screws quickly bit into the frozen wall. I relaxed, and the climb flowed – this was how it should feel! The grade eased at an ice gully after 50' – ice on the right and snow in the center. I'd no desire to slog through snow, but it was easy to keep ice under foot by following the bulges along the right. These led to a steeper finale.

I had to search for a strong enough belay point in the loosely knit mountain ash, birch, and evergreens. Where was the dense krummholz when needed? Icy ledges higher on the mountain loomed behind as I belayed Nolan. We rappelled down the 120' route in two sections. A stand of cedars halfway down on the climber's left of the gully was integral to the second rappel.

We heard a distant thumping in the air as we tied into the cedars – helicopters. They flew over the Gorge and around Mt. Haystack as gray clouds blew high overhead. The sound echoed from the various cliffs. We surmised that there was a rescue underway and this wasn't just a search. I later learned that someone with a leg injury was hoisted off Little Haystack. In the end, the event inspired Nolan to suggest *Fly By* (WI3) as a route name. On a sadder note, this day also marked when the DEC found the body of a hiker who died of hypothermia on MacNaughton Mountain. Life is fragile in the mountains, especially during winter.

Left: Nolan standing at the base of Orson's Tower. **Right:** Kevin leading Fly By. Photo by Nolan Huther.

We were satisfied with putting up two lines though it was only 3:30 p.m. Darkness would encroach upon further climbs. Lines on the *Ramp Wall* about 100' south were viable options, but would be on thinner ice and more difficult (Alan Wechsler and I returned for these in 2017). The day had gone well, and there was no reason to push the envelope, so we followed our trail out – again falling through the snow to our waists. I took solace in knowing that we were not deep in the Gorge and the bushwhack was relatively short. It would be a relatively early finish.

Nolan published an article about our outing soon after the trip. The following quote encapsulates his appreciation for the wilderness experience:

As we passed through the Gorge and ascended smears and cascades of ice, I felt as though I was in another time, and throughout the day there were feelings of such nature quietly playing in the back of my head. A set of three forty-foot free-standing pillars of rock we encountered proved to be particularly provocative. Kevin told me that these were described by the Adirondack guide Orson "Old Mountain" Phelps while passing through the region back in the 1800's. I distantly wondered how many people have stood at the base of these towers between the time of the guide and that of ourselves. It is surely well-guarded, for here there are no trails, no evidence of the passage of man in the thick forests under the looming cliffs and hanging ice. The experience brought feelings unusual in daily life, for it is rare that I can have the feeling that if I were to reach out and place my hand on some section of rock, that no one had ever placed their hand there, or ever will again.[2]

Pioneer Anomaly and Belshazzar's Fate

With: Adam Crofoot (lead) & Alan Wechsler on 2016 May 28
Area: Marcy *Agharta Wall* & Marcy *Panther Den*
Routes: *Pioneer Anomaly* (5.8) & *Belshazzar's Fate* (5.8)
Duration: 4:00 a.m. – 9:30 p.m.
Reference Plates 1, 2

Some people may define "a long time" as years when referencing the time between visits to an area. I tend to define it in months. The last trip was in March, and I felt driven to surround myself with forested slopes, birdsong, and the whispers of the wind. My wife had noted the tension building over the previous months.

"You need to get out for a long day," she encouraged.

The timing was right; the snow and ice had melted, so we hoped the rock would be dry enough to get something done. Thus began the rock climbing season of 2016. While every trip is unique, this was one of the most relaxing.

The season's wish list contained about a dozen unclimbed lines some of which included ones discovered by Adam Crofoot and Bill Schneider. I had my eyes on several moderate options for days when they were busy. Waiting for perfect weather is often easier said than done. Late May is usually a crap-shoot, and the long-range forecast seemed unstable leading up to this trip. One misses opportunities by being too conservative, so we rolled the dice when the storm probability dropped below 90%.

Left: *Adam looking for gear on the first pitch of Pioneer Anomaly. Photo by Alan Wechsler.*

Above: *Adam leading the second pitch.*

The Chronicles of Panther Gorge

Our stakes were higher this time. Adam and I planned to introduce Alan Wechsler, a friend/climber/journalist, to the Gorge. He hoped to participate in a first ascent and walk away with photographs and a story for an upcoming article. We started early in hopes of getting a jump on possible rain showers. Alan intermittently interviewed us during the approach. We began the traditional bushwhack from the Marcy/Haystack col at 8:30 a.m. and arrived below our first target on the *Agharta Wall*. One of our hopeful choices was home to an appealing cascade, but we had several backup options in mind. One was dry and positioned to the left of a huge overhanging buttress on the left side of the wall. Adam planned to lead and scoped the possibilities as Alan and I trekked south to explore another option in the *Huge Scoop*. It looked feasible though slightly wet. Discussion and agreement focused our attention on the *Agharta Wall*. The "game was on" by 9:45 a.m. – it felt good to be climbing again.

The proposed line followed a right-facing corner formed by a vast detached flake, a stunning feature with appealing geometry. The minutiae were unknown, and we expected surprises. Most of the rock in the Gorge is clean, but loose blocks are common objective dangers. Adam meticulously worked his way up the corner, tapping on a stone that answered with a ring – a disconcerting sound to both climber and the belayer some 50' below. He deposited small loose stones in recesses or tossed them aside. Once above a grungy corner, the line was clean and followed a deep handcrack that terminated atop a pinnacle to the left of a series of overhanging cracks. A flared chimney, handcrack and a vertical fingercrack were among the options. Our route would follow the latter.

Alan photographed the action from the north while "entertaining" a cloud of curious blackflies. They merely swarmed around his head, but they'd be interested in feeding in a few short weeks. I planned to be back around that time, but not as a blood sacrifice.

Adam set up an anchor, and I called to Alan. It was his turn. The pitch was straightforward, and it didn't take long before it was time for me to follow. The ledge at the top was narrow, so their respective stances left Adam better suited to play photographer. After a winter of ice or snow climbing, I often forget how sharp the small feldspar crystals in the anorthosite can be. Pondering such thoughts, I climbed past loose stones in the corner and arrived at the gong-like rock that Adam tapped while leading. I couldn't resist giving it a light hit with my knuckles. The flake rang loudly, but it was interlocked with much larger pieces and presented no danger.

The crack above swallowed my hand while the sharp edge of the 60' flake was easy to grip. I was satisfied with the quality thus far. I crawled up onto the belay ledge below a vertical wall, the next challenge. Adam had built the anchor in a fingercrack, the beginning of pitch 2. I looked around and noticed that *CrazyDog's Halo*, a route from 2014, was located 20' to our left. Though nearby, this climb was entirely different in style. The similarity was the view. The proximity of *Halo* reminded me that the routes on the wall were getting more crowded and keeping them independent in the future would require forethought.

Alan was in a semi-hanging belay, and I was seated on the ledge overlooking Haystack where a small cumulus cloud threatened from the east. My thoughts drifted to possible stray showers or storms mentioned in the forecast. It wouldn't be the first time we were caught in the rain, but I had no desire to climb a wet fingercrack or deal with the dangers of lightning on an open face.

Adam started pitch two via the fingercrack while I shot some blind photos of his lead, extending my arm as far as was comfortable while trying to frame him against the cliff. Any good images could be chalked up to chance. Alan and I chatted as Adam vanished

Left: Adam belaying Alan on pitch one of Pioneer Anomaly. **Right:** Alan following Belshazzar's Fate.

from view, the rope slowly disappearing from underfoot. Alan's last venture with me was a couple of years ago during the winter: a hike over Haystack, Basin, and Saddleback. This was the perfect adventure to get the ball rolling again. Two hundred feet of rope and several conversational topics later, it was time for Alan to climb. I broke down the anchor and followed some 50' behind; Adam belayed both of us simultaneously. The fingercrack and dimpled stone created a secure climb with big exposure.

A second crack peeled off to the left. It was good for placing a cam, but not where we wanted to take the route as it led toward less appealing options. The primary crack petered out at what became the crux move. Only small divots in the face bridged a span between the crack and a higher ledge. Several additional ledges led to a 10' tall overhanging wall with an obvious crack and chunky holds.

Once above, low-angle slab led to the belay station of *CrazyDog's Halo*. Déjà vu! We decided that extending our present line was impractical; the *Cloudsplitter* route was close to our right, and we'd likely have to join with one of the existing lines to breach the headwall. Thus we made the call to end our route after two pitches and 350' of climbing. *Pioneer Anomaly* was up. It had taken 3.5 hours to climb: 9:30 a.m. to 1:00 p.m. We rappelled and enjoyed the views that make climbing in the Gorge so dramatic and rewarding. We feel free and relaxed in this environment. Hikers on Haystack looked like groups of ants – our only indication that the outside world still existed.

Adam and I studied another line while we ate lunch in the glade. I said a prayer of thanks and Alan scribbled notes before we moved north to the *Panther Den*. Was the climbing over? Of course not, even if Alan was hoping to finish before the local restaurants closed. Upon arrival, Adam studied a difficult line that was on his to-do list. It was soaking wet – a characteristic of some of the hard crack lines. I, on the other hand, studied the glade. It showed evidence of an ice fall and heavy runoff from the winter melt...heavier than average from a winter conducive to building ice. A significant portion of vegetation had been removed.

We walked north to a 6' deep right facing corner, one that seems to be forever wet and grungy. Adam and I had previously discussed a nearby chimney 20' to its right – our new target. It would be a single pitch, but short is what we often look for when climbing a second route during the same day. Besides, it was 3:30 p.m. and the clouds were building.

Adam climbed a short face to a ledge then entered a flaring chimney. It looked awkward yet fun. He wriggled his way up and switched his position 180 degrees halfway up to a prominent roof. He warned us about a small "death block" that needed to be trundled by the last person. Removing it would make the route safer for future climbers. It would likely be displaced in the near future by natural forces. Adam worked through the roof and again shouted a warning about a large stack of blocks.

"I don't know how this is even staying in place," he quipped before climbing a crack off to the left.

We knew to pass with care based on how delicately he moved around the stack. The crack finished the route. Locating a proper belay station took time and may have been the crux! The krummholz above was dense, but the trees were small and insecure near the edge. Two nearby cracks in a mossy slab offered a secure option from which to belay.

I climbed next. The moves in the chimney were challenging, but a crack in its back created secure hand jams. This was a nice juxtaposition to footholds that were more difficult to locate. I felt the strain of a second climb as I used full body tension to remain in the chimney. I awkwardly wriggled my way upward to more apparent holds and neared the roof. I moved out to the right and face climbed past the 10"x 20" "death block." It must have fallen from above and, by luck, landed on end. It was precariously balanced and teetered when touched. I continued up the face beyond the roof. A long step to the left led to a ledge beyond Adam's gravity-defying blocks.

The vertical crack led to exposed face climbing and the finish of the route. I clipped into the master point of Adam's anchor before rappelling partway down to photograph Alan's ascent. Leaning away from the face, I captured some of my favorite photos of the day as he moved in and out of the chimney, the ragged anorthositic wall contrasting against the green valley. We were surprised by the quality of this climb. What looked like a consolation prize from below was, in reality, a worthwhile climb. The Gorge surprises us over and again which keeps us coming back each season.

We regrouped at the base and, after a quick discussion, named the route *Belshazzar's Fate* after the fate of an ancient Babylonian king. The biblical reference is a reminder to keep one's pride in check in all facets of life – including climbing. The name, *Pioneer Anomaly*, was Adam's brainchild. It's both an allusion to an anomaly experienced by the Pioneer spacecraft as well as how we're pioneering the Panther Gorge routes. New routes in the Adirondacks are rarely on-sighted from below in today's age; it's more common to rappel and explore it from the top-down.

It was satisfying to take a chance on a sketchy weather forecast and beat the odds. One can't always come out on top; future outings proved that! In the end, Alan's story was entitled "Panther Gorge Rocks" which appeared in the September/October 2016 issue of *Adirondack Explorer*. We were collectively thrilled to start the season on a high note. I prayed that logistics would allow us to chase the dream throughout the summer.

Embracing our Predatory Instincts

With: Bill Schneider (lead) & Nolan Huther on 2016 June 4
Area: Marcy *Huge Scoop*
Route: *Predatory Instincts* (5.9)
Duration: 4:00 a.m. – 9:00 p.m.
Reference Plate 1

It had only been a week since the last trip to Marcy's cliffs. No, I'm not insane though a few friends and family members might disagree. It seems that my body has finally adapted to high-mileage trips with heavy packs on consecutive weekends. The continued fair weather added incentive to pushing forth. Bill Schneider and I had already planned to visit the area when I invited Nolan Huther for his second trip to the area, this time for rock climbing. Repeat partners in the Gorge are a premium! Our target was the southernmost prominent line in the *Huge Scoop*. I'd brooded over the details of the cliff for most of the winter – how hard would it be? Would it go at all? The details looked interesting – especially the cracks in the left wall of the scoop and several small roofs above the great depression.

Nolan overnighted at my house, and the alarm went off at 3:15 a.m. The temperatures were moderate and a nice change from the prior week's heat. Our pace placed us at the base of the *Huge Scoop* before 9 a.m. Nolan had seen the northernmost wall (*Panther Den*) from atop an ice route on Haystack the previous March but hadn't explored the

Kevin leading the runout slab of the Huge Scoop. Photo by Nolan Huther.

Bill leading the second pitch. Which crack to follow? Photo by Nolan Huther.

larger cliffs on which we'd be climbing. A week of warm temperatures and little if any rain offered us the chance to climb an ordinarily wet area in potentially dry conditions. This was a golden opportunity.

We passed the second wall of Marcy – the *Feline Wall* – it was wet. My heart grew heavy, but I tightly gripped a thread of hope. The next wall was mainly dry. I rushed downhill and bushwhacked up the tedious slope to the base of our quarry. I found an answered prayer – dry anorthosite. A long-awaited plan coming together is a beautiful thing. I offered to lead the runout slab start; terrain on which I'm comfortable. Bill would lead the hardest pitches so we could put up the most appealing line. The blackflies had transitioned from annoying pests to voracious vampires in a week's time. Perhaps the wind would dissipate them as we climbed? Hindsight showed that to be wishful thinking. We'd donate a bit of blood to the cause.

Rumours of War, the obvious central route of the *Huge Scoop* starts near the center of the slab. I started the new route to its left at a four-foot high pancake of rock. The black slab in the *Scoop* is a technical step above friction climbing. One must use the edges of small features in the face. The only daunting issue was a lack of cracks to protect against a tumble. Twenty, thirty, forty feet higher I found a narrow fissure and placed the first small piece of gear. I could almost hear, *Kevin and his darn runout routes*, echoing in the wind.

I then followed a line up to a small overhang and ended the pitch below an overhanging crack in the headwall. It gave me butterflies based on how difficult it appeared. About 30' to the left were the easier and appealing twin cracks on the right-facing wall – the dream line I'd studied during the winter. I set up an anchor with tricams under an overlap and simultaneously belayed Bill and Nolan. Nolan had been photographing from below; his keen eye for perspective yielded several shots that captured the feel of the arena.

It was Bill's turn to pick a line. He studied the overhanging crack in the headwall, and we collectively agreed to give it a try. I belayed as he climbed up the slab to explore the wall's base. We were climbing on unknown terrain save a few photographs, so there's only one way to understand the details – to try it. Bill's effort testified to the crack's difficulty. A crux partway up turned him back after several tries. The main complication was that the crack was wet and slippery where it constricted – something we couldn't see from below. In the end, he fell lightly on a well-placed nut, and we continued to the original objective. I don't mind admitting that I breathed a sigh of relief. I wanted to climb the new route cleanly and questioned whether I'd be able to do so with a wet overhanging crack in the mix. He estimated the grade at roughly 5.11a.

Nolan enjoying the incredible cracks of pitch two.

Bill, still grumbling that he had to turn back, traversed south to the right-facing wall and up to a set of twin cracks. The wall overhung slightly with cracks that tilted about 10 degrees to the right. From my perspective, they looked deep. Once Bill gained the cracks, he lit up like the finale of a fireworks show. Phrases like "This is amazing!" and "This would be a classic at the *Spider's Web* (a crag across from Chapel Pond)!" echoed in the *Scoop*. His excitement was contagious. Every few feet, he re-emphasized just how good the route was. The holds were bomber up to a chockstone where he stepped left and climbed to a comfortable belay ledge – but not before hanging backward by his right hand and laughing like a backcountry madman! Nolan continued to photograph the action with my camera. Unfortunately, it jammed – the Gorge had killed another piece of equipment.

I climbed next. The cracks were as thrilling as advertised. They enveloped my hands. The footholds were good until the crux where the crack constricted. My arms lost strength as I worked through this section and found the next substantial hold or "thank God bucket" to quote Bill. I gained the face, clipped into the anchor and took Bill's camera as Nolan climbed. He traversed the slab and worked his way up to the crack as I leaned out to photograph. Each of us approached the ascent differently since there were a variety of holds (except at the crux). Bill dubbed the pitch *double chocolate love*. Nolan climbed quickly to our position where we jockeyed around to fit three people on the ledge. We then strategized about where to start pitch two.

The broken ledges and roofs were foreshortened from our perspective – a hundred feet looked like fifty. Comparing our position on the cliff to the position of the features in the photograph produced a tentative plan. Bill led the way since efficiency counts and the day was wearing on, as were the biting blackflies. The wind wasn't strong enough to keep them at bay.

Memories of double chocolate love were replaced with questions about what we'd find in the roof systems. I followed when Bill shouted, "Off belay!"

The Chronicles of Panther Gorge

Getting onto the line involved a slight down-climb onto a 65-degree slab leading to an overlap. Then it got steep. I face-climbed up to a small corner with a fingercrack and over to more slab. Unique pockets in the face, not the typical pitted moonrock, led to another crack and a prominent roof. I looked up with a bit of apprehension but decided to just climb rather than make a study of it. Copious features made it exhilarating rather than daunting. I buried my hands in the crack between the roof and the face. I then laid back from it thus pushing my feet into the surface. Hand-jams and abundant edges kept me in place as I rounded the lip and ascended the crack to another run of slab. I found Bill anchored below another roof above a tree island. Nolan quickly followed, and we restacked the rope for the final pitch.

Our choices included a short chimney directly above, a corner in the center, or another short corner to the right. We agreed on the central corner with horizontal cracks on the left-facing wall. It seemed like the most challenging and most aesthetic option. Based on our beta photo, this would be the last obstacle before finishing the route. Above was a tree island and low-angle slab, some of which I'd rappelled in 2015. There was no lack of gear in the wall, and Bill made short work of it as the clouds blew overhead. The time was nearly 3:00 p.m.; we'd been on the wall for a long time. He yelled to be careful of the loose pancakes of stone as he stepped onto the low-angle face. I paid out the rope as he climbed ever higher before finally setting up an anchor. I went next using a combination of the deep horizontal cracks and the crack in the corner. The moves seemed intuitive. Within minutes I was on the upper face avoiding the loose rock. I drifted right, past a large tree island from which Bill was belaying. I stopped and waited for Nolan…it didn't take him long to catch up. We then traversed across the top of the island while avoiding a huge ant hill that Bill had stirred up. They were angry at the intrusion and searched a broad area for the perpetrator (who was hiding far away in the trees). A large spruce marked the end of the route where we prepared to rappel down the face along *Twin Fracture Gully*. Two rappels placed us close to the bottom of the *Scoop* where we could safely walk back to our packs.

It had taken roughly 7.5 hours to put up the route – a new on-wall duration record for our trips. After so many outings to the Gorge, you'd think that the exit would become easier. No. If there was a lesson to be learned from this trip, it was that the possibilities are seemingly endless and each outing renews my feeling of exhilaration. Conversations regarding the route name ensued immediately after the rappel but weren't finalized until Bill came up with the name *Predatory Instincts* a few miles from the trailhead. He managed to encapsulate the feel of the route with one of his classic feline allusions.

Bill climbing the final pitch of the route.

Lost in a Galaxy of Tears

With: Dustin Ulrich (lead) on 2016 June 17
Area: Marcy *Feline Wall* Buttress
Route: *Galaxy of Tears* (5.9)
Reference Plate 1

Dustin approaching the crux of the route on pitch two.

Our "galaxy trip" marked one of the trips where camping was part of the itinerary (June 17-19). Bivouacking between the jaws of Haystack and Marcy is surreal and magnificent though it takes a tremendous amount of energy to bushwhack into the Gorge with such a heavy load. I yearned to experience the cool evenings, birdsongs, and relaxation associated with the cliffs so close at hand. Friday's plan was to attempt a new route with local guide and climber Dustin Ulrich. His would be a day trip, but I planned to bushwhack back to the Phelps Trail to meet another friend, Loren Swears, who planned to spend Friday night through Sunday evening climbing and exploring.

My pack was 65 pounds with the overnight gear, but we managed to maintain a steady pace and arrived at the base of the *Agharta Wall* before 9:00 a.m. The blackflies buzzed a greeting as the summer heat rose with the sun. It was forecast to be in the 80's with a light breeze. I'd pre-selected a new line on the fringe of the *Agharta/Feline Walls*. To set the stage, the southern edge of the *Feline Wall* is a buttress that delineates it from the *Agharta Wall*. We were inclined to begin a route on the southern side of the buttress using a rising handcrack to reach a 20-foot flake that seems to defy gravity. It seemed as if a sneeze might topple it.

Attaining the crack was a difficult task even though it began at the forest floor. It was wet and, in hindsight, I wonder if it ever completely dries. But I'm ahead of myself.

Left: Weathered anorthosite on the final pitch.

Above: *Galaxy of Tears* follows the top of the buttress.

Dustin tried various options and backed down after encountering either wet or crumbling rock. He settled on a precarious face climb to gain the line a little higher up—the dripping crack in a slightly overhanging wall. Carefully ascending, he slowly progressed as the water soaked his arms and chilled his hands. Rather than describe the next hour and a half, I'll merely say that we had to retreat. I suspect that water enters cracks hundreds of feet higher and trickles under the buttress before exiting in this area. The dry weather of late did little to diminish the flow. I looked at it months later, and it was still wet. He was frustrated with the retreat, and I was disappointed that I didn't account for this kink in the plans. That's how it sometimes plays out.

I had a viable backup plan in my pocket and said, "Don't worry about it. There's another option around the corner that will be just as good."

He seemed a little perplexed as we walked north. An obvious crack rose 100' up a steep featured face. Our frustrations evaporated in contrast to the dripping water around the corner. Dustin meticulously climbed up a fingercrack leading to a face with nubby chunks of feldspar below a handcrack. He cleaned small bits of moss out of the way and continued. Meanwhile, the sun baked my neck and blackflies swarmed. He disappeared over the top of the wall and set up an anchor – I prayed that he did it quickly. My immediate urge was to climb fast to be rid of the vicious bugs, but I could only maintain a steady pace at the bottom. The handcrack required thought; the moves weren't as intuitive as I'd envisioned. I enjoyed having to think about each hand and foot placement. Cerebral climbing's better than simply muscling my way up – the deep crack and featured face created such a climb. What we preliminarily graded as 5.7 was harder in reality.

I found Dustin at an anchor built in several cracks next to a three-foot wide flake that overhung the *Agharta* amphitheatre. The 10' deep crack was partially filled with pieces of stone, large and small. Someday this detached flake will fall to the forest. I looked up and gasped in awe of the *Agharta Wall*. I'd never seen it from this angle. The exposure to the south was intimidating and inspiring. It also gave me a good vantage point to photograph three prospective new routes.

Pitch two appeared to be the most straightforward section based on my photographs. I assumed it was a low-angle slab. The reality was a complete surprise. A defined fingercrack paralleled an arête that fell away 100' to the base of the *Agharta Wall*. My original thought was to follow the crack then break right at a large overhang. Dustin envisioned a more exciting option. He gained the crack and stepped left over the edge and out of sight (which was also a roof over the large flake). Reappearing, he yelled that there was a hard line under the roof – info for the future.

"Yes, I bet there is," I mumbled.

He continued up the crack and explored left around the overhang which placed him 100' higher along the same roof. The stone above him looked sheer and featureless from my stance. He methodically climbed, glancing and tapping to the left and right, before disappearing above a ledge at the next belay point. My heart rate quickened as I tried to work out the movements of what he had climbed. It wasn't straightforward.

"On belay," heralded my turn as I suppressed a ping of apprehension before embarking up the line.

The sharp edge and excellent finger jams boosted my confidence. I slowed my pace as I followed left below the overhang and stepped down into a corner that led to the sheer seemingly blank face. I felt like I was stepping into the void.

Dustin's voice calling over the wind jolted me from my thoughts, "Is this excellent or what!"

He warned of an exposed hand traverse to the left of the overhang. A fall could send me over the roof into the open air. My screams echoing off the walls might be amusing to anyone watching from Haystack if I peeled from this area. The next section was up what's called an "open book" (a type of inside corner). The gear was good and positive handholds helped though I felt my fear of heights rising. I was clear-headed enough to realize that Dustin had picked a spectacular line! It had high exposure, thoughtful moves, and offered an expansive view to the south.

I found my partner standing on a large ledge belaying from horizontal cracks. Our next pitch began with a right-facing flake. He climbed it and grumbled when the flake closed to a mossy corner. If he fell, he'd hit the ground next to me. Upon climbing, I found that he'd buried a yellow alien (cam) into the corner as protection. I extracted it only after a tedious battle. One might say I was fighting aliens in Panther Gorge.

We crossed the top of *Kat Nap*, a route that follows a dominant corner far below. The route then toned-down on a low-angle slab. A short bushwhack led to the upper cliff band where we planned to finish the new line via a fourth pitch. I'd never been here. Such unexplored terrain always ignites my curiosity. We arrived under a 75-degree face 50' left of a large left-facing corner. The corner was mossy and the face beyond was less appealing than the cliff overhead. A series of vertical cracks and a textured face led up to a small wall. It didn't take long to realize that this was an excellent addition to the first three pitches. We climbed stone that was similar to a large cheese grater. Differential weathering had transformed the face into something far more featured than the typical moonrock often found in the High Peaks. Instead of finger-sized divots, we enjoyed two-inch deep pockets that overlapped and formed large jugs with sharp edges. There were infinite possibilities either in the crack or on the face. The funky face climbing led to a short traverse below a minor wall. Dustin broke left, ascended a small chimney, climbed more slab, and crawled into the krummholz.

We'd put up a quality route, more so than I initially imagined. What a pleasant surprise. At 600' long, it was one of the longest routes in the Gorge. I felt relieved and thrilled that Dustin experienced the Gorge at its best after the wet start to the day. The blackflies were voracious as we rappelled the cheese grater and bushwhacked down and left to the top of the *Feline Wall*. A single rappel of 200' placed us in a third class gully where we down-climbed to the glade and back to the base of the route.

We had chatted during the week preceding our climb – another mass shooting had just occurred. The insanity that's so common in our time left me feeling sad and distressed. The route name – *Galaxy of Tears* – seemed an appropriate tribute to the fallen victims of these senseless crimes.

Our exit together was brief...only to the Phelps Trail where I met Loren at the Haystack Trail junction. Dustin, who carried only a light pack since I kept the gear, ran back to the trailhead in two short hours. Loren descended with me for his multi-day adventure. I knew it would be fun since he's up for nearly any experience during summer or winter.

Over the following two days, we explored possible routes, ascended *Grand Central Slide*, crawled amongst the talus fields to find thick ice sheets, and enjoyed the views from the beaver ponds. Even with all of this diversity, it was the camping that remained fast in my mind. Sunset found us watching the hulking shadow of New York's highest peak creep up the flank of its eastern counterpart until darkness ruled. Songbirds sang melodies until ceasing with the fall of night. The ensuing silence seemed overwhelmingly loud (if that makes sense). Deer mice scampered nearby if there was so much as a morsel of food that had escaped the bear canisters.

Moonless nights are ones of inky darkness untouched by village lights while the Milky Way sprawls overhead like a galactic dragon. We, however, enjoyed full moon camping. It seemed other-worldly in this setting. We sat below the silhouetted cliffs of Marcy and watched a dim lunar glow steal up Mt. Haystack's ridgeline until it grew into a bright orb. It seemingly balanced on the summit before traversing across the valley. The great eye slowly scanned the wilderness on its trip west. Only the scurrying creatures of the night, wind, water, or an occasional shifting rock in a streambed broke the stillness. In a word, the experience was sublime.

Moonrise over Haystack's summit.

Sometimes it Takes a Woman to Put up One for the Boys

With: Allison Rooney (lead), Adam Crofoot (lead on Agharta Wall project), Bill Schneider on 2016 June 25
Area: Marcy *Panther Den*
Route: *One for the Boys* (5.9)
Duration: 4:00 a.m. – 8:00 p.m.
Reference Plates 1, 2

Left: *Allison crushing the new route. Kevin on belay...notice the headnet.*

Above: *Bill and Adam relaxing on the glade.*

Every day in the backcountry has a unique feel even though the general location may be the same. The collective energy during this trip was one of the strangest to date – not bad, just odd. Speaking for myself, I attribute it to the fact that I'd trekked into the chasm during four of the five previous weeks. I was exhausted.

I also noted that it was becoming more difficult to run into the Gorge and expect to climb a new route every time. I'd recently explored several possible lines and found them unrealistic or unworthy. Success has never been absolute, but a feeling of doubt had eked its way into recent trips. Nearly 30 rock and ice climbing routes were added between 2012 and this outing. Some of the remaining lines were chronically wet, difficult (5.10+), short, or of mediocre quality. Mt. Haystack's lines were practically limitless but usually less than 100' in length. Climbing the primary lines was our goal, but the result of nearing one's vision required a mental shift. We needed to be more strategic in planning the trips.

We were a party of four this time: Bill Schneider, Adam Crofoot, Allison Rooney, and me. This combination guaranteed a high heckling to hiking ratio. It also meant bringing a single rope as well as doubles (the leader belays two followers then one of the followers belays the fourth person as the leader continues up the next pitch). Our energy seemed fine for the approach though my knee and hamstring protested – a gift from carrying a heavy pack the week prior. A brief respite at Slant Rock reinvigorated me and provided humor. Unseasoned campers are sometimes good for that.

A man emerging from the woods announced, "By the way, *this* [said with confidence bordering on arrogance] is the last water," to Bill and Allison. He was incorrect by about one half mile, 600 vertical feet, and a dozen springs. "Last water of the day" became one of several recurring phrases.

We bushwhacked down to the *Agharta Wall* where our ambitions were focused. The blackflies were ferocious on this windless weekend. The 50+ bites I'd endured a week ago were just healing. The winged demons seemed much worse than last year. Bill announced that his energy was "off" and that he planned to follow rather than lead. That is, in part, how one stays alive in the mountains – by honest self-assessment and following one's instincts. We always leave ego at the trailhead.

Adam approached a route we nicknamed *Orange* since I used an orange route line on the beta photo. A car-sized, loose block moved when he placed the first cam and tugged. Allison was positioned below and felt sand fall on her arms. He retreated to a different position and reviewed the options. Without the crack associated with the block, there was nothing except unprotectable slab on which to begin the route. As a result, we moved over to an equally appealing line downhill to our right. Like *Orange*, it too started under the *Agharta* roof system. Adam ascended to a horizontal crack, traversed right and placed gear in an overhanging handcrack. Both the background and foreground positioned him in a fantastic area that spotlighted the ruggedness of the cliffs. A photo of this would later appear in *Climbing* magazine.

After a cumulative two hours of examining new lines and testing the waters, Adam down-climbed and we reassessed. The day was beautiful, and the scenery alone was worth the walk even with thin gloves and head nets to ward off the swarming blackflies. Yes, we're a dedicated if not slightly crazy little group! We decided to head north and attempt an unclimbed single-pitch crack on the *Panther Den*.

Allison planned to lead while I belayed. By 12:30 p.m. she was ready to ascend while Adam and Bill relaxed off to the side. The crack seemed straightforward and was located slightly downhill of a large and usually wet corner of the wall. Looks can be deceiving so I thought it might be more difficult than it appeared. Allison climbed to a small terrace below an overhanging segment of the crack and tossed pieces of stone into the woods to mitigate a few objective dangers. The overhang was the crux, but nothing she didn't handle with grace. There were tricky areas, however. Meanwhile, Adam slept on a small labradorite-riddled ledge near the glade, and Bill sat silently wearing his headnet. I quietly tended to my belay duties in order to let her focus.

Allison quipped, "Thanks for all the encouragement from below!" As stated earlier, the collective energy was low.

I threw out a sincere, "Good job," every now and again until she reached the top some 30 minutes later.

Bill, Kevin, Adam, and Allison on Haystack with Panther Gorge in the background. Photo by Allison Rooney.

I climbed next and found out why the crux looked somewhat daunting. It wasn't an obvious crack climb, and I was forced onto the face more than I envisioned. There were several apparent choices higher along the route including adhering to the crack or using nearby edges. I topped out, and she lowered me. Bill climbed next, followed by Adam. *One for the Boys* (5.9) was a reality by 2:00 p.m. This was a fun route up another plumb line on the *Panther Den*...kudos to Allison for the leading her fourth 'first ascent' in Panther Gorge.

Ambitions waned to the point where we no longer had the desire to climb, but we also felt no immediate need to hike back to the Garden since the weather was idyllic. Allison mentioned ascending either Marcy or Haystack. The latter sounded most appealing, so we exited the Gorge, lightened our packs, and climbed to the summit. Leisurely enjoying the views with good company was one of the most rewarding parts of the day. We relaxed for 30 minutes while a light breeze licked the ridge. Our vertical home away from home sat across the abyss – our spirits lightened. We left the mountain, smiles all around, at 4:00 p.m.

Much blood, sweat, and energy have been donated to these cliffs. Time feels like it has evaporated like a morning mist when I reflect upon the last few years. I remember trip each as if it was yesterday. I'm thankful for the unique imprint that each leaves in my mind, a set of memories that sustain me when concrete walls and a computer screen are my weekday companions.

Persistence Leads to a Tail of Redemption

With: Bill Schneider (lead) & John Pikus on 2016 July 30
Area: Marcy *Agharta Wall*
Route: *Tail of Redemption* (5.7+)
Duration: 4:20 a.m. – 7:30 p.m.
Reference Plate 1

The weather pattern during July was frustrating for climbing at elevation. Some of the remaining obvious lines on Mt. Marcy are a nightmare to climb with the mildest pre-trip rain showers. Heavy mid-week storms shut us down for four weeks – no sense marching back to look at waterfalls! When the weather turned for the better, Bill Schneider and I commandeered a Hamilton College student named John Pikus and set plans in motion to revisit the roof system on Mt. Marcy's *Agharta Wall* where we were shut down a month earlier.

The raspy sounds of an agitated saw-whet owl and a barred owl resonated through the pre-dawn woods at the trailhead. Given equal start times, the first light in June usually arrived after we passed Johns Brook Lodge. We were closer to Bushnell Falls when it crested the ridgeline and lit the canopy – days were getting shorter once again, but that's where a headlamp comes in handy. Nine-thirty a.m. saw our arrival at the *Agharta Wall* with our game faces on.

Looking back at June: the weather was warm, and the blackflies were terrible. I tolerated them reasonably well, but they'd started to gnaw away at my patience. This outing found us under partly cloudy skies with temperatures in the 70s and only the stray

Bill scouting for a safe start to the new route.

Kevin climbing textured slab to a crack. Photo by Bill Schneider.

blackfly passing within earshot. They didn't seem to be interested in feasting on climbers' blood. Other years have found them biting in late September.

The cliff seemed dry – perfect. Our first target and Bill's lead was below the largest roof in the center – an elongated triangle set into the cliff face. A daunting roof capped the feature. One can study beta photos all day and not account for the nuances of what lies within such a feature. I belayed while Bill worked his way up an ever-constricting vertical seam at the back of a corner. It disappeared as did the footholds on the adjacent walls. After an hour, he called for me to lower him – a tough, but smart choice. Like a line he attempted to climb in the *Huge Scoop*, he estimated the grade around 5.11. It will be there another day, and there was another option nearby.

Bill put up *Cloudsplitter* on this wall during the early 2000's. He noticed a crack about 20' to the right of his old route while studying our beta photo. It completely avoided the roof system by skirting its southern edge. Photographs and common sense hinted that there might be cracks above. Only the quantity and quality was a mystery. We scrambled up a precarious grassy slope and found a comfortable spot from which to belay. A nearby roof would protect John and me from any stray rocks knocked loose by the rope. Bill organized the gear and began the route at 11:15 a.m. He tested the rock with his nut tool.

"Tap, tap, tap, thud," answered the rock. Small areas around the cracks were loose but manageable.

It wasn't long before Bill climbed up to a chimney/corner on the left-hand side of the *Agharta* roof system. He shouted not to touch anything below a small outcrop near the corner and disappeared. In contrast to past trips with strong winds, we could hear each other well as he climbed.

I paid the rope out slowly before it stopped. I later realized that Bill was trying to connect seams and cracks on a face with sparse protection. He's meticulous, and his patience paid off. The familiar "off belay" then "climb on" phrases triggered me into motion. I climbed about 40' before stopping at a good stance to take photos of John before letting him

John Pikus on pitch one.

pass so I could continue to play photographer. Upon climbing, I left the small ledge, moved to the right and found myself on an exciting face climb. Bill had only managed to place a small micro-nut in a seam, but the edges were perfect for crimping so there was little risk of falling. Rather than ascending a scary pitch, I found myself in my element on the steep slab. Another 50' placed John and me along a left-facing corner/overlap. We stepped right onto a short runout pitch before the overlap arched left at its top. The next 30' ascended a deep handcrack. One would have to work to fall from this area! Bill was near its top taking photos from a small depression.

I led the top pitch which added another 170' to the 150' of the first pitch. I followed the crack to its end and climbed low-angle slab over a few bulges to a left-facing corner. The upper portion wasn't always clean but was still enjoyable. The opposing corners marking *Cloudsplitter* and *Agharta* were 50' to my left. This was a dramatic arena. A prominent corner had deep cracks in which to place gear. I then climbed diagonally right to steeper slab below a table of stone over a four-foot deep hollow. I tapped it a few times to make sure it was stable – the stone was firmly set. A stout tree then served as a convenient belay station.

Our route was up – John's first in the area. His expressions betrayed his excitement which, in turn, excited us. We opted for the latter of two decent options – bushwhack south to the *Wreck of the Lichen Fitzgerald* area or work north to the top of the *Feline Wall*. I led in hopes of finding the belay tree that Dustin Ulrich and I used in June. The bushwhack fell short of heinous and wasn't pleasant in climbing shoes. A few ledges and 15 minutes later, I located the red cord and carabiner around a thick spruce.

We discussed putting up another route and assessed two single pitch possibilities. The route had only taken two hours to climb – one of our fastest times. Instead of pushing ourselves, however, we decided to leave the Gorge early and relax the pace during our exit. It was 7:30 p.m. when we "clocked out" after 15.25 hours. I felt amazingly fresh, and thoughts of the next trip subtly invaded my thoughts. As for the route name; we decided on *Tail of Redemption* about .5 mile from the parking lot after several hours of tossing ideas back and forth. This line redeemed several failed attempts, has religious overtones, and incorporates a feline theme.

Climb After Slime and You Moss be Kidding Me!

With: Alan Wechsler (lead) on 2016 August 6
Area: Marcy *Panther Den*
Routes: *Climb After Slime* (5.8) & *You Moss be Kidding Me!* (5.7)
Duration: 4:30 a.m. – 10:00 p.m.
Reference Plates 1, 2

A flash of lightning startled me awake at 1:30 a.m. Wind-driven rain tapping against the window brought me to a conscious state.

"Give me a break," I muttered. The radar showed a dozen thunderstorms moving east across the High Peaks – spawned by a cold front.

The bottoms of the green amorphous blobs only brushed Keene Valley, so perhaps Mt. Marcy remained dry. So much for my statement in the *One for the Boys* chapter. We'd be throwing strategic planning around the weather to the wind. My climber/journalist friend Alan Wechsler had driven up and was car-camping nearby, so we were committed to our plans regardless of conditions. He didn't come only to climb but to write an article for the November 2017 issue of *Climbing* magazine.

I fell back into an unsettled sleep and rechecked the radar when my alarm sounded at 3:15 a.m. It couldn't be worse – two large cells were located an hour to the west and targeting Mt. Marcy. My enthusiasm ebbed, but I readied myself (walking around under a black cloud) and met Alan at Rooster Comb Trailhead.

Left: *Kevin getting ready to lead pitch one. Photo by Alan Wechsler.*

Above: *Alan taking notes at the base of the Panther Den.*

Alan traversing after the handcrack.

The first drops of rain spotted the windshield as we drove to the Garden Trailhead at 4:15 a.m. It was pouring with lightning flashing in the background by the time we began the slog. I don't mind objective challenges, but this bordered on the absurd. It was one of those "God has a sense of humor" moments. The deluge turned into a light rain a few minutes later. None-the-less I silently brooded in the knowledge that our day was likely going entail a long hike with little climbing unless we targeted Haystack's *V Wall* which would be fun, but of lower angle. The dew point was notably high so the stone would also take longer to dry.

Showers eventually moved out of the area to assault Vermont and the first rays of soft morning sunlight crested the ridge as we walked up the incline between Hogback Brook and Johns Brook, about halfway through the approach. The dim light in combination with valley fog produced a beautiful scene – a consolation prize, perhaps. Climbing conditions continued to seem bleak as I glanced up from a clearing .25 mile past Slant Rock. A hanging cloud stubbornly hugged Mt. Marcy's ridge. Wet trees in the Gorge foreshadowed what was to come. Or did they? The gloomy conditions of the north side miraculously disappeared as we descended south.

Sun and strong winds rekindled my enthusiasm as we erupted from the trees at the top of the *Panther Den*. It had rained, but the rock was dry except for the usual seepage from some of the cracks. Our target was on the obvious prow at the bottom of the first glade. I looked up, and there was no water on what I perceived to be the crux. The natural outlet at the bottom of a technical gully would serve as the start to keep the line independent though one could begin to the left on the runout start of *Cat on a Wet Tin Roof*. The prow looked imposing and, at a glance, was the undeniable highlight of the route. A dominant flake about 60' up looked aesthetic if we could attain it. Photographs suggested a deep crack behind it, but it didn't connect with the gully.

Alan took the first pitch, placed a couple of cams and stopped to reconsider. The first 15' were vertical and spotted with wet moss and algae – easy in dry conditions. I offered to take over. I was used to climbing blocky unclean stone. I lowered him and took over. The wet moss likely upped it a grade, but good feet and gear gave me the confidence to ascend without issue. The unappealing moves off the ground transitioned to a "fun-five" gully with copious cracks. I followed them and set up a belay below the flake for Alan to get some lead time. He climbed to my position where we studied the proposed line. *Note:* one can combine the gully and flake into a single pitch without incurring rope drag. Keeping them separate during the first ascent seemed prudent, however.

Attaining the twin fingercracks below the flake was the crux. Small crimps on a near vertical wall offered the only holds. Alan tried several strategies before gaining the cracks and climbing up to the large right-facing flake. The crack behind the flake ate small to mid-size cams as he ascended 30' up to its top where he found two choices: move left to a questionable overlap or right via a horizontal. This is where studying beta photographs proved valuable. I noticed a black line on the photo several months prior, but couldn't ascertain whether it was a useless seam or deep crack that we could use as protection. We needed to choose well since Alan was running out of gear.

We discussed the options. Alan had a first-hand perspective, but couldn't see the outcome of either, and I was tossing out ideas based on reasonable assumptions. The horizontal turned out to be a deep, appealing crack leading to a wide arête. This added an airy traverse into the mix and made the route more appealing – perfect.

At the end of the traverse, he followed a couple of right-facing overlaps, broke onto low-angle slab and built an anchor somewhere out of site before yelling, "Off belay!"

The first moves helped me understand why Alan tried several options to attain the fingercracks near the flake. The traverse felt insecure, like I'd peel off and tumble down the gully (which was impossible as the second climber). A ring-lock at the first crack boosted my confidence. I stepped out onto the most exhilarating portion of the trip. The moves up the flake were easy and fun – a series of hand jams and laybacks from the sharp edge of the flake. The fracture was unweathered and sharp like a giant force had recently detached the massive piece and left thousands of razor-sharp tips. They added several small cuts to my growing collection. Mixing my blood with the mountain was a regular event and a small price to pay.

Edging out onto the horizontal was a completely different experience. I inched out onto the prow with nubs of feldspar serving as good stances while my fingers grasped the edge of the crack. It ended all too soon. I looked down where the 80-degree arête turned vertical a few feet below me. I couldn't see the bottom of the wall, only the grassy slope on the edge of the balsam forest. As counterintuitive as it may seem for non-climbers, there's nothing as peaceful as dangling from a wilderness cliff...feeling the void below, yet knowing you're secure. It's not an adrenalin rush (a signal that I'm doing something wrong), but a relaxing moment when I wish I had the power to slow time.

Haystack's cliffs glowed across the valley when the sun penetrated the fast-moving clouds. A stray shower or thunderstorm was possible, so I kept a close eye on the weather after I felt the wind shift direction. The sky to the north looked ominous at intervals and showers spotted the landscape to the south near Allen Mountain. I hoped to avoid being drenched in the Gorge again especially before we finished the route. In the end, we remained dry, but I was later told that we received an inch of rain 10 miles to the north. God was on our side from start to finish.

Back to the climb – I ascended the face to the slab and stopped at Alan's belay station in a chimney formed by a free-standing pyramid and the cliff. Bill Schneider and I used the other side of this feature as the final pitch of *Cat on a Wet Tin Roof* in 2015. A belay this soon wasn't necessary, but it made communicating easier with the wind. I took the lead and scrambled up the remaining slab to a ledge and into the woods where I belayed Alan. A few minutes later Alan came up with a name...*Climb After Slime* (5.8), a play on the song "Time After Time" by Cyndi Lauper.

Our descent options were to either walk off or find a rappel station. I knew the top of *Panther's Fang* was about 75' north of our position. The bushwhacking was heinous atop the cliff so the shorter, the better. Ten minutes later I found a stout tree and prepared to rappel. I laughed as I descended when I noticed that the tree was only about 15' from the piton atop *Panther's Fang*. I didn't realize we were that close. We rappelled down the *Fang* and discussed our next option while re-nourishing. Alan wanted to try the *Fang*.

After discussion, we decided to top rope it and sought an easier line of ascent. Yes, it would have been better had we thought of this before rappelling. I suggested a crack 20' north might be an option – another unclimbed line. By the looks of it, there was a reason it hadn't been climbed. It was mossy yet amazingly dry. I had climbed the first 10' of it during Alan's rappel and was already contemplating it as a future option regardless of the moss. I didn't

Looking at the north end from the cliff.

expect to do it during this trip. We studied it for a few minutes, and Alan decided to give it a try. The crux appeared to follow a small chimney in the center. The entire ordeal took Alan 30 minutes; it looked like a surprisingly fun line. The route started in a 10-foot chimney which led to a ledge. I was surprised by the quality of the climb. It looked unappealing, but the handholds in the crack, jams in its back and secure feet made it well worth the effort – looks can be deceiving. Sometimes jewels don't glimmer as expected.

As Alan stated, "You don't notice the moss, and it doesn't get in the way."

A deep chimney at the top with solid blocks in the back and featured sides ended the real climbing. We topped out in a low-angle gully that led to a left-facing corner where I found Alan belaying. I suggested *You Moss be Kidding Me!* as a name and thought, *Next time, I'm leading it*.

We moved back to the top of *Panther's Fang* and rappelled again before Alan top roped the 1963 route. Given the time and possible showers, I decided to forego an ascent. Besides, I'd previously climbed it and planned to lead it when I had the opportunity. It had been a fruitful day by any standard! The days of beginning and ending under the light of a headlamp were upon us again. We began the outing with a horrendously wet slog and ended 17.5 hours later under a clear sky with stars twinkling overhead. Sometimes one rolls the dice and finds a winning combination.

Stunning Revelations on the Slabs of Marcy

With: Nolan Huther (lead – pitch 4) & Loren Swears on 2016 August 27
Area: Marcy *East Face*
Route: *Revelations* (5.8+ X)
Duration / Mileage: 4:20 a.m. – 2:00 a.m. the next day / 19+ mi.
Reference Plate 5

It is difficult to accurately describe the diversity, beauty and utter brutality of this trip. Many outings over the last decade have tested me, but never to this degree. The psychological demands were as grueling as their physical counterparts over almost 22 hours. It was a perfect storm of adventure. Nolan Huther and Loren Swears were my "partners in climb." Both were veterans of the Gorge though this would be Loren's first technical climb in the area; it was Nolan's fourth. The target was a line I'd been contemplating since Anthony Seidita and I retreated from it in 2014. I wanted a change from the northern cliffs to something seemingly easier (insert a hearty laugh here). I was in for a surprise – a revelation – regarding the grade.

The high dew point was unpleasant, but the temperature was fair as we departed the Garden. To my surprise and dismay, the trail seemed wetter than I expected. This sent my mind racing in various directions. It had rained more than I realized so I pondered whether the face would be dry. There are many places from which the top seeps so avoiding water can be challenging. There's no place to inspect the *East Face* except from inside the Gorge or from Haystack's summit. Sometimes you work with what you're given; we don't give up easily based on "what-if" concerns.

The excitement of the day started after Basin Brook. Nolan had encountered several black bears over the previous week at a climbing area called the *Beer Walls* – four encounters to be specific! I spotted fresh bear scat about a mile from Slant Rock and paw prints a few hundred yards later. I mentioned that we were close to a bear and Nolan balked; he was tired of dealing with them – the novelty had worn thin. We then arrived at Slant Rock and found a man and woman who asked if we were "feeling strong." I had a hunch what was going on. I wanted to see a bear and the devious/humorous part of me wanted to see Nolan's reaction.

"There's a bear," he stated.

Yes! I excitedly thought. I know that sounds counterintuitive to most people that aren't accustomed to spending time in the woods, but I only see bears at my house, not while on trips. We asked where it was located.

He responded, "Eating our breakfast over there near the rock."

We chased it off (not a recommended tactic). It growled then disappeared into the forest.

A few minutes later two men screamed, "Hey bear, hey bear...!" It had taken their pack and run off into the woods. It soon circled back to Slant Rock, however. By then we'd filtered water and moved on as they continued to deal with the issue. It's sad to see so many habituated bears.

Once at the col I contemplated the bushwhack. It would be longer than usual; even the deepest of the northern Marcy walls fall over .25 mile short of the *East Face*. That may seem like a short distance, but one must consider the terrain. To get to the face, we had two realistic choices: hug the cliffs to *Grand Central Slide* or cut through the talus to the slide drainage stream then follow it up to the face. I opted for the latter option in hopes of finding an accommodating corridor through the forest – I'm always trying to ferret out the best way to this or that. Sometimes it works, sometimes it fails.

We arrived at more loosely knit forest after twenty minutes of crawling through the talus. We replenished our water at *Grand Central Slide*'s base and traversed the *East Face* in a comical series of trips and falls. The ferns were almost five feet high, and the underlying grass was slippery. I watched Nolan slip and disappear just as Loren fell while I laughed… before falling. This continued for a few hundred yards. Less amusing were the wide swaths of seepage on the face. I couldn't bear the thought of walking this far only to be defeated by water. None-the-less, I felt excited to see what we could get done. I was home once again and hoped to finish what Anthony Seidita and I started years before. We arrived at our quarry at 10:30 a.m., 6.5 hours after leaving the trailhead. I said a prayer of thanks that most of our line appeared dry from below.

The first pitch began all too easily on low-angle slab leading to a crack with tufts of grass growing here and there. I didn't bother placing gear since this was akin to slide climbing but waited until it got steeper at a series of overlaps with a handcrack underneath. The climbing was fun though I wondered how a nearby traverse to a giant arrowhead-shaped flake would pan out.

Nolan called out, "150 feet!" all too soon as I neared the end of the protection.

I looked to the right and spotted a few nubs of stone that I could connect and delicately worked my way to the "money pitch" of the lower face. Until this point, I'd only guessed about what type of climbing the giant flake offered. A four inch crack rose upward at a 75

Kevin leading the runout pitch. The north end cliffs are in the background. Photo by Loren Swears.

Loren approaching the large blocks at the belay.

or 80-degree angle to a tiny tree island. Small ledges for my feet and hand holds along the edge of the flake created a fun, effortless climb. I set up an anchor above the shrubs after 190'. It was time for Nolan and Loren to get a taste of the magnificent *East Face*.

They climbed without difficulty to the belay station. Once they were secure, I continued up the crack to the top of the flake. The huge piece of stone was detached from the mountain; a feature that's easy to see even from Mt. Haystack. The wide crack it formed seemed to continue back forever into the blackness. Above the arrowhead, the angle eased, and there were several cracks in which to place protection. A combination of slab/face climbing with some wet areas led to a last steep move before a nearly level terrace. Pitch two was about 130' long; its end placed me below a vast overlap with a small shallow crack. It initially seemed to be a good place to build a solid anchor, but it took me far too long since I had to clean it out to find cam placements. Nolan and Loren followed easily. I awaited their arrival to discuss the options. Above me was a face without protection, but with plenty of features. It was slightly lower to my left, but climbing it would require a long traverse with uncertain results.

Pitch 3 was the undeniable crux, something I suspected from studying the face over the last few years. The large bulge I just described was always the great unknown—how steep, what protection, etc.? Photographs suggested that there was a corner or crack in the face to the right of the tree island on which to start the next pitch. Finding such a crack would allow me a protected start with only the slab above as a question mark. I knew that my experience soloing the area's slides would help me keep my head if the exposed slab above was unprotectable for long distances. I stepped behind the tree island and studied the vertical face. Divots, embedded feldspar clusters, and a couple of small edges looked reasonable to connect, but the wall was high and convex, so it disappeared from view after 20'. It looked fun, but not 350' up the face with an impending ledge-fall if I slipped.

Thus I opted to climb the aforementioned corner where I saw a 1 ½ inch crack in the dihedral. I only had to traverse a small slippery rail of grass to reach it. A mantra of breath in, breath out, breath in played in my subconscious as Nolan belayed. I relaxed slightly after placing a cam. Then I noticed water running out of a seam around the corner. The bomber crack wasn't solid at all but formed by a large block sitting in place. If I fell on it, the piece could move – it was useless at best and dangerous at worst. That ended my plan to climb the corner and left me with the unprotected face as my sole option (except rappelling to the base).

I inhaled a few deep breaths to regain focus and committed myself to the task at hand. I secured a sling to a tree so if I fell I wouldn't pull my partners from the face. I then marked some critical nubs of stone with chalk and took a first tentative step up. I ran out of good finger holds three moves later. Searching left and right, I located various possibilities. I was committed after the next move – no down-climbing. The initial moves seemed to take forever, but probably took no more than a few minutes.

During this time I concentrated on the texture of the rock, the position of my body, and my breath. I blocked all negative thoughts. There was no question of whether I would make this go, I had to. A large jug of stone about 20' above my partners eased my concerns as I grabbed it. I then heard a sound and realized it was a loud "Whew…" escaping my lips. The slope eased beyond the hold; a few additional moves led to the first piece of protection – yes, the first piece! I couldn't afford to feel complacent since there was also wet stone to contend with. This was a runout line (a route with a long distance between one or more pieces of protection) – a fact Nolan reminded me of for years to come.

As if to say, "It's alright, dude," a salamander walked lazily through the water as I ascended the dimpled anorthosite and small overlaps.

I had my eye on the prize – two adjacent room-sized blocks sitting high up on the face. I hoped to climb a crack between them but first had to reach them. The approach slab was less featured and quickly became a friction climb up wet stone.

I've done this on slides a hundred times, I thought.

My legs shook from exertion as I made the final push to the soaked cracks underneath the blocks. I set a large cam in place and knew the worst (or perhaps best) was over. The junction of the blocks, the crack, was filthy and the nearby stone hosted a carpet of lichen – so much for that option. This forced me to undertake a sketchy traverse below the right-hand block. I jammed my arms in the space under the monolith to compensate for a lack of friction. The far side had chockstones wedged in a two-foot wide crack which created the perfect belay station. I breathed a sigh of relief and felt the thrill of realizing my *East Face* dream line. The route had my personality written all over it.

Reality intruded when I realized that I hadn't protected Loren's climb as much as I needed to (there were two ropes, and I didn't clip his in all the placements). If he fell, he'd slide sideways. Grumbling, I self-belayed back to the large cam and clipped his rope through the carabiner. Once that was over I again relaxed and focused on belaying Loren and then Nolan. They climbed as I enjoyed the views while working the ropes. There was only one more pitch up moderately sloped slab to the cliff band and large trees.

Nolan exclaimed, "Kevin…," in exasperation.

He loved the line but was less than happy about the wet traverse under the blocks. I snickered. Once they were both tied in, I asked Nolan if he wanted to lead the final pitch. I'd let my mental guard down, though I could raise it again if needed. Besides, I thought it would be nice for him to lead a portion. I knew the top wouldn't be as runout. He agreed and explored a few possibilities including a mossy off-width crack and a moderately clean face before 80' of "easy" (5.5) fifth class slab. He ended up following the large crack along the block and disappeared from view.

It seemed to take quite a long time before he yelled, "Off belay!"

We realized the reason when we stepped around the corner. Everything was running with water. He admitted that the exposed wet climbing with intermittent protection spooked him. A small broken cliff band at the top looked less than pleasant to climb so he'd set up an anchor on its left. We climbed to his position, and I led the final couple ledges to a stout tree where we sorted gear and coiled the ropes.

The most straightforward rappel was to bushwhack several hundred feet north to a large cleft in the center of the *East Face*. It would require three 200' rappels. I thought that down-climbing the *Margin Slide* along the south side of the *East Face* might be easier, so we trekked north 75' and found a nearly vertical vegetated ramp that led up to the next cliff tier. This forced us to solo a 15' wet slab to more trees. Was the fun over? No, it had just begun! We found ourselves in a gully, and the only way out was via another mossy corridor – you guessed it, a vertical one. A few off-the-cuff remarks added some humor, but we pulled it off and bushwhacked south to the top of the *Margin Slide*. Its top was low-angle and ledge-ridden. We only entered the woods after the ledges became too precarious to descend safely. Down we went into a narrow mossy gully – again, nearly vertical. All forward motion stopped at a cliff.

It was time to rappel – Loren's first time. Nolan descended first and had the pleasure of unwinding the rope from the trees as he progressed. The edge of the slide was overgrown – helpful for bushwhacking but problematic when trying to throw the ropes cleanly. Meanwhile, I explained the procedure to Loren. This was not the ideal venue for a first rappel, but a prusik backup would help if he lost control. A second rappel led to the glades 100' from our gear. In its entirety, the climb and rappel took eight hours, from 11:00 a.m. until 7:00 p.m. We named the route *Revelations* which was another biblical reference (all the glory goes to God for another exciting route). The name also hinted at the surprise 5.8+ runout pitch.

I previously noted the arduous nature of this expedition; we were still nine miles from the trailhead and, in many ways, the worst was ahead. We were already tired – the thrill of the climb soon wore off. I was mentally drained and could have slept standing in place. We stumbled our way north through the slippery grass and arrived at *Grand Central Slide*'s drainage stream as dusk settled in. We needed water, and I needed to raise my blood sugar

Nolan flaking the ropes at the top of the East Face.

level. The ensuing 2.5 hours would be beyond grueling. It was time to navigate the talus in the dark. The talus fields of Panther Gorge are beautiful during the day, but not at night after a strenuous climb. Our position at the slide drainage stream gave us choices. We could either climb to the waterfall then contour north or try to find our way below the talus field before crossing through it. I chose the latter option, but hindsight made it clear that the first choice was the best.

With headlamps aglow, I led us up a small drainage stream and then stayed on an even elevation. This led into some of the most massive talus of the area. Walking over deep voids was inevitable. After stepping over such a gap (surrounded by moss), I decided to descend east to free us from the maze. It was now completely black under a moonless sky. An oppressive inky darkness swallowed us. We crept slowly down through the corridors until the rocks loosened their grip ever so slightly. Just when I thought we were in the clear, we found ourselves surrounded by more. I knew our approximate position and silently berated my poor judgment. We needed to continue lower which would make our eventual exit harder, but I felt that it was the only safe choice. The terrain then flattened, and our way became more evident as we hooked north.

I focused on silently counting drainages to track our progress – I didn't bring a GPS, and my compass was in the pack. Several slides and gullies drained the cliffs from the west. Each time we crossed one, I visualized where we were in relation to the cliffs. A comparatively large stream meant that we were somewhere near the *Huge Scoop*. The terrain eventually began to steepen – a positive transition that meant we were on target and in for a beating. The forest tightened its grip, and stacked boulders became the norm. We sometimes climbed the rocks and other times used trees to gain the next ledge while avoiding the underlying caverns. Our headlamps illuminated the needles thus making it difficult to see more than a few paces ahead. Every now and again the tree growth would loosen, and our lights would shine on a 20' tall monolith blocking our way.

Against all the odds I rounded a stone and found myself in a small talus cavern... one that Loren and I had visited months earlier. What were the odds? I knew exactly where we were...directly below the *Huge Scoop*. Instead of making a hard left at the next passage I stayed right hoping to take us in the direction of the more northerly cliffs. Some 20 minutes later, we found a dry streambed and ascended northwest. My eyes had adjusted to the darkness, and a slight glow in the sky helped me recognize the silhouetted stone above—the *Agharta Wall*. The faint herdpath never looked so inviting. It was 9:30 p.m. when we reached the *Panther Den* and fell to the ground like sacks of flour. We extinguished our lights. Without lamps, it was as black as death. Loren eventually turned his headlamp back on which illuminated a bat as it patrolled the cliff.

The final 20 minutes of bushwhacking were a challenge in the dark, but we emerged on the Phelps Trail at 10:00 p.m. I hoped that the bear at Slant Rock had found other places to patrol and other people to harass. Like Nolan, I wasn't in the mood to deal with it. Our pace was slow and deliberate. The exit through the talus had been mind-numbing. I speak for each of us when I say that it sapped much of our strength and left impressions that would reach far into the future. Even following the Phelps Trail seemed like a mental burden. Words were few and long periods of silence were the norm. If one of us took a break, the others quickly sat or reclined to sleep. Time seemed to warp as we staggered nearer and nearer to the trailhead until we finally reached the vehicle at 2:00 a.m. after almost 22 hours of intense exertion. Our limits were tested and tempered however unintentionally. It took me over a week to recover. Sometimes one asks for an adventure, and God answers in the affirmative!

On the Wind with a Prayer: Psalm 23 and Windjammer

With: Jaryn DeShane & John Pikus (lead on Windjammer) on 2016 September 17
Area: Haystack *V Wall*
Routes: *Psalm 23* (5.7) & *Windjammer* (5.7)
Duration: 4:30 a.m. – 9:30 p.m.
Reference Plate 8

Left: *Low clouds hanging on Marcy.* **Right:** *A fin balancing at the edge of the cliff.*

    Ah, the weather – the deciding factor that can change the fate of a trip. It seemed like it might play along with our goals on September 17th after spoiling plans to venture into the Gorge the week prior. Showers were forecast to hold off until the evening – it would be another race to the finish. The target was on Mt. Haystack – the *V Wall* on which Adam Crofoot and I put up a route called *All Things Holy* a couple of years prior. Studying photographs of the wall fanned the flames of curiosity; I wanted to see what was in the center and along the left side of the V-shaped wall. The left side hosted a series of corners and cracks which looked particularly enticing. The secondary goal was to scout a more direct route from the Marcy climbing walls. Local climber, Jaryn DeShane, and John Pikus opted to accompany me. This was Jaryn's first time into the Gorge; a subject we talked about at length while slide climbing on Giant Mountain's *Diagonal Slide* the week before.

    The first words out of Jaryn's mouth upon seeing the Gorge were, "I understand now!"

    The last time Adam and I went to the *V Wall*, we took a comparatively long route across the talus to the base of a large slab on Haystack. We then followed the bottom of the cliffs which involved some nearly vertical bushwhacking and precarious maneuvers over the contours of the mountain. This time we hugged the cliffs down to Marcy's *Feline Wall* and descended into the talus fields via a dry streambed. The contour of the terrain funneled us down the center once we descended Marcy's slopes. We climbed through dense talus while navigating around a large wooded buttress of Haystack. The terrain

Jaryn following Psalm 23.

eventually flattened, and Marcy Brook became more pronounced. It was bone dry, and I was counting on the brook to replenish our water supply. We were frightfully low and had to follow the streambed down a couple of hundred feet past the pronounced drainage from the *V Wall*. Hindsight is 20/20; it would have been easier to navigate to the boulder from the *Agharta Wall*, not the *Feline Wall*.

With a few liters safely tucked in our respective packs, we ascended the steep drainage stream from the *V Wall* avoiding talus and deadfall whenever possible. It was an arduous but safer approach than threading through Haystack's cliffs. It was 10:30 a.m. when we arrived at the base of the wall above the wooded intersection of the gully and trap dike. We re-nourished and watched the clouds lazily drift by Marcy. There was an oppressive feel to the backcountry vista with clouds low enough to obscure most of Marcy's *East Face* and northern walls.

The sides of the *V Wall* were vertical, but the bottom was blocky and of lower angle. This is where our new route began. Small ledges broken by grassy bands led to a terrace where John prepared to belay me. I knew this wouldn't be a multi-pitch route and thus hoped it would be the first of at least two climbs. I started up and stepped back down.

Jaryn dryly proclaimed, "You're off route."

Yup, he fit in well with the rest of the Panther Gorge crew. Sharp stone, dozens of cracks, small ledges, and pockets made climbing the first 100' seem easy. It then morphed into a sloped terrace below a short vertical section.

Above led to more cracks and the crux where John yelled, "You've got about 20' of rope left (of 200')."

That should work fine, I thought.

I studied two cracks. An option to my right was wet and vertical, but the one above was overhung and looked enticing if not a little dirty. I'd set 8 pieces of protection to this point and added another to protect a fall if my hand slid out of the somewhat moist crack. The last 15' took me about 1/3 as long as the rest of the climb. The crack ended in a fist-sized crevasse capped with a nearly vertical slope of blueberry bushes. I jammed my arm in and groped around for a fistful of roots and tugged to test their security. Satisfied, I crawled up to an ash tree where I belayed John then Jaryn. They simultaneously climbed about 75' apart while I scanned the Gorge. The clouds had lifted 1,000' higher, and the wind stirred the trees except in our protected alcove.

John reached the crux – the rope went snug as he yelled, "Rock!"

He hadn't fallen, but his foot broke a piece of stone loose and sent it down past Jaryn. The entire affair took slightly more than an hour, about what I'd hoped. The hour was slightly past noon, so we had time to rappel down the northern side of the wall and explore the cracks and corners. John set up the rappel from a stout tamarack and descended a gully. He passed over the crux and said it looked like a fun climb though it was wet – what I expected on both counts. Below, we enjoyed the aesthetic geometry of the gully. Up to our left sat a broken fin of rock precariously perched on a narrow wall. What forces might cause it to tumble? How long had it been in place? Geologic wonders are among the incentives to explore, and this area did not disappoint.

John wanted to lead a route in the Gorge and jumped at the opportunity to give this line a go. We chose the most dominant (and driest) line between opposing corners – a crack that followed the left-facing corner (right side). This crack was continuous and led to a small gully above. He worked his way up the intermittently wet line using solid hand jams and copious jugs. The obvious crux was up a vertical wall where the crack widened near a chock-stone. I was tall enough to place a foot on either wall while climbing though shorter people might have to use a different strategy. The angle decreased above the chockstone before increasing again in the gully. "Fun five" climbing led back to our rappel station at the tamarack. Fast forward to our hike out for a moment – hours of discussion and bouncing names back eventually led to the name *Windjammer* – a perfect name given the techniques used and conditions of the day. Our first route assumed the biblical reference *Psalm 23*.

During my climb of *Windjammer*, Jaryn was bouldering on the opposing wall of the gully and found what would have been a fun line if it was longer. There are thousands of similar options in the Gorge, but only some are gems and worth the effort. It was 2:30 p.m. by the time we each had a turn at climbing and rappelled. We then walked to the other side where *All Things Holy* began and scouted a third line. The only appealing option was wet; disappointing in a summer of near-drought conditions. We were tired and knew that the long bushwhack across the talus would slow the exit. Thus we called it a day at 3:30 p.m.

Jaryn led the way and side-sloped across the wooded buttress that we'd skirted on the approach. This worked well and seemed like a more direct route back to Marcy though it included the risk of running into small ledges. Our tactic after the buttress was to aim for the *Agharta Wall* using line-of-sight navigation. Remarkably, we found a loosely-knit section of trees between the upper talus field and the large boulders below *Agharta*. We exited the woods at the glen below our target and felt the first drops of rain. Timing is everything!

Another 15 minutes found us at the *Panther Den* shooting video of the clouds whipping north out of the pass. Foul weather had found us. The scene reminded me of Alfred B. Street's ominous description of the Gorge in his book, *The Indian Pass*. With the climbing over, watching the dramatic cloud-play was a relaxing counterpoint to the beautiful weather I've enjoyed on many of our trips. It added a more profound sense of adventure to the day. As for John and Jaryn...they voiced a desire to return! Their enthusiasm made me smile. I felt like I was passing, or at least sharing, the torch with a new generation. I was happy to close the Panther Gorge rock climbing season on such a positive note. The Gorge isn't something that we (Bill, Adam, etc.) want to keep to ourselves. We hope other climbers with similar passions and respect for the wilderness will embark upon adventures with fresh ideas and explore with new eyes.

Top: John leading Windjammer. The ice route called John 3:16 follows the wet streak.
Bottom: An interesting view of Marcy's East Face from the top of Psalm 23.

A Birthday Celebration on Kitty Cake and a Second Ascent of By Tooth and Claw

With: Doug Ferguson (lead) & Walker Wolf Bockley on 2017 January 14
Area: Marcy *Panther Den* and Haystack *North End*
Routes: *Kitty Cake* (WI2), 2nd Ascent of *By Tooth and Claw* (WI4)
Duration: 4:00 a.m. – 7:00 p.m.
Reference Plates 1, 3, 11

Doug during the second ascent of By Tooth and Claw.

    The winter adventure season of 2017 began with storms and created a snowpack more significant than the prior year. I'd skied Whiteface Mountain's toll road by October 23 and held little hope of heading into Panther Gorge until a warm front brought howling winds and an inch of rain. Last minute plans to invade the Gorge materialized when I connected with Mountain Skills Climbing Guides owner Doug Ferguson and his client Walker Wolf Bockley. I'd met Doug on Gothics' South Face a half-decade earlier, but our schedules never synced for us to climb together. The temperature registered at roughly 5 degrees at 4:00 a.m. as we walked the icy trail to Johns Brook Lodge – an excellent way to start my birthday. After two hours of walking under the light of headlamps and a nearly full moon, the blue-black glow of the rising sun dimly silhouetted the ridgeline. I pondered the viability of crossing Johns Brook at Bushnell Falls given the recent rain. It was frozen solid. Blocks of ice along the trail and gullies through frozen snow were telltale signs of the recent high water.

    Low humidity and cold temperatures along with layer management helped keep moisture to a minimum though Doug's pace bumped against my limits. We reached the Haystack/Marcy col after 3.75 hours minutes of hiking. It was time to test the snowpack

Doug looking down from the belay below the chimney.

for bushwhacking. Did the rains and sudden freeze harden it or had it been a snow event at this elevation? We put on snowshoes and stepped off-trail. The snow was hard enough that we barely dented its surface. Descending was easier than during summer – a nice bonus! The winds whipped my face as we exited the snow-encrusted balsams along the *Panther Den*. I sensed that it was going to be a good day; the Gorge was loaded with fangs of ice and distant smears. Nothing is more inspiring and humbling than seeing acres of ice flows. Wind-whipped creations in various colors looked like the tentacles of translucent sea monsters. The flows were fatter than during any of my previous visits.

Kitty Cake

Moving forward in time to noon – our second climb of the day and a new route: We walked from Marcy to Haystack and added a short line immediately to the right of *Orson's Tower*. From Marcy, it looked like an easy target to climb during our exit. Walking across the center of the north pass was pleasant on the consolidated snowpack; so much so that it hardly seemed like the Panther Gorge with which I was familiar. The "thrill" of avoiding the man-eating holes between talus blocks was lacking! There was, of course, a pre-requisite thrash up through Haystack's lower crown of flesh-flaying spruce. Once at the route, blue-white ice beckoned; the group of free-standing pillars was only 20' to our left (north).

We knew it would be easy, but that played into the strategy of an early exit – Doug had to drive three hours after our trip then guide the next day. Choices of either a steep or moderate stepped bulge led upward. He quickly disappeared from view without placing any screws. This was an easy solo for him. He set up an anchor and belayed Walker and I a few scant minutes later. The top had a short vertical step before a good belay tree located 15' into the woods. Doug named the 60' route *Kitty Cake* after his cat which is reportedly not as laid back as the route.

What can I say – it was fun but hardly epic! Its value is in its proximity to several nearby routes. While it would be unworthy of a trip to the Gorge in and of itself, it is worth climbing when combined with the adjacent routes on Haystack (*Orson's Tower, Fly By, Ride the Lightning* or *Skip the Lighting*). They vary in grade from WI2 to WI5- and all boast inspiring views of Marcy.

By Tooth and Claw

...back to 8:30 a.m. The highlight of the trip was not the new route as usual, but the second ascent of *By Tooth and Claw*, a route tucked in a northeast facing corner that's proven reliable each year. We descended along the *Panther Den*, assessed a couple of lines and stopped at the corner 300' down the glade. Tiers of yellow and white ice blanketed the ledges below the crux 150' higher. After three months of being away from the Gorge, I was ecstatic to be back. I thought back to last February to when Bill Schneider, Devin Farkas, and I added this little beauty. Instead of the windy conditions present during the first ascent, we enjoyed a calm day with blue sky and temperatures hovering between 5-10 degrees.

Doug looked up the route, dropped his pack and said, "Let's climb this!"

Game on. The dark stone was covered in thick ice; conditions were considerably fatter than a year ago. It almost seemed like a different route. This is one of the reasons I'm drawn to ice climbing – conditions differ according to the humidity, temperature, and recent precipitation. I looked up at the crux, a vertical chimney largely hidden from view. Parasols of ice decorated the cliff, intimidating structures formed by recent rains in combination with strong winds. Doug began climbing, deliberately and efficiently – as one would expect of a seasoned guide. There were four or five tiers to climb before the crux

Left: *The Kitty Cake ice flow.*

Above: *A delaminated curtain of ice on Marcy.*

View south from the route. Marcy's East Face and Allen are in the background.

of the first pitch. Walker belayed while I scooted up a tree to photograph from a better vantage point than the ground. Haystack loomed to the east with its cliffs glistening as ice fell from Marcy – small chunks chipped off by Doug's tools. There was little sound other than the axe strikes and the occasional shout of, "Ice!"

Given the chilly temperature, I felt exceptionally comfortable. Only my toes grew cold, but that would change with the exertion of climbing. We readied ourselves as Doug approached the belay corner. I climbed first and felt a bit of déjà vu as I followed the familiar line. The difference was that the brittle ice of last year was replaced with hard ice that didn't easily shatter. A small trickle of water ran down the surface in some areas and created sections of softer ice – the route was still building! In fact, one of the ice screws that Doug placed was already entombed in 1/8" of ice after 30 minutes. I tried to keep both myself and the rope out of the water.

The last tier was 10' high and wet which allowed my axes to stick effortlessly. Long icicles decorated its right edge. Above, Doug was clipped into an anchor he'd built in the chimney. I tied into it, and Walker began to climb. This gave me time to continue reflecting. I felt warm and comfortable which is rare during an ice climb. The entire scenario was different from last year when 40 m.p.h. winds swirled the spindrift and drove stinging ice crystals into our faces.

A mackerel sky covered us like a woven blanket. A large ice curtain clung precariously to the cliff immediately overhead. There was a 4" space between it and the black stone of Marcy – the sheet had delaminated. Wind-contorted icicles near the curtain appeared especially intimidating. It looked as if the slightest breeze might break the structure free and cause it to come slamming down like a medieval fortress gate.

Doug led the next pitch up the chimney and crossed onto low-angle ice at its top. The transition appeared easier than the last time. Again, conditions change ice routes by the day. Both walls of the corner held ice, and the chimney was all but sealed shut. Climbing up to an obvious ledge led to an exposed step to the left where the angle decreased. The rope disappeared along another corner and up a short gully. I chipped at the ice to gain a placement. The movement spooked a mouse that ran up into the krummholz. Doug was belaying from a pinch-point in what we named *Bill's Man-Cave* – a small ice-veneered talus cave at the end of the gully.

I believe many of the routes we've added are quite worthy of second ascents though I'm a little biased since I enjoy any climbing in the Gorge. It was music to my ears when Doug stated that he thought that this was a great route and climbers would be lined up for it if it was located closer to the road. True. A short time later we'd rappelled and were en route to *Kitty Cake*. We turned the day around in roughly 13.5 hours, a few hours faster than the average Panther Gorge foray.

A Mythical Melting Beast: Chimæra

With: Matt Dobbs (lead on crux) & Jace Mullen on 2017 February 18
Area: Marcy *Feline Wall*
Route: *Chimæra* (WI3-)
Duration: 4:40 a.m. – 8:00 p.m.
Reference Plates 1, 10

The *Feline Wall* sometimes hosts a thin ice smear down its center. It forms every year though there is a caveat, so it's best to have an alternative goal in mind. The smear is most robust at the top where the water seeps from the krummholz. The slab faces southeast, so the sun heats the underlying stone and often delaminates the bottom portion where it is considerably thinner. Whether it is bonded to the dark anorthosite when one visits is a persistent wildcard.

Warm February temperatures were forecast to be in the 40's in the Keene Valley. Temperatures at 4,000' in elevation should have been in the 30's when I and friends, Matt Dobbs and Jace Mullen, went searching for ice. Jace was a St. Lawrence University student and new to Panther Gorge – he'd heard my stories. Only when I returned home did I find out that ambient temperatures had jumped to nearly 60 degrees. Such high winter temperatures explained the conditions we encountered, but I'm ahead of myself.

We walked up the Phelps Trail; I scanned the cloudless sky as daylight illuminated the forest in the soft light of early morning. Would the bright sun destroy the route? Perhaps, but it seemed worth investigating, plus Matt and I had our hearts set on this particular

Left: *Matt getting ready to lead.*

Above: *Jace and Matt on the second pitch of a melting route. Photo by Brent Elliott.*

Kevin climbing hollow ice on pitch two. Photo by Jace Mullen.

line. We tried for this last year, but conditions were unappealing, so it didn't go. The first three hours' hike was on a hard-packed trail – easy walking which conserved energy for later. Only the last .6 mile was covered with fresh powder. Once at the col, I added tails to the snowshoes and plunged into two feet of fresh snow over a supportive rain-crust. The overall bushwhack was pleasant, and gravity was on our side. The strenuousness of this section can make or break a climb depending on how far the route is located in the Gorge. Slow and steady won the day. Only the occasional snow-laden tree hampered progress. They served as wrestling partners in the tighter areas.

We stepped out from the canopy to the base of the *Panther Den* and were lashed by strong gales. The forecast called for 55 m.p.h. winds on the summit, but our target was over 1,000' lower and more protected. I scanned the Gorge and noticed that some of the ice was thinner than last month...hmm. Matt broke trail the rest of the way to the *Feline Wall* where the snow slope below the slab was speckled with fallen debris: it had recently been warm. Climbing the steep incline was tedious work of one step forward/two steps back, but its top offered us the best perspective from which to view the smear. Thankfully it was "in" though the ice appeared thin and soft. Much of the slab was barren.

A loud crack from the nearby *Agharta* route brought me to attention. Ice had broken off or expanded. It seems like the exception when I don't hear that noise during a winter visit. Meanwhile, small ice plates intermittently fell from the top left of our planned route. They shattered on the exposed slab before rolling by. Only a few pieces remained whole and precipitated the occasional exclamation, "Ice!"

Small rivulets of water also ran down the face. The sun was punishing Marcy's ice. On the positive side, I noticed that my usual battle of fighting cold toes and hands wasn't an issue. It was much warmer than I anticipated. We were protected from the aforementioned wind at the base, so I didn't even need gloves. This was both pleasant yet disconcerting given the rills that seemed to grow in volume by the moment.

Matt said, "Ok, decision time."

After assessing the risks, we decided to give it a try and began gearing up. Voices suddenly distracted me. Were they whispers carried on the wind from one of the nearby summits? No, that was too far away given the gusty conditions on the ridge. I asked Jace if he heard them when, on cue, two people materialized from behind a buttress. Our first thought was, *Oh no, they followed our tracks by mistake!* Surprise...they were here to climb. Thus we made the acquaintance of Brent Elliott and Laura Duncan. They looked at *Agharta*, but settled for climbing *Sorry, Kevin* – an icy gully 75' north of us. Matt and his friends had added the route to the growing collection during 2016. To my knowledge, this was the first time that the Gorge has seen two separate ice climbing parties on the same occasion. The chance meeting was rewarding!

It was 11 a.m. when Matt climbed onto the line. Slushy ice along the edge broke underfoot. After finding a sketchy tool placement, he put a chock in a vertical crack and attained the center of the smear. The ice was 15' wide and only 50 degrees in slope at the bottom. It sat to the right of a large flake of stone with a ledge at its top. The slope increased thereafter. He placed a screw before climbing to the ledge in search of more solid gear. After several attempts, he hammered a short piton into a crack. He later confessed that the piton was a critical piece; he didn't know if it would have been wise to climb higher without it.

The next section was delineated by two runs of parallel ice separated by a small island of rock; he climbed along the left-hand side toward a stone outcrop 175' above the base. It looked like an obvious belay station from my perspective. Solid thudding sounds signaled that his tools found adequate purchase. I felt restless as I waited. The sun was quickly destroying the line; small pieces continued to calve off. I distracted myself by watching Brent ascend the tiers of their chosen route. It seemed intact if not a bit wet.

Note: Given the conditions I just described I feel it's necessary to note that we didn't recklessly throw caution to the wind. We continually assessed the risks. I wouldn't touch a more vertical run of ice in this condition; the entire piece could slough off. The sketchiest area of this was at the bottom where the angle was low. The top was held securely in place. I knew that we needed to move quickly, but that we would be safer on the thicker ice above. In the end, it's a personal judgment call.

Matt built a suitable anchor by slinging a protruding ledge backed up by clipping ice tools stuck in frozen dirt. It was soon our turn to climb, and I went first. With a questionable axe placement in ½ inch of ice for balance, I front-pointed across the slush-covered slab and began climbing adequate, yet soft, ice. I didn't dally. The ice screws that I removed had melted the surrounding ice in only 30 minutes' time. They sat in a watery hole and were useless as protection by the time I reached them. The route grew steeper and thinner until a corner with more solid ice. The face was convex and gradually cruxed at nearly 80 degrees. I'd only been climbing about 10 minutes when I reached steeper terrain and comparatively harder ice. Miniature cascades flowed on either side of me as gusting wind blew the water in all directions and effectively soaked our shells and gloves. It didn't take long to reach Matt's position where I clipped into the anchor and photographed Jace with Mt. Haystack's ledges glistening in the background.

Warm sun over Haystack as seen from the Feline Wall.

I led the second pitch. Water running out from under the ice did nothing to boost my sense of security though my rational side knew it was solid enough for climbing. The ice was as thick as we expected, but air pockets under the ice were common. Many of the ax strikes made a disconcerting hollow sound. The first reliable protection was about 15' up from the anchor. I fiddled with an ice screw and chock but settled for placing a cam under a small overlap of stone. My aforementioned shower was merely a prelude to the one I received here! It may sound a bit absurd as a reader, but I was having fun dealing with these conditions, and it was considerably drier than a recent winter climb up Mt. Colden's Trap Dike.

The remainder of the ascent was straightforward – bury the tools in the soft ice, bounce test, and step up. Rinse and repeat (literally). The ice was tiered at the top before ending in the krummholz. Three screws and 75' later I was swimming through waist-deep mashed potato snow searching for a tree from which to belay. I clipped one of the small spruces with a quickdraw to redirect the rope since the safest anchor tree was angled away from the finish. Jace later noted with a facetious grin, that the snow slog might have been the crux of the route! Matt snickered at my creative redirect. Once anchored, I gave a few hard tugs as a signal for them to begin climbing. Meanwhile, I received – you guessed it – another shower. As we'd realize during the rappel, the runoff was increasing, and the wind blew the water upward. Gortex and waterproof gloves made this a mere inconvenience rather than an uncomfortable issue.

Readying for the rappel involved the usual rope tangles in unsupportive snow amongst grabby tree branches – a three-ring circus. Matt went first and disappeared over the edge. I went second and received a final bath of the day below the first ledge at the top. We angled south to a gully, set up another anchor and performed a last rappel to the base. There was no rush to leave, so we loitered to enjoy the warm weather. Matt refilled his water from one of the rills flowing down a crack. He was effectively drinking our route.

I scanned the panorama. Critical sections of previously fat routes on Marcy and Haystack (potential targets) had calved or become thinner. The sun had, by now, changed its hot stare to Haystack. While it doesn't receive the same heat as Marcy's southeast facing slabs, all the cliffs were flowing with runoff. Even shaded ice flows were melting. I looked up at our route, which we named *Chimæra*. It was aesthetic and, in better conditions, would have been a straightforward climb. Much of it had disappeared in the hours it took to climb. Our timing was perfect, and we'd made the right call.

Exiting up the consolidated herdpath was pleasant especially since Brent and Laura had compacted it even more during their exit. The day was memorable if not wet and offered us another chance to introduce "fresh blood" to the area. As for Matt and I, well, this was high on our respective winter tick lists for Panther Gorge. It was satisfying to finally put a somewhat elusive goal to bed though I'd still like to climb it in drier conditions.

Time to Ride the Lightning on Haystack

With: Alan Wechsler (lead) on 2017 March 10
Area: Haystack *Ramp Wall*
Routes: *Ride the Lightning* (WI5-) & *Skip the Lightning* (WI3+)
Duration: 4:15 a.m. – 9:45 p.m.
Reference Plate 11

Moderate March weather in the 70's was followed by a couple of inches of rain before it cooled to more seasonal temperatures. The reprieve created a veneer of hard crust and consolidated the high-elevation snowpack by two feet. Such conditions made visiting the Gorge exceptionally appealing. Area veteran Alan Wechsler jumped on board for the backcountry ice hunt. As usual, we watched the forecast during the preceding week. Predicted temperatures for the weekend dropped daily and, accounting for wind-chill, settled at roughly -40 at the elevation where the climbs are located. I had no desire to suffer in such Arctic-like temperatures, so I took a day off from work. There are always objective dangers to consider. At least we wouldn't find the route melting out from under us like *Chimæra*!

The alarm sounded at 3:15 a.m.; we were walking an hour later. I wondered if the Johns Brook crossing at Bushnell Falls had refrozen after being open earlier in the week. That could end the day after five miles. Additionally, I didn't feel on top of my game, but that's how it sometimes rolls – you learn when to push through moderate illness and pray for the best. Meanwhile, Alan fought his own physical demons. A large blister formed on his foot soon after departure. Would we even make it as far as the crossing? So many things were amiss that I wondered if God was sending a hint. Alan tried a variety of blister remedies before a 3" square piece of mole-skin provided relief. We later found the crossing at the falls was well frozen – I'd worried about nothing.

Left: Kevin walking on a glade near the Feline Wall. Photo by Alan Wechsler. **Right:** Icy fangs on *Skip the Lightning*.

Persistence and a rock-hard trail eventually got us to the jump-off point at the north end of the Gorge. The depleted snowpack and a bullet crust allowed us to walk down the center of the drainage without snowshoes, a narrow sloped glade that descended into an arena of possibilities. It was time to explore! We hoped to find moderate multi-pitch ice line. As usual, I had a couple of new ones in mind, but the ice at the top of the pass was thin. This didn't bode well for the most sensational possibilities. We spent an hour and a half walking to the *Agharta Wall* where *Agharta*, the largest of the routes, looked relatively thin though climbable. There were several challenging unclimbed routes to the south, but nothing looked like a sure bet. Ambition and common sense fought in my mind, but the latter won as usual. We wanted to exit at a decent hour given the encroaching cold weather. After some discussion, we bushwhacked across to Haystack's *Ramp Wall*.

The wall's obvious left-rising ramp is about eight feet wide and 50' long. It divides the wall into a slightly off-vertical bottom section and a vertical top pitch. The top left (north) corner usually has ice as does the bottom right side below obvious opposing corners – the main seepage lines. I liken it to a miniature version of *Upper Washbowl Cliff*'s ramp, home of the famed *Weissner Route*. This trip, it hosted an aesthetic possibility that I'd coveted for two years. It was fatter than I'd ever seen it thanks to the recent rains and cold snap. We crept up to its base as Alan noted that the line running directly to the top would be the best and hardest option.

We reached the wall at 11:30 a.m., but it was noon before we were ready to climb. I knew I could lead the section below the ramp, but questioned my ability to lead the top safely. I'm not stupid enough to push my limits this deep in the backcountry – especially feeling less than optimal. I told Alan that we should put up the best line possible and that he should lead if he wanted to try the plumb line. Thus began the start of *Ride the Lighting*, a name I had tucked in my mind for a worthy route. He wanted to name the route, *Oops*, but that would necessitate explaining a small mishap that happened during the climb.

Alan leading the final few feet of Ride the Lightning.

It was vertical with good stances off the deck though it gradually decreased in grade on approach to a series of ice bulges which led through the corners and onto the ramp. Alan placed the first screw in the upper wall after 20 minutes; something that would save him from sliding off the slope if he fell (the aforementioned "oops"). Meanwhile, the weather began playing games. Intermittent snow showers seemed to be more on than off in nature. Moderate winds swirled the snow south down the ramp. The magnificent views of the lower Gorge and Mt. Skylight disappeared as the sun transmuted into a vague orb of light. It was an eerie scene complete with a hawk soaring high above – a phantom sailing through the snow.

Alan slowly progressed up the remaining 50' of the route – ice climbing isn't about speed. It looked short from below, but I knew that to be a trick of perspective. He climbed along a 10' hanging ice spear and moved right to a small bulge before finishing the line. The spear reminded me of Verplanck Colvin's description of huge yellow icicles draped on Haystack's cliffs. The one above us was one of hundreds.

As if to celebrate Alan's success, the sun came out to spotlight his finish. With temperatures comfortably in the 20's, I felt warm and ready to climb. As expected, I was comfortable climbing to the ramp. Hard, but not brittle, ice took the tools well. I relaxed as the sound of metal striking ice echoed off the broken crags of Marcy. Once on the ramp, I looked north. What a view! The ice in the corner formed a series of parasols (hollow formations sculpted by strong winds blowing under quickly freezing water). Small icicles, which Alan later described as dragon teeth, rimmed the hollows. Looking up the line above was both inspiring and intimidating even though I wouldn't fall far if I came off. It was a two-foot thick wall of mostly-vertical crystal beauty.

Breathe in, breathe out. Start. I began a measured series of movements that would take me to the first screw on the upper wall. Once there, I held on with my left hand, front-points digging into small bumps in the surface, and unscrewed the protection.

This route felt more strenuous than anything I'd previously climbed. Forty more feet to the top, I thought.

I immediately berated myself for such considerations. I didn't want to rush the experience; I wanted to savor it without negative self-talk about my stamina. Higher up, the sun broke through the veil again. The ice glistened as I worked up to the fragile hanging dagger. I tried to focus on the surrounding beauty, not the desperate feeling welling up inside or my strained technique (over-gripping). I seemed to be fighting the ice and the tools. Rather than berate myself again, I accepted that not every trip is one during which I can attain inner peace. Moments when one's "game is off" are also part of the journey.

Enough of the retrospective analysis – persistence paid off when I topped out and drove the pick into a fat ice bulge. I was out of breath and shook my head as I looked up at Alan who was tethered to a few small spruces 10' left of a rock wall hosting a small ice flow. I bushwhacked past to lay down in the snow and enjoy the view. The spruce covered platform on which we sat belonged to a fin of rock separated from the Haystack massif by a wide corridor – I'd been here before. The fin was attached only on its north side. Features like this are among the reasons why Panther Gorge is so alluring.

We rappelled down as a band of heavier snow moved in to mask the world in white. Back at the base, we noted a mixed climbing option (rock and ice) up to the ramp. We hoped to climb an entirely independent line up to the ramp then left to the highest corner with the parasols of dragon-tooth ice. Alan gave it a go before backing off some

30 minutes later. It was harder than it looked. We instead used the start of the first route to attain the ramp. The ambitious side of me wanted to lead, but I knew better based on how I was performing, so Alan took the sharp end and made short work of the easier line.

By 3:30 p.m., the snow was getting heavier, the winds were whipping, and the temperature began to drop. It was again my turn to climb. I buried my axe into a void in some soft ice 20' up and spent five minutes trying to extricate it while hanging on with my left hand. I snickered at having a problem again – all's well if one can laugh at the situation. The pick was caught on the sharp teeth along its bottom edge. Enough surrounding ice eventually melted to remove it and, with cold hands, I climbed up to the ramp and into another predicament.

Kevin rappelling during a snowstorm. Photo by Alan Wechsler.

This route meandered, and it included two perpendicular angle changes. Alan had left one of the ropes free of the clips to avoid rope drag. Unfortunately, the blue rope caught on a horn of stone which brought me to a standstill. There's nothing like the disconcerting feeling of being immobilized as spindrift blows by – until you realize that you can safely untie from one of the ropes. Without further ado, I climbed the ramp and stopped to enjoy a close-up view of the ice formations. Multi-tiered hollow parasols of translucent yellow-white ice looked magical. Delicate rime covered icicles hanging in haphazard directions lined the edges of the hollows. From a practical standpoint (and as Alan had proven), the parasols were supportive enough to climb. I followed the rope and ascended ice bulges to Alan's position in another snag of spruce trees.

With the second route complete, we moved 20' south to the rappel trees of the first route. I rappelled last. By then it was snowing hard, and Alan captured a dramatic mid-rappel photo – a bad weather souvenir. The warm weather in the mid-20's was being pushed out by the cold front; it was 5:00 p.m. and time to retreat. We'd accomplished our objectives. We discussed the routes as we packed and decided on *Skip the Lighting* (150'/WI3+) for the second, easier route. *Ride the Lighting*, the first route, was 110' long and considerably more difficult at WI5-. We felt blessed since it usually sets up as a thinner line.

Our exit was made easier by trekking back up the bullet crust in the center of the drainage. The temperature had dropped significantly by the time we arrived at Johns Brook Lodge. We chilled quickly without motion to keep our blood flowing, so the typical break on the porch was short. Such is the way of winter mountaineering. Activity equals warmth. I always say that the best days begin and end under cover of darkness. This was no exception. We were fatigued but delighted that we'd added a more difficult route to the Gorge.

All Ryled Up About Marcy's Great Chimney & Slacker Cracker

With: Adam Crofoot (lead on *Slacker Cracker*) &
Jaryn DeShane on 2017 June 3 & 15 (DeShane)
Area: Marcy *Chimney Wall*
Routes: *Slacker Cracker* (5.9) – June 3,
Marcy's *Great Chimney* (aka *Empty Tomb*) (5.8) & *All Ryled Up* (5.7) – June 15
Duration: June 3 – 15.5 hours, June 14 – 16 (camping trip)
Reference Plate 4

One of the best-kept backcountry secrets is a large vertical trap dike capped with a diagonal car-sized capstone on Mt. Marcy. It is set in a northeastern facing cliff called the *Chimney Wall* and resembles a pencil-thin shadow from the summit of Mt. Haystack. This is Marcy's *Great Chimney*, first ascended in 1978.

St. Lawrence University Professor of Geology, Jeff Chiarenzelli, described the dike as follows, "The dike is composed of metamorphosed basalt with fine to medium-grained, interlocking, crystals including the metamorphic mineral garnet." It is very similar to the larger and coarser-grained gabbroic dike on Mt. Colden in terms of its mineralogy and chemistry. Since they cut across the anorthosite, and retain their straight-walled boundaries, they have apparently escaped any major deformation that may have occurred after their intrusion. It is thought they represent samples of magma similar to that which allowed the formation of plagioclase feldspar as found in great abundance in the Marcy anorthosite massif. Such mafic rocks originate from partial melting of the Earth's mantle and make their way into the crust along fractures or faults. Both dikes trend WNW providing a clue to the direction of extension the area was experiencing during their intrusion."

Jaryn at the top of Marcy's Great Chimney. A giant chockstone is behind him.

The basalt eroded and formed several vertical to slightly overhanging sections in a deeply inset six-foot wide chimney. Unlike Mt. Colden's Trap Dike which is generally considered fourth class terrain, Mt. Marcy's dike is significantly more difficult.

I noticed the chimney several years ago when camping in the Gorge with friend Anthony Seidita. We didn't venture near enough to realize it was a trap dike and I didn't have the skills to climb it. None-the-less, the dark cleft inspired me. When local climber and friend Adam Crofoot mentioned scaling it, my curiosity jumped to anticipation. He'd noticed it over a decade earlier. It was prime real estate for exploration and, in my opinion, one of the most unusual jewels of the Gorge. We didn't realize it had been climbed until the first ascensionist responded to an online article about the chimney.

Adam leading the crack on Slacker Cracker.

We tried to climb the beast several times and were turned back by inclement conditions each time. Two attempts during the winter of 2014-2015 were thwarted by thin, dry ice – the first known winter attempts. For all things, there is a season and not every outing ends as anticipated, but ascending the chimney had evolved into a battle.

Slacker Cracker – June 3

It was early June, and we had a four day clear weather window ahead of our outing. Late May/early June is always a crap shoot for climbing at elevation. The trails were muddy but not as bad as I expected. We found a few pockets of snow as we neared the 4,000' elevation contour though we found nothing in the Gorge except an exceptional amount of evergreen pollen. A stream draining one of the technical slides between the *Huge Scoop* and the *Overhang Slide* was flowing strongly, so we refilled our water bottles before moving on toward our objective. I was disappointed, but not surprised, when the chimney was flowing as well. The cascading water emphasized the overhangs. There'd be no climbing it this day without a snorkel, but I remembered an appealing crack downhill.

The line looked deceptively easy which made me apprehensive, so Adam racked up and took the sharp end. There was a roof overhead with a small chimney harboring a dead tree to its left. I was sure there was another route hiding up there (We affirmed this in September)! Our objective started by face climbing to a fingercrack with good gear. This led to a long right-rising crack. It was larger than it appeared from afar, a tiny shadow in my photos. Adam protected himself and back-cleaned gear to conserve the cams; we had a limited supply of the right size, and he used them quickly. An interesting move up and over a discontinuity in the face led to even nicer climbing. Luckily the lip of the crack formed a positive edge on which to grab. This was reassuring since we needed to smear our feet on the rock rather than rely on edges. The crux involved crossing an area of the crack where the lip was less acute and where it was filled with dirt. Adam engaged in a little Adirondack "gardening" and moved past it before he disappeared from view. At the crack's end, he climbed blocky stone up to a small tree covered terrace and set up an anchor in the cracks of a wall.

I climbed, then Jaryn. Once comfortable on the ledge I looked up to see what might be next. A 20' broken wall led to a large tree covered terrace. There was more cliff beyond, but Adam explored the broken wall and climbed back down. We decided to end the route on the first terrace. Climbing higher would simply create an annoying bushwhack. There was surely a better way to breach the cliff and climb to an interesting feature – a 10' free-standing pillar. We rappelled, and Adam noted that it would be a 4-star route along the road. It was a good line. Adding routes to this wall (such as the chimney) would cluster good climbs together and make visiting this crag worth the long approach. *Slacker Cracker*, a tip of the hat to both *Dacker Cracker* at the *Spider's Web* and a *Joshua Tree* route, was up.

The Great Chimney

Tenacity often pays dividends in the discipline of climbing, so I planned another trip and asked Jaryn DeShane to join me. Several days of hot, dry weather preceded our trip. I prayed for a safe, successful climb. We began our trip early on the evening of June 14 and bivouacked under a moonlit canopy after a five hour trek from the Garden Trailhead. The usual late spring serenade of birdsong awakened me at 5:00 a.m. I contemplated what might happen in the coming hours – not a good habit since it drains energy and blurs one's focus. Jaryn's light-hearted quips and amiable personality kept the mood light during the ensuing bushwhack. We reached the *Huge Scoop* at 8:30 a.m. Our next stop was a stream to refill our water bottles. The dry weather had all but dried up what was a flowing stream two weeks prior. We had to climb uphill to find even a small trickle. This was a good omen for climbing the chimney; it would likely be dry. Another 20 minutes of threading our way through the forest and navigating moss-covered talus led to a grassy glade below the *Overhang Slide*. Our quarry was several hundred feet uphill.

Kevin getting ready to lead the chimney. Photo by Jaryn DeShane.

We reached the trap dike/chimney at 9:15 a.m. A vertical cliff, the *Chimney Wall* – harbors its namesake feature. The sheer wall of anorthosite is spanned along the base by a 45-degree gully that rises north into the forest. Various other crags sit to the south and east while Mt. Haystack looms across the valley. The chimney was lit by the sun and bone dry – perfect! What little moss or algae that grew on the trap rock would be easy to avoid. Conditions were ideal, but that didn't mean we had the ability to climb it. It also didn't minimize the objective dangers such as loose rock, my foremost concern. If I committed weight to a hold without evaluating correctly, I could pull a boulder loose on myself or Jaryn. The chimney would direct all rock-fall out its bottom, so we found a protective ledge where Jaryn could safely belay.

It was time to get down to business, so I organized the gear on my harness – everything from a 5" cam to 1/8" chocks. I took a few deep breaths and climbed up the grassy slope to the bottom of the chimney. The trap rock was broken by numerous cracks and a few pieces were loose. I knew I'd find good gear placements in the wall after 15'. I arrived at a slab of trap rock with spots of lichen and a huge crack on its left. The piece slightly overhung as I expected from watching water cascade over it two weeks earlier. A variety of solid hand-holds boosted my confidence as I stemmed upward, one foot on the left wall of the chimney and the other on the right. I pulled up and found a comfortable foothold. After repeating the process several times, I was on top of the block and placed a cam to protect myself before resting to take in the scenery. I was positioned roughly 20' into the cliff and felt strangely secure. The rugged brown walls framed a sliver of Haystack. The southerly wind created an updraft in the chimney which kept the blackflies at bay but blew the chalk into my face when I reached into the bag.

The crux that Adam reached in December of 2014 was roughly 1/3 of the way up and about 10' above my stance. I spotted a couple of chocks and a spectre ice piton in the wal – the pieces from which I'd lowered him. Maybe this would become a historical artifact in a few decades if we didn't remove it! He'd spent nearly two hours in this area grappling with the crux. Memories of watching him climb up then back down precariously thin ice on the vertical wall jumped to mind.

The next large block also overhung, but flakes in the adjacent anorthosite created excellent footholds. Thus I was able to ascend above a small roof to another rest in a squeeze chimney. It gave me a chance to take a few photos though dislodging myself was a chore. I couldn't have fallen out had I tried. I wriggled up to a more comfortable stance inch by precious inch. There were more challenges above, but nothing appeared as difficult as what I'd just climbed. The next section looked like it was plugged with jagged unattached boulders, but I soon realized that this was a trick of perspective. They were firmly locked in place. A small terrace gave me a chance to study the surrounding walls which looked as appealing as continuing up the chimney. A plumb crack ran up the left-hand side. Other cracks and features adorned the right. Each was a potential variation. However, I wanted to ascend the pure line of the dike.

Climbing higher also brought the diagonal chock-stone into perspective. It was 12-15' long, split across the bottom and tightly lodged in the chimney. It looked like the open door of a tomb. I'd been curious about the stone for years – what would it look like and how I would get around it. Another short climb placed me at the base of the monolith where I found two choices that led up to the forest: ascend the left corner up piled basalt or climb up a vertical crack in the right corner. I chose the right. It was an exhilarating exit that necessitated using the edge of the chock-stone to apply pressure with my left foot. Twenty feet higher I topped out, built an anchor from a spruce and gave a hoot as a three-year dream materialized. I thought, *For all things, there is a season.* The route was 165' long.

I tossed names around in my mind as Jaryn began to climb. I lean toward route names with Christian themes but also wanted to note the uniqueness of the feature. Marcy's *Great Chimney* (aka *Empty Tomb*) seemed appropriate. As mentioned, we didn't realize it had been climbed in the 70's, but the first ascendant agreed to keep our name. What had taken me almost two hours to climb while placing 14 pieces of gear took Jaryn about 30 minutes to follow. He recorded his climb using a selfie-pack equipped with a gopro camera. I made a few quips about the setup, but it worked well in the end. We sat atop the wall and enjoyed the satisfaction that comes from executing a plan without mishap.

The dike didn't look impressive from the top down, but it was a stiff diverse climb that employed an arsenal of techniques – stemming, lay-backing, face-climbing, hand/finger-jamming and even a restful kneebar. As for the views – they were spectacular from our cliff-top perch. We could scan the western flank of Haystack and the largest of Marcy's northern climbing walls.

All Ryled Up

The day was young. It was only noon. Jaryn wanted to lead a route in Panther Gorge so I suggested that we rappel back into the dike so he could lead the aforementioned crack on the left-hand wall. He rappelled first and set up an anchor on the terrace below the chock-stone. I would belay him from there. Once on belay, Jaryn stepped confidently into the crack and began to climb. It was an

Jaryn leading All Ryled Up. Haystack's ridge is in the background.

appealing handcrack to its top. He placed cams every body length until reaching two obviously loose blocks. He then stepped left and face-climbed up to the trees. I followed and measured the route at 40' long – a nice exit variation. He named his first Panther Gorge lead *All Ryled Up*.

We had climbed on a single 70-meter rope which means we could rappel half that length. Double ropes would have made it easy to rappel from trees at the top of the chimney to its base, but not a single rope. Thus we bushwhacked 50' south to the corner of the wall (the cliff has a southern and northeastern aspect) where I hoped to find a shorter drop. Nearly an hour later, I realized that there was no easy way off of the corner, but we located a stout tree above a large grassy terrace 100' below and rappelled. We descended past the free-standing pillar and down an overhanging wall (what would become pitch 2 of *The Panther's Pinnacle* later in the summer). We reached our packs at 2:30 p.m. after two rappels.

There was a weather change in the forecast, and the clouds were coalescing to the south, so we bushwhacked back to camp and cooked a hearty meal. We felt the first drops of precipitation at 8:00 p.m. and endured a steady rain until noon the following day. We slogged out in a blowing fog at 3:30 p.m. The weekend had been cut short, but this mattered not. It is all part of the game we play to recreate in the Gorge.

Anorthofright: Breaking Through the East Face Roof System

With: Steven St. Pierre (swapped leads) on 2017 August 27
Area: Marcy *East Face*
Route: *Anorthofright* (5.9-)
Duration: Saturday 4:20 a.m. – Sunday 12:20 a.m.
Reference Plate 5

The theme for the summer of 2017 was rain, rain, and more rain. Weather thwarted efforts to climb in the backcountry most of the weekends between mid-June and late August. Just a week before this trip, Ken Hebb, Steven St. Pierre and I walked to the *Panther Den* only to find that the warm, humid air over Elk Lake blew up the valley and condensed on Marcy. We stood shivering for two hours in hopes of catching a break – an optimists' club if there ever was one. In the end, climbing was not to be, and we walked out with our tails tucked. It was a good reminder that man "conquers" nothing and the mountain decides when it will be climbed.

Steve signed on for this trip as well – he's a tough bugger. He bore witness as I broke a vow that I took after putting up *Revelations* – precisely one year before this climb. I swore to never again day hike a route on Marcy's *East Face*. Pulling off a day-climb in this area exacts an enormous toll afterward, at least on this aging body. The *Revelations* trip took nearly 22 hours, but the negative memories were fading as is typical of a mountaineer (the "short memory of an alpinist"). The hours of light in each day were also growing shorter, so it was high time to focus on the roofs and steep slabs located on the north side of the *East Face*. Above, I hoped to scale the last pitches via the white streak from the rockfall. I also hoped we could get the line up and exit to the car in a reasonable time frame – say 18 hours. I hear you laughing. Yes, it's subjective.

Steve rifled through his gear at 4:00 a.m. at the Rooster Comb parking lot while scarfing breakfast down. He put his pack in my car for the ride up to the Garden, locked his door and shut it. Silence. He then uttered, "I think I just locked my keys in the car..."

My thoughts shot to and fro, but he didn't seem distraught, so we decided to deal with it later...much later. Temperatures were cool, the humidity was comfortable, and the stars twinkled brightly overhead. I felt good about our decision to take on the route. It had exciting potential. We crested the Marcy/Haystack col around 8:15 a.m. and descended. Skies to the south were slightly hazy, but it was forecast to remain clear.

Bushwhacking in the Gorge has been a series of navigational experiments over the years. The closer one stays to the cliffs, the "easier" the terrain. We walked far too low in August of 2016; this added to the overall time of the trip. Steve and I passed the various walls and entered thicker forest beyond the *Huge Scoop* where we maintained the same elevation until reaching *Grand Central Slide*. We crossed the streambed, trekked downslope around a buttress, and up to a raspberry bush covered glade below the *East Face* and our target. It was around 10:45 a.m. when we reached the base of the face.

I've often commented that photographs can be deceptive. Reality often unveils surprises even after dozens of study sessions. I anticipated that the start would be on a slightly off-vertical wall with suitable edges leading to a series of cracks. I was correct in a

Steven belaying below the roof system of Marcy's East Face.

sense. It was off-vertical but overhanging rather than positively sloped. I studied the stone and tried a couple of options near some loose blocks before getting frustrated with wasting time. Steve had an idea, so I offered him the lead of pitch one. It was 11:30 a.m. when he bouldered up, gained a narrow ledge, and traversed left on a grassy rail. There was a little seeping water, but it was dry overall which was a nice change!

He disappeared from view after climbing a vertical crack and, a while later, yelled, "Off belay!"

I readied myself and climbed. I didn't make it look as natural as Steve, but I gained the ledge and eventually the pitted slab atop the overhanging wall. The first thing one sees when cresting the lower wall is a broad set of roofs that looks like an impending gray tsunami. The roofs dwarfed Steve's frame. Easy technical face climbing and cracks led up to a foot-high left-facing corner and his anchor. The wall above was dead vertical below an overhanging roof with a horizontal crack in between.

We swapped leads, so I grabbed the gear and added a traverse to the mix. I knew there was a breach in the wall to the south, so I followed a small crack toward my target. The slab underfoot varied from about 50-75 degrees as I worked my way across, placing cams where I felt it necessary to protect against a bouncing pendulum-type fall. I stepped over a corner and scanned the area in hopes of a clean crack upward. I instead found a somewhat mossy corner. There was enough clean stone with which to work, so I placed some sketchy protection above my head and committed to the move. Exiting the corner required the use of several blueberry bushes before I flopped onto my stomach and crawled up to the roof to create an anchor.

The scenery was breathtaking. A series of steep grassy ledges led to the south, and a broken roof system swept north. Blocks under the roof were held in place by constrictions in the cracks. It was reminiscent of climbs on the *Agharta Wall* and the *Huge Scoop*. The northern jaws of Marcy and Haystack flickered light and dark as the clouds passed. Steve was in the background below a roof that looked ready to crush him. If I could only make a moment last forever…

I belayed Steve to the ledge and quipped that he'd probably hate me for the last move. Instead, he commented on another harder option that I'd apparently missed while focusing on the traverse. There's always another day, and fresh eyes often find alternatives. Pitch three was Steve's to lead – the money pitch of the route. A dark line in one of my beta photos betrayed a visible crack where I knew we could breach the roofs. I didn't expect it to be as aesthetic as it was. There was an arm-deep crack behind an overhanging flake on a slightly overhanging wall. Small blocks locked in place created thin cracks that were equally useful. He reached its top and vanished from sight. I paid the rope out in small increments until 180' disappeared from my terrace. We couldn't hear each other. A scream sounded like a faint echo bouncing off Mt. Haystack. I couldn't tell if it was him or a hiker yelling from the eastern summit. A tug on the rope and faint, "...belay," signaled that I could take him off belay so he could pull up the remainder of the rope.

I climbed the flake, laying back from its edge while "walking" up the wall, my body horizontal. The overhang tilted me back awkwardly at its top, but my arm in a crack – sharp crystals drawing a little blood – held me in place. I expected the slope of the face to become more moderate as it did below, but found a pleasant surprise. It was much steeper than I expected. I didn't want a "walk-up." A deep crack in the 75-80 degree slab provided excellent protection. The following 30' was up a dimpled face of the same angle – thrilling exposed climbing! The grade moderated as I crossed several horizontal cracks and a tree island. Higher, I noticed Steve belaying me from a vertical wall with a large black crack near another tree island. The route was all I'd envisioned and more.

I led pitch four which was comparatively easy climbing. We followed a short grassy ramp to large cracks that led to the clean white streak created by the rockfall. I'm accustomed to soloing this type of terrain, but doing so above an ever steepening face that terminates with a roof wasn't appealing. The pocketed stone, rough surface, and cracks allowed me to climb fluidly. I placed gear every 40'. I'd scaled 200' before I found a large bowl near the edge. I was literally at the end of my rope and needed to set up a belay. Steve

Dramatic scenery below the roof system with Marcy and Haystack in the background.

then followed and passed my position after a short time. We soloed the last 120' of "fun five" friction slab to its top below the terminal cliff. I'd walked across this section with Ranger Scott van Laer almost half a decade earlier. It was still sparkling white.

It took 4.5 hours to climb the 710' route – *Anorthofright*. We "merely" had to navigate down to our packs and bushwhack out before dark to avoid a mind-numbing night exit through the talus. Options included setting up multiple rappels down the face, rappelling down the central gully, or walking off to the north. Having descended *Grand Central* several times, I decided the walk-off would be the most expeditious option. We scrambled across the face, weaving through small tree islands until I could see the slide. The angle of the *East Face* continued to lessen though we remained roped together. The edge of the face was only about 15' high when we reached the forest. A short bushwhack led to the slide.

The many hours in tight climbing shoes had taken a toll. Our toes were downright angry with us! Thus we

Steven traversing under the roof system.

walked down the slide barefoot, each sighing with relief. Visiting *Grand Central* was like seeing an old friend. This trip marked my fifth visit to the slide, and it's likely not the last. We entered the woods before the lip of the waterfall and bushwhacked to the top of a 30' ledge from which we planned to rappel. Bushwhacking in rock climbing shoes is always "interesting," and the blackflies had their fill of my blood while preparing for the rappel. If you ever hear someone say that those winged devils are dead by the end of June, don't believe them!

Progress abruptly halted when Steve noticed that he'd lost a rock climbing shoe (probably when he fell backward into a sod-hole). He decided to mount a search while I dangled near the edge of the cliff feeding the blackflies…for 20 minutes. He bushwhacked back up to the slide and re-climbed/re-descended it in search of the elusive shoe. It was futile in the end. The mountain had claimed another piece of gear much like Mt. Colden "stole" my GPS in 2002.

We reached our packs at 6:00 p.m. and I contemplated the three-quarter mile bushwhack back to the col (and how he was going to get into his car). The exit bushwhack was a daunting aspect of climbing so far south in the Gorge. We had daylight on our side, but we needed to maintain a steady pace. Navigating terrain with gullies, talus, and sod-holes while carrying the rope and metal on our backs wasn't fun after a hard day's climbing. We reached the northernmost cliff as twilight overtook the cirque and stepped onto the Phelps Trail as darkness swallowed the valley.

Steven breaking through the roof system on the start of pitch three.

Steve said he felt strong (I hid a smirk and had a hunch that assertion might change). I felt OK but knew the next eight miles would wear me down. He was 20 years younger, so maybe he was more resilient. To say the last four miles was arduous is an understatement. Rests became longer, and our pace slowed. Steve mentioned that his eyes were bothering him, but I didn't understand his context. There wasn't urgency so much as exhaustion in his tone. A few hundred yards before Johns Brook Lodge (3.6 miles from the trailhead), he said he was falling asleep while walking and had to take a break…just five minutes. Thus we rested along the trail with headlamps extinguished. Steve reclined with a deep sigh that quickly morphed into a resonating snore that drowned out the relaxing sound of crickets. I shook my head – if only I could fall asleep in 30 seconds. I, on the other hand, re-nourished while contemplating the logistics of how we'd get into his car. I knew the adventure was far from over.

I woke him up 15 minutes later to continue our death march. We passed a hiker at 11:15 p.m. – Ranger Scott van Laer. We talked about the day, and he offered to call AAA from the Interior Outpost. With any luck, we'd beat the tow truck to the trailhead. In the end AAA was unable to verify my account and sent no aid. Nevertheless, it was a blessing to reach the trailhead at 12:30 a.m. A short drive down to Rooster Comb led to the next brief escapade. I called AAA then waited until 1:30 a.m. when the bright lights of the truck rounded the bend. The driver retrieved the keys after 20 minutes of finagling. Success!

Afterthoughts:

The *East Face* hosts a variety of lines ranging from steep friction climbs to intimidating roof bands. The central gully roughly bisects the face. The most technical terrain and best future potential, should anyone want to push the grade, is north of the gully. There are harder possibilities than *Anorthofright*, most likely to the right of the route. As of this date, however, I believe that I'm finished new-routing on the *East Face*. My curiosity was satiated. The route surpassed my expectations and held several surprises. Is a 20-hour day worth the reward? Absolutely – to me, in any case. Exceptional beauty sometimes comes at a cost.

The Panther's Pinnacle

With: Steven St. Pierre (swapped leads) on 2017 September 16
Area: Marcy *Chimney Wall*
Route: *Panther's Pinnacle* (5.9)
Duration: 4:00 a.m. – 11:15 p.m.
Reference Plate 4

Several features in Panther Gorge stand out to the keen observer. Some of the gems are hidden unless one is looking from the correct perspective. When Adam Crofoot and I walked down the gully in front of the *Chimney Wall* in 2014, it was impossible to miss the free-standing needle perched high on the cliff. It looked fragile, but it's difficult to assess the stability of an object that's located so far above the ground. I fancied seeing it up close. How interesting would that be! In 2014, however, it was merely a dream on a long list of priorities.

Steven St. Pierre and I set out in mid-September to see if we could climb the southeastern arête of the *Chimney Wall* and incorporate the pinnacle into the route. I knew we were setting ourselves up for a long day, but autumn was knocking on the door. I didn't want to wait another winter to explore the feature. I thought it would be an easy to moderate climb (perhaps 5.7 or 5.8) and admit to dreading the extra bushwhacking required to attain the wall. The 20-hour trip we took two weeks earlier was still fresh in my mind.

The Phelps Trail seemed damp on approach to the Marcy/Haystack col, more than I expected after a recent stretch of dry weather. I didn't fear that the cliffs would be running with cascades like other times, but I also wasn't surprised to find several of the cracks seeping. I knew this wouldn't be a problem on the sun/wind-blasted southern aspect of the *Chimney Wall*. The most significant question in mind was how to begin the route. There were mature trees along the base of the arête and part of it was overhung and shaded – moss heaven! We wouldn't know the best start until we explored the options.

Views at the top of the first pitch of Panther's Pinnacle.

The author leading the runout start of pitch three while clouds build over Haystack. Photo by Steven St. Pierre.

We reached our target at 10:30 a.m. I was weary from weaving over the talus and falling into a couple of small holes – the same thing we did two weeks prior in the same area. We explored south around the buttress and up a grassy fourth class gully where we spotted an option. We wanted something better, so we tried starting via *Slacker Cracker*. Steven saw a possible line, so he led the first pitch. He followed a thin crack to a small roof then continued up *Slacker* when an option to the left didn't look viable either. The holds were dirty and sloped downward. Nothing to the right seemed promising. I lowered him so we could re-strategize.

Up we trekked to the first option where I took the lead. Two large cedars blocked an off-width crack (about 6-8 inches wide) above mildly sloped slab. It would be an easy way to kick off the route and traverse to the "real" climbing. The wide crack led to a chossy face. I looked down into the void then back at the broken rock in front of me. I groaned but found solid cracks amongst the crumbly rock in which to place gear. This boosted my confidence, so I decided to give it a go however carefully. I didn't want a rock to peel from underfoot. I knew the climbing above would be better.

Small ledges led to a band of cedar and the main gully (to the right) where multiple cracks ran up the center and edges. Red autumn colors lit a mountain ash growing from a chimney near an obvious roof that loomed above. The shadowed anorthosite of the nearby *Chimney Wall* framed the north end of Panther Gorge – a dramatic view well worth the climb to this point. The perspective was similar to the view along the overhangs on Marcy's *East Face*.

Steve took the next pitch. He quickly dismissed a potential line up a wide overhanging crack into the squeeze chimney – too much lichen. He, instead, chose to ascend a 3" crack in the left corner. The slight overhang pushed him into an uncomfortable stance while trying to place gear. The crack was arm deep and secure but wet in the back – an additional challenge. A few moves later he stepped left over the edge and out of sight. It wasn't long before the rope stopped moving and he'd set up an anchor. Unlike the last trip, we were within earshot of each other with no communication challenges. I followed and found him standing on a low-angle ramp at the end of a handcrack. We were situated near the lower rappel station (a large pine) that Jaryn DeShane and I had set up after climbing the chimney.

I looked up at the wall and asked Steve if he wanted to finish the route since the second pitch was short (50'). He declined, and I set about finding the best way up. There were multiple choices, but the wall slightly overhung in some areas. Hmm... I saw a seam leading to a fingercrack above a large flake near Steve's anchor. It looked nice, but near my leading limit. I took a few hesitant steps upward and studied the face for what seemed an eternity. It was a hard line, but one I could protect if I could reach it. I took another step, tugged on a critical hold, and overcorrected my balance when it peeled off in my hand. My stomach flip-flopped, and I took a few deep breaths. It wasn't worth the time or effort, so I backed down and studied further.

Meanwhile, our beautiful day turned ominous as a dark cloud moved in from the north. Haystack's shadowed massif looked like the malevolent Titan described by Alfred B. Street, though I'm sure it wouldn't spring to life and cast stones at Marcy like he described. The wind shifted, and the temperature dropped. I wrestled with second thoughts about climbing further (wind shifts often foretell rain), but the forecast called for good weather through the day and evening. I decided to bet on the forecast this time.

A handcrack located to the right provided a viable fallback option, so I placed a small nut behind a corner to protect the anchor and began the next pitch. The vertical face was unprotectable for 10' beyond the nut. After that, I could get a stance on a ledge of sorts to reach the crack. I stepped out onto a ½" edge, side-pulled on another edge, and halted again. I can't remember all the moves, but I ended up performing a partial split and still felt reasonably comfortable (however counter-intuitive that sounds). A final committing maneuver set me on the ledge, and I jammed my hand deep in the crack with a sigh of relief. There was no turning back without leaving gear. I was concentrating too intently to notice Steve snapping photos with my camera. He captured several inspiring images in which I somehow looked relaxed on the multi-colored cliff face. He and Haystack, topped with layered clouds, were my only witnesses. This is one of the great joys (and potential dangers) of backcountry climbing – solitude.

The crack led onto a much steeper ramp. I worked my feet into the now slightly rising crack and stood up. A span of classic Panther Gorge moonrock led to the base of the free-standing pillar. There was abundant gear, so I protected myself and absorbed the moment. The base formed a 4' square that was slightly offset from the platform on which it stood. The outside edge arced up to the top while the side facing the cliff was relatively straight. A horizontal crack split it halfway up, and patches of lichen grew on its surface. The view through the 6" void between the pillar and the cliff created a unique perspective of the *Chimney Wall*. I could see the arête of the chimney proper flaring out which emphasized the verticality of the overall area.

Uncertainties regarding the stability of the anorthositic spike evaporated as I studied its structural integrity. It would take a hydraulic jack to move the beast, at least from its bottom. I spied an alternate way to finish the route via a large flake to its left, but I hoped to incorporate the pinnacle to create an exposed route. This thought also took my breath away as I contemplated the quality and features of the cliff above the pillar.

The first few moves refocused me. I couldn't resist slinging a sharp horn of stone sticking out from the spire's base. It would both protect me and save a piece of gear. I was running startlingly low on cams. My climb up the spike can only be described as a graceless wriggle with my left leg jammed between it and the cliff. Its upper half was detached and sitting firmly atop the broader base. It still wouldn't budge as I pushed using the cliff as leverage. I soon stood on the rounded top of the needle. There are no words to describe the feeling of balancing on a rounded eight-inch point situated on an arête falling away for 150'. It was breathtaking and surpassed expectations!

Left: *View from the top of the free-standing pinnacle. Photo by Steven St. Pierre.* **Right:** *Profile of the Chimney Wall and the pinnacle of the route.*

I stepped off and onto a ledge. A series of subsequent ledges led up to the krummholz. I could see the options, but connecting them involved awkward moves especially since the cliff overhung by a few degrees. The first few were wide, but moving up required committing to less than ideal handholds.

I felt like it was taking forever to get the job done, but there was no way to safely rush the ascent. Brushing off critical cracks for gear with just my fingers took time and trying to connect it all required thought, trial and error, then more thought. Nothing felt intuitive. The last six feet of climbing presented the most significant problem. I couldn't find a way that felt secure and stood on a narrow rail. I focused on the stone in front of me to calm my nerves. I then placed a small cam in a crack, tugged to test it, and leaned back to gain perspective. Ha! There was a broad ledge to the right. I moved over to it, cleaned it off, mantled up and was within feet of the trees when my left hand slipped. I backed down and took a breath. Darn overhanging cliff! I moved left and committed to the corner of the arête, my left hand pulling on a small rounded horn of stone below the woods. My grip held this time.

I grabbed a handful of blueberry bush roots once at the top. A bushwhack up an 80-degree slope led to a wooded terrace. I collapsed in the forest duff at the end of the 250'/three-pitch route. My face was coated in debris from cleaning the ledges; enough that I probably looked like a miner resurfacing after working underground. I gave a hoot and set up an anchor from a small cliff in the woods.

I screamed, "On belay!" This set Steve into motion.

It wasn't long before he crested the edge and climbed the ramp. He had my camera and continued to shoot breathtaking photos of the route including several from the top of the pinnacle. He made the climbing look easy; was I that much of a chicken or just slow? He climbed past the anchor and quickly found the tree from which Jaryn and I rappelled a couple of months before. There were only a few stout trees close enough to the edge to be useful.

The route took over four hours to put together which was longer than I originally planned – so much for an easy day. That's what backcountry on-sighting is about – exploring and safely adjusting to ever-changing variables. At least we had the approach and exit bushwhack dialed in! It was 5:30 p.m. when we finally reached the packs after rappelling. I'd envisioned climbing another short line on the way out, but such thoughts evaporated partway up the *Panther's Pinnacle*. We were tired and had only enough ambition for the exit. Our day ended at 11:15 p.m. – and this time, Steve didn't lock his keys in the car.

Dragon's Breath

With: Jaryn DeShane on 2018 February 1
Area: South of the *Chimney Wall*
Route: *Spiritus Draconis* (WI4+)
Duration / Mileage / Elevation Gain: 4:45 a.m. – 4:30 p.m. / 14.75 mi. / 4,400 ft.
Reference Plate 10

The winter of 2017-2018 began harshly with extended periods of sub-zero temperatures. There was enough snow to deter me from pushing the limits of backcountry climbing, so I stayed along the road and practiced leading. A short January thaw and rain increased the possibility of finding a crust at elevation. That was all the incentive I needed to tromp into Panther Gorge with eyes on a stout line south of the *Chimney Wall*. The outcome was uncertain, but the adventure was intrinsic.

Jaryn DeShane signed on when I took a last minute vacation day to leverage the warm weather window. We used the "Crofoot Approach" – a route that Adam Crofoot scouted several years earlier. It allows one to enter through breaks in the clifftops after bushwhacking one-third of a mile from the Van Hoevenberg Trail. One just has to hit it dead-on or be ready to rappel. Trust me when I say that unless you're carrying technical climbing gear and know how to use the equipment, you don't want to test this approach.

We departed from the Adirondak Loj at 4:45 a.m. We hoped to be back to the trailhead by dark. Jaryn wasn't feeling 100%, and I needed to keep some energy in reserve for the rest of the week. This objective was wise in hindsight since I was called to participate in a Great Range rescue a few days later. The winter was marked by the injury of many hikers, and a contributing factor was obvious during the first several miles. The trail was covered in ice. The first snow-cover over the ice was near Tabletop Mountain. We reached the cloud ceiling near the Phelps Trail junction. Our bushwhack would be a blind approach with no line of sight navigation. I thought of the people who have gotten lost near this area while hiking Marcy. It's treacherous terrain.

View from the glade below three routes--Spiritus Draconis on the left, Apex Predator in the center (first climbed in 2019 by Aaron Courain, Kevin, and Alan Wechsler), and Panther's Pinnacle (5.9) on the right.

Kevin leading Spiritus Draconis. Photo by Jaryn DeShane.

We bushwhacked east from the trail a little farther up toward the summit and wove through the ice-entombed trees on a modestly firm snowpack. It was not the hard crust I envisioned, but we only plunged a foot deep except for the occasional spruce trap. The trees were tightly woven for the first 800 ground feet, but they loosened as the grade increased during the descent.

I joked, "I hope there's ice down there."

Jaryn retorted, "Kevin, there better be ice!" Neither of us wanted to be turned back by poor conditions.

Ghostly ledges riddled with thick flows sat to our north – a good sign for our concerns. Roughly 45 minutes later, we found a break in the trees as we approached the cliffs. We climbed down an icy ledge in search of the gully atop the *Chimney Wall*. Nothing looked familiar though we were near the GPS point on Jaryn's device. Hmm...north or south? We were close. Jaryn suggested that we skirt the nearby cliff. At worst, we'd need to climb back up and search more or rappel and scan from the bottom.

As it worked out, we contoured around the cliff and "fourth-classed" our way to the *Chimney Wall* – the chimney was directly in front of us; the little detour hadn't stymied the day. We slid down the gully to look up the dike. More ice (albeit thin) was in the chimney than during my previous winter visits, but a full rack of rock climbing gear was still necessary to climb it. I spotted our potential line to the south. There seemed to be ice, and my pulse quickened.

The line may have been in sight, but the bushwhack wasn't over. The side of Marcy is a rugged area with small ledges and gullies down which we needed to navigate. My hopes evaporated as I assessed the condition of the dual pitch climb. Wind and the contour of the cliff left the lower run of ice in a poor state. It was thin, hadn't touched down, and was slightly overhung – scary and out of our league. Thin vertical ice delaminating from the underlying black bedrock sat above. Only after 30' did the grade ease slightly. The upper column was climbable – a vertical pitch of blue/yellow ice some 50' in height with parasols at the top. Looking wasn't enough, so I donned crampons and walked up to the base. I tapped, and it resounded like a drum – hollow. I chose to live and climb another day.

We turned our gaze 100' to the south. Beta photos showed a northeastern aspect pitch of ice that I knew would be in climbable condition – a consolation prize of sorts. I usually hike in with a backup plan. It looked like a comfortable lead from below (famous last words) though few things truly feel "comfortable" this far into the backcountry. The yellow flow topped out in the trees a few hundred feet north of *Grand Central Slide*. The time stood at 10:30 a.m., so we had plenty of time to climb this and a second line if we had the stamina. It appeared to be a solid WI4 pitch, at least from below.

Packs dropped to the ground, and we set to the task of putting on harnesses and organizing the gear. The first swing of my axe was at 11:10 a.m. I knew several things by 11:11 a.m.

- The ice was bullet hard and brittle.
- The route was more difficult than it looked (as is usually the case).
- I might tuck tail and back off.

I climbed the first 10 vertical feet to a short run of low-angle ice and placed a screw. The sharp screws took time to bite into the surface. I sat for a few moments and collected myself after realizing that I couldn't simply muscle my way up. Placing protection from strenuous stances would take time. I had to think and move slowly. While I was out in the backcountry a fair amount, I was still a relative "newbie" on vertical ice compared to those who have been climbing for decades. This fact resonated with each swing of the axe and kick of the crampons. I didn't want to underestimate the route or overestimate myself. I often space protection far apart – not today. A couple more moves placed me at the bottom of the vertical wall of yellow "china." Such was the sound when we struck the ice where it was hollow.

I briefly thought, *Why am I doing this?* Should I have Jaryn lower me from a screw and call it a day? I reconsidered the thought. I was well protected and I had spotted enough of a line where I could stand on small though uncomfortable stances to place more protection. Similar thoughts have crossed my mind throughout my sojourns when

Jaryn nearing the gully at the top of the route. Apex Predator sits in the background.

Jaryn ascending the steep gully below the Chimney Wall.

I rub against my comfort zone. These are learning moments. I hooked (placed the pick in a hole in the ice) and struck my way up a hollow curtain. I then found a slightly better stance from which to look around.

I started up again and broke a large plate off onto my shoulder, "Ice!"

Higher was a larger ledge where I found a small ice cave from which the lower part of the flow was building. The formation was interesting and harbored the only "soft" ice of the route. Most people associate all ice with the term "hard." Soft ice only makes sense when you climb it and realize that they are relative terms. One can feel the density of ice that's seen little sunlight and has been subjected to sub-zero temperatures with little water seepage.

I was above the crux and had a good spot to rest, so I took a moment to soak in the scenery. I had a much better view of the monster to the north, but Haystack's cone was vanishing in the mist. The cloud ceiling was getting lower, and it was snowing harder though I could still see the lines on Marcy (*Agharta* and a few others) as well as a half dozen unclimbed lines on Haystack. The gullies were swollen with ice, and most of the cliffs had at least a thin tier of crystalline daggers decorating the edges. The entire Gorge seemed to be in prime condition. What a spectacular sight!

A short vertical pitch led to easier bulges at the top where I felt more in my element though I didn't let my guard down. The ascent wasn't over until I slung a stout evergreen at the top and shouted, "Off belay!" roughly 45 minutes after starting.

It seemed like it had taken hours, but perspective is an odd thing. Every trip is a learning experience, and the 90' of ice below was a strict teacher with a stiff ruler. It was now Jaryn's turn to get a taste of Panther Gorge ice for the first time. I couldn't see him on the vertical sections, but I could sense what he was doing by a few choice words carried on the wind and the tension on the rope. The occasional strike of a tool echoed off the nearby cliffs. I scanned the immediate scenery; the area was now socked in. The rope disappeared over the gray bulges and into the abyss. Eventually, Jaryn's face popped into view with a smile. He was standing on the largest ledge. The perspective was particularly dramatic, so I took a few photos. It was turning out to be a good day!

He reached my stance and yelled, "That was a lot harder than it looked…what the…?"

"Yeah," I snickered, "I noticed that on the way up."

Our route was just one of the possible lines in the deep Gorge. With the right conditions to build the ice, there were many short (100'-200' range) potential new routes (WI4 to 5+ at a glance) on the immediate cliffs. It's a difficult area to access, and it's frustrating when one arrives only to find that the ice hasn't fully formed. In any case, an interesting name seemed in order: *Spiritus Draconis* (Dragon's Breath) with a rating of WI4+ and probably a 5 if one adhered strictly to the climber's left.

Jaryn rappelled first, and I heard him say, "Holy crap, this is dead vertical." I laughed again.

We wanted something challenging relative to our skill level and the wish had been granted. In the end, brittle ice increased the difficulty, but this is often the case with "high elevation" water ice. We decided against hunting for a second route. Both of us wanted a shorter than normal day. It was only 12:30 p.m. when we finished the rappel, so we were on track if all went well. There was just the issue of bushwhacking up to the Van Hoevenberg Trail.

Back at the *Chimney Wall*, it was the usual slog up a 45-degree slope with various forms of underlying ice. Thin smears and curtains adorned the cliff on our left: God's water-art. A flow ending in wind-whipped formations that looked like viper fangs guarded the exit. We changed into snowshoes once in the safety of the forest and began the slow task of trailbreaking. We then angled north to intersect our approach path. The track had consolidated which helped save energy during the ascent.

Back on the trail, we glissaded down the steep sections and made good time as the weather warmed to 40 degrees. Light rain was in the forecast, but we didn't experience much precipitation other than the snow during our time in the Gorge. I knew we were on pace for the quickest turnaround time of any one of these trips (personally speaking). Outings have always been longer than 12.5 hours with an average of 16.5. We arrived at the trailhead at 4:30 p.m. Exiting with daylight to spare seemed strange. In the end; our pace, the "modest" itinerary, decent bushwhacking conditions and a "short" approach relative to our target cliff helped us finish the day in 11 hr. 45 minutes. It was a nice change, but not anything I expected to duplicate in the near future.

Jaryn taking in the view with Haystack in the background and the beaver ponds in the valley.

Between Scylla and Charybdis

With: Laura Duncan (lead P1) & Brent Elliott (lead on Scylla) on 2018 February 17
Area: Marcy *Twin Fracture Gully* (Southern edge of *Huge Scoop*)
Routes: *Charybdis* (WI4) & *Scylla* (WI4)
Duration: 4:15 a.m. – 10:30 p.m.
Reference Plates 1, 10

Twin Fracture Gully is a deep gash that slices into the side of Marcy along the southern border of the *Huge Scoop*. The distinctive feature is 20' wide and deeply inset into the southeastern aspect of the ridge. The main channel splits into dual gullies amidst roof systems at its top. As a drainage for the ridge, it is a chossy wet mess during non-winter seasons, but that sets it up for fat ice when the snow flies.

It was on my winter tick list for a few years, but the thought of trudging that far into the Gorge was unappealing. I kept it in my pocket as a backup option in case a target line wasn't fully formed. Enter Laura Duncan and Brent Elliott, two climbers I met in Panther Gorge during February of 2017. They drove seven hours to share in an Adirondack adventure. We met at the Garden Trailhead at 4:15 a.m. Our primary target was a smear 100' north of the *Agharta* ice route. The potential line looked fat from afar during the *Spiritus Draconis* trip. I questioned whether the bottom of the curtain had touched down and, if not, whether we'd be able to find a way up to the ice. Recent rain followed by a flash freeze sparked my hopes, but longer daylight hours and the dark anorthosite of Marcy were working against it. The only way to find out was to visit.

Hard-packed trails aided with the trek to the col but the crust off-trail wasn't bulletproof as I had anticipated. We endured some bushwhacking acrobatics in the talus and walked out on the snowfield below the *Agharta Wall* 45 minutes later. Its namesake route and *Just Nickel and Iron* were fat. The blue sky and warm stare of the sun were in contrast to the

Laura leading pitch one with Brent belaying.

Laura and Brent enjoying the scenery from the top of pitch one.

forecast which called for partly cloudy skies with 15-20 m.p.h. winds – not good for the smear. Our hopeful line looked terrifying. Melted daggers were 15' from the ground, and there wasn't enough feature in the rock to climb up to their start. The middle of the line was nearly melted out. I grumbled to myself, reset my hopes, and suggested that we trek 15 minutes south to *Twin Fracture Gully*. If that wasn't in, we could throw new-routing to the wind and climb *Agharta*.

The snowfield showed evidence of the recent warm spell – a spear of ice sticking out of the surface. A few minutes later, we were catching our breath in the snowfield near the gully. I climbed up high enough to view the top, and my heart jumped with excitement. I could see ice capping the cliff at the top of the gully. It wasn't simply climbable; it was fat. The six hour approach suddenly seemed worth the effort. I said a quick prayer for a safe climb before the action started.

Laura tied in and zipped up the first pitch. Several women have made their mark in the Gorge including Emilie Drinkwater who climbed *Panther Gorge Falls* during her historic solo of Joe Szot's *Trilogy*. To my knowledge, Laura is the first woman to be part of an ice climbing first ascent in the area. She took the first pitch 180' up to a bulge below the confluence of the dual gullies. It didn't take long before she had Brent and me on belay.

Marcy enveloped us as we climbed side by side on the blue ice. Upon reaching the anchor, we climbed another 50' up to a stance that was protected from icefall. We assessed the options and discussed strategy. Our initial thought was to put up a single long line, but it was early, and there were two obvious choices. After discussion, we agreed that I would lead the left, we'd rappel, and Brent would lead the right. The terrain beyond our view was likely just low-angle ice.

With the climbing logistics under control, I looked around at the amazing ice formations: ramps, bulges, smears, hanging spikes and wind-whipped icicles. The arena had several similarities to *Multiplication Gully* as well as *Haggis and Cold Toast* (on steroids). There were a multitude of other route possibilities. I ascended the first bulge, placed a screw and entered an ice-entombed chimney. A fat curtain on the right, several inches

An icy chimney is one of the highlights of Charybdis.

of clear ice on the left, and a thick ramp underfoot set the stage for comfortable, if not occasionally awkward, climbing. Higher, the right-hand wall opened for an unobstructed view to the north. Large black roofs and hanging daggers were overhead.

I rested in a spacious cave under the roof system. Curtains of clear ice continued north, but I planned to take the line straight up an exposed vertical section. Twenty feet higher, I worked my way into a squeeze chimney of freshly formed ice. The route was still building. I didn't expect to find "plastic" during the climb since we're usually fighting bullet ice at this elevation. I stemmed and squirmed my way into a good stance for another rest. I looked down, and Laura and Brent were back into view (we had lost sight of each other after the first bulge). Another short vertical tier led onto a gleaming white bulge and into the trees. I was near the end of the rope, so I slung a solid spruce and set up an anchor. The length of the new route was 400' with three pitches. It was thrilling to find such a challenging and aesthetic line to lead.

Laura, then Brent, followed. It was impossible to see her progress until she entered the upper chimney.

Her smiling face popped into view and she yelled, "This is the best pitch of ice I've ever climbed!"

That statement alone made my day. I love sharing these experiences with people who appreciate the rugged beauty (and a bit of suffering). Brent soon appeared, and Laura took photos of him cresting the top. Instead of climbing directly to our position, he explored right to see if we should continue the line. A low-angle snow gully led to another short bulge, but it didn't seem worth the effort, so we rappelled down to the confluence and prepared to take on the northern gully.

Our warm, cozy nook turned into a blustery freezer as high-level clouds and a moderate breeze moved in – the conditions of the original forecast. Accounting for wind chill, the temperature was in the single digits. Laura and I were shivering even while wearing belay jackets. She decided to rappel to the packs to heat some soup and take shelter. Brent and I continued the quest though I admit that at the time I'd have been just as happy to have descended with her. I knew the climbing would eventually reanimate my hands. I watched the cedars whip back and forth along the cliff top and shivered again.

It was easier to watch the leader on this line although showers of ice chips occasionally sent me scrambling for protection against the right-hand wall. A few short vertical sections led to a ramp below a vertical curtain. The crux was at the top.

A half hour later Brent reached the trees and yelled, "Off belay!"

I tried to climb fast enough to regain feeling in my fingers. It worked just as I reached the curtain. I stopped to rest and deal with the "screaming barfies" – a painful condition. It was a visually intimidating arena with a few columns that had touched down and plenty of free-hanging mass. One could put up a WI5 here if they were so inclined. A line up the right side offered a more comfortable option. It had the requisite awkward exit into a dense cedar grove – classic Adirondack adventure climbing. Brent's line was 180' long.

Two rappels later found us back at our packs and behind the shelter of a small ridge. Laura emerged from the trees looking reinvigorated from a hot meal. It was 4:30 p.m. and the waning sun behind the clouds looked like a soft orb as it moved toward Marcy's ridge. My motivation shifted from new-routing to something more simple – bushwhacking back to the trail before darkness swallowed the Gorge. I knew the way, but trail-breaking out through the north pass in the dark is dispiriting. We slowly followed our tracks, connecting glades until we reached the *Panther Den* at the top. We then diverged from our entry path to avoid the talus in the center of the drainage. *By Tooth and Claw* (2016) was thin but climbable. Several new possibilities including what looked like a WI5+ on the *Panther Den's* prow were in as well.

The situation became humorous during the final push to the Phelps Trail while Laura broke trail. She did a fine job of finding the powder stashes which brought her to a screeching halt on the steeper slopes. Brent quipped that she was a skier at heart. At least I knew where not to step. It was 5:30 p.m. when we reached "civilization." With eight miles to go, the day was far from over.

We named the routes *Charybdis* (WI4/400') and *Scylla* (WI4/180') during a discussion at Slant Rock. Twin monsters of the deep Gorge seemed appropriate, and Laura appreciated that Scylla is depicted as a female in Greek mythology. A warm fire at Johns Brook Lodge seduced us into another rest before reaching the trailhead at 10:30 p.m. Thus closed the "calendar winter" ice climbing season in Panther Gorge.

Left: Ice on all sides and a roof at the top of Charybdis. **Right:** View of Haystack from a cave along the route.

Endnotes

Introduction and History

[1] "Gleanings from Old Fields. Rainbow Falls – The Ausable Ponds – Panther Gorge," *Plattsburgh Republican*, October 12, 1872, http://nyshistoricnewspapers.org/lccn/sn83031979/1872-10-12/ed-1/seq-3/.

[2] *New York State Conservation Department, Thirtieth Annual Report for the Year 1940*, no. 38 (New York: Publishers Printing Co., 1941): 50-51, accessed November 29, 2016, http://nysl.cloudapp.net/awweb/guest.jsp?smd=1&cl=all_lib&lb_document_id=115179.

[3] New York (State), Department of Environmental Conservation, *Draft High Peaks Wilderness Complex Unit Management Plan: Wilderness Management for the High Peaks of the Adirondack Park*, (Albany, N.Y.: December 1994): app. 5, 4.

[4] E.R. Wallace, *Descriptive guide to the Adirondacks, and handbook of travel to Saratoga Springs; Schroon Lake; Lakes Luzerne, George, and Champlain; The Ausable Chasm; Massena Springs; and Trenton Falls* (Syracuse: Watson Gill, 1894), 341.

[5] Robert W. Carroll, Jr., *Notebooks of Robert W. Carroll, Jr.*, 1941-2005, Courtesy of the Northeastern Regional Organization of the National Speleological Society and Chuck Porter.

[6] "Gleanings from Old Fields," 3.

[7] Wallace, *Descriptive guide to the Adirondacks*, 314.

[8] James A. Goodwin, *And Gladly Guide: Reflections on a Life in the Mountains* (Self-published manuscript, c2003), 32.

[9] Alfred Billings Street, *The Indian Pass* (New York: Hurd & Houghton, 1869), 97.

[10] John Warren, "The Big Blowdown of 1950," *Adirondack Almanack*, November 15, 2010, accessed January 15, 2017, http://www.adirondackalmanack.com/2010/11/natures-wrath-the-big-blowdown-of-1950.html.

[11] Wallace, *Descriptive guide to the Adirondacks*, 311.

[12] Phil Brown, "The Map of Adirondack Remoteness and Boreas Ponds," *Adirondack Almanack*, May 9, 2017, accessed March 20, 2017, https://www.adirondackalmanack.com/2017/01/boreas-ponds-map-remoteness.html.

[13] Sandra Weber, Mount Marcy: *The High Peak of New York* (Fleischmanns, NY: Purple Mountain Press, 2001), 69.

[14] Street, *The Indian Pass*, 3.

[15] Tim Tefft, "Mount Marcy," in *Heaven Up-h'isted-ness!: The History of the Adirondack Forty-Sixers and the High Peaks of the Adirondacks* (Cadyville, NY: Adirondack Forty-Sixers, 2011), 173.

[16] Street, *The Indian Pass*, 97.

[17] Ibid.

[18] Ibid., 98.

[19] Ibid., 99.

20 Ibid.

21 Ibid., 20.

22 Ibid., 99.

23 Laura Waterman and Guy Waterman, *Forest and Crag: A History of Hiking, Trail Blazing, and Adventure in the Northeast Mountains* (Boston: Appalachian Mountain Club Books, 2003), 116.

24 Weber, *Mount Marcy*, 76.

25 Margaret Sidney, *An Adirondack Cabin: A Family Story, Telling of Journeyings by Lake and Mountain, and Idyllic Days in the Heart of the Wilderness* (Boston: D. Lothrop, 1890), 218-219.

26 "Finding Aid Orson Schofield Phelps", *Adirondack Research Library of Union College*, last modified July 12, 2016, accessed March 13, 2018, https://libguides.union.edu/arl/ARL-finding-aids.

27 Benson J. Lossing, *The Hudson, from the wilderness to the sea* (New York: Virtue & Yorston, 1866), 37.

28 Orson S. Phelps, "Keene Flats," *Essex County Republican*, September 29, 1870, accessed October 10, 2017, http://nyshistoricnewspapers.org/lccn/sn84031741/1870-09-29/ed-1/seq-3/.

29 Edith Pilcher, *Up the Lake Road: The First Hundred Years of the Adirondack Mountain Reserve* (Keene Valley, NY: Centennial Committee for the Trustees of the Adirondack Mountain Reserve, 1987), 182.

30 Verplanck Colvin, *Seventh Annual Report on the Progress of the Topographical Survey of the Adirondack Region of New York: To the Year 1879. Containing the Condensed Reports for the Years 1874-75-76-77 and '78. With Late Results in Geodetic and Trigonometrical Measurements, Magnetic Variation, Hydrography, River Surveys, Leveling and Barometric-hypsometry, Meteorology, Rain-fall, Botany, Zoölogy and Geology. With Maps, Engravings and Chromo-lithographs* (Albany: Weed, Parsons & Company, 1880), 91.

31 Ibid., 93.

32 Orson S. Phelps, "Keene Flats," *Essex County Republican*, June 8, 1871, accessed October 11, 2017, http://nyshistoricnewspapers.org/lccn/sn84031741/1871-06-08/ed-1/seq-3/.

33 Weber, *Mount Marcy*, 112-113.

34 Ibid., 130.

35 Orson S. Phelps, "New Trails to the Summit of Mount Marcy," *Essex County Republican*, July 8, 1875c, 3, accessed March 1, 2017, http://nyshistoricnewspapers.org/lccn/sn84031741/1875-07-08/ed-1/seq-3/.

36 Ibid.

37 Orson S. Phelps, "Mountain Camp Building," *Plattsburgh Republican*, July 3, 1875b, 1, accessed August 15, 2017, http://nyshistoricnewspapers.org/lccn/sn83031979/1875-07-03/ed-1/seq-1/.

38 Ibid.

39 Orson S. Phelps, "Among the Adirondacks," *Plattsburgh Sentinel*, September 19, 1873, 2, accessed January 28, 2015, http://nyshistoricnewspapers.org/lccn/sn85026976/1873-09-19/ed-1/seq-2/.

40 Orson S. Phelps, "The Rivers and Brooks of the Adirondacks," *Orson Schofield Phelps Collection*, Adirondack Research Library of Union College.

⁴¹ "'The Stroll of the Tahawus Club," *The Plattsburgh Republican*, September 4, 1875, accessed January 24, 2015, http://nyshistoricnewspapers.org/lccn/sn83031979/1875-09-04/ed-1/seq-1/.

⁴² Ibid.

⁴³ Ibid.

⁴⁴ Seneca Ray Stoddard, *The Adirondacks: Illustrated* (Glens Falls: Stoddard, 1891), 170-171.

⁴⁵ Verplanck Colvin, *Report on the Topographical Survey of the Adirondack Wilderness of New York* (Albany: The Argus Company, Printers, 1873), 5.

⁴⁶ Ibid., 33.

⁴⁷ Verplanck Colvin, *Report on the Topographical Survey of the Adirondack Wilderness of New York for the Year 1873* (Albany: Weed, Parsons and Company, 1874), 33.

⁴⁸ Colvin, *Report on the Topographical Survey*, (Printed 1873), 20.

⁴⁹ Verplanck Colvin and Paul Schaefer, *Adirondack Explorations: Nature Writings of Verplanck Colvin* (Syracuse, NY: Syracuse University Press, 1997), 226.

⁵⁰ Colvin, *Report on the Topographical Survey*, (Printed 1873), 21.

⁵¹ Colvin, *Report on the Topographical Survey for the Year 1873*, 33.

⁵² Ibid., 35.

⁵³ Ibid., 36.

⁵⁴ Ibid., 35.

⁵⁵ Ibid., 35-36.

⁵⁶ Ibid., 37.

⁵⁷ Ibid., 38.

⁵⁸ Colvin, *Seventh Annual Report*, 12.

⁵⁹ Ibid., 93 app.

⁶⁰ Ibid., 96 app.

⁶¹ Ibid., 98 app.

⁶² Ibid.

⁶³ Ibid.

⁶⁴ Ibid., 99 app.

⁶⁵ Ibid.

[66] Orson S. Phelps, "Finding the True Height of Tahawus," *Plattsburgh Republican*, November 20, 1875a, accessed January 14, 2016, http://nyshistoricnewspapers.org/lccn/sn83031979/1875-11-20/ed-1/seq-4/.

[67] Colvin, *Seventh Annual Report*, 91 app.

[68] Ibid., 99 app.

[69] Ibid., 100 app.

[70] Ibid.

[71] Ibid., 101 app.

[72] Ibid., 31.

[73] Colvin, *Report on the Topographical Survey for the Year 1873*, 34.

[74] Russell M. L. Carson, "Snow Climbing in the Adirondacks," *High Spots*, January 1932, 3.

[75] Waterman and Waterman, *Forest and Crag*, 213.

[76] Newell Martin, "Six Summits," *High Spots*, July 1931, 4.

[77] Ibid.

[78] Ibid.

[79] Waterman and Waterman, *Forest and Crag*, 395.

[80] Martin, "Six Summits," 6.

[81] Harold Weston, *Freedom in the Wilds: An Artist in the Adirondacks*, ed. Rebecca Foster (Syracuse, N.Y: Syracuse University Press, 1971), 49.

[82] Tony Goodwin, "Alderson Camp," e-mail message to Richard Tucker, June 25, 2017.

[83] Martin, "Six Summits," 3.

[84] Christopher Shaw, "At Panther Gorge with William James," *New England Review* 33, no. 4 (2013): 86, accessed November 17, 2016, doi.10.1353/ner.2013.0011.

[85] William James and Henry James, *The Letters of William James* (Boston: Little, Brown, 1926), 76-77.

[86] Shaw, "At Panther Gorge," 91.

[87] James and James, *Letters of William James*, 78.

[88] Shaw, "At Panther Gorge," 97.

[89] Goodwin, *And Gladly Guide*, 32.

[90] Pilcher, *Up the Lake Road*, 182.

[91] Goodwin, *And Gladly Guide*, 32.

[92] Ibid.

[93] James A. Goodwin, "Rock Climbing in the Adirondacks," in *The Adirondack High Peaks and the Forty-Sixers* (Adirondack, NY: The Adirondack Forty-Sixers, 1970), 141.

[94] Ibid.

[95] Ibid., 142.

[96] P. F. Loope, "Marcy via the Ausable," *Adirondack Daily Enterprise* (Saranac Lake), June 27, 1955, 8, accessed January 15, 2016, http://nyshistoricnewspapers.org/lccn/sn86033360/1955-06-27/ed-1/seq-8/.

[97] Gerald D. Murray, "Panther Gorge," *High Spots*, July 1934, 20.

[98] Ibid., 19.

[99] Ibid., 20.

[100] Alfred L. Donaldson, *A History of the Adirondacks*, vol. 2 (New York: The Century Company, 1921), 257-259.

[101] Alfred L. Donaldson, *A History of the Adirondacks*, vol. 1 (New York: The Century Company, 1921), 58.

[102] Pilcher, *Up the Lake Road*, 7.

[103] Ibid., 28.

[104] Weber, *Mount Marcy*, 151.

[105] Pilcher, *Up the Lake Road*, 53.

[106] "Marcy Purchased for State Park," *Massena Observer*, March 26, 1908, accessed August 17, 2017, http://nyshistoricnewspapers.org/lccn/sn84031311/1908-03-26/ed-1/seq-1.pdf.

[107] Pilcher, *Up the Lake Road*, 54-55.

[108] Tony Goodwin, "Panther Gorge Trail, 03-05-2016," e-mail message to author, March 5, 2016.

[109] Pilcher, *Up the Lake Road*, 56-57.

[110] Goodwin, *And Gladly Guide*, 124.

[111] Chuck Porter, "Robert W. Carroll, Jr. Obituary," *National Speleological Society News*, September 2005.

[112] Ibid.

[113] Robert W. Carroll, Jr., "Mount Marcy Cavern," *The Northeastern Caver*, January-February 1977, 10.

[114] Carroll, *Notebooks*, 174.

[115] Ibid.

[116] Ibid., 253.

[117] Ibid.

[118] Ibid.

[119] Ibid., 254.

[120] Ibid., 265.

[121] Colvin, *Seventh Annual Report*, 96 app.

[122] "Perilous Trip, A," *Elizabethtown Post and Gazette*, October 18, 1883, 2, accessed March 17, 2017, http://nyshistoricnewspapers.org/lccn/sn92061912/1883-10-18/ed-1/seq-2/.

[123] "Rangers Rejoining Mt. Marcy Search," *Press-Republican* (Plattsburgh), March 27, 1973, accessed April 4, 2017, http://nyshistoricnewspapers.org/lccn/sn88074101/1973-03-27/ed-1/seq-2/.

[124] Charles Decker, "Identification Made of Atkinson's Gear," *Adirondack Daily Enterprise* (Saranac Lake), June 16, 1976a, 1, accessed December 26, 2017, http://nyshistoricnewspapers.org/lccn/sn86033360/1976-06-16/ed-1/seq-1/.

[125] Charles Decker, "Solution of Mystery Nears as Skeleton is Discovered," *Adirondack Daily Enterprise* (Saranac Lake), July 28, 1976b, 1, accessed April 4, 2017, http://nyshistoricnewspapers.org/lccn/sn86033360/1976-07-28/ed-1/seq-1/.

[126] Ibid.

[127] Gary Spencer, "We Just Couldn't Go Anymore," *The Lake Placid News*, January 15, 1976, 1-2, accessed April 4, 2017, http://nyshistoricnewspapers.org/lccn/sn86033359/1976-01-15/ed-1/seq-1/.

[128] Ibid.

[129] Ibid.

[130] Ibid.

[131] Kate Gurnette, "Recalling Fruitless Search on Cold Mountain," *The Baltimore Sun*, May, 20, 2001, accessed April 3, 2017, http://articles.baltimoresun.com/2001-05-20/news/0105200003_1_mount-marcy-paul-thomas-ken-sherwood.

[132] Ed Hale, "The Search for Steven Thomas," *Adirondack Life* (web log), April 1982, accessed March 3, 2017, http://www.adirondacklifemag.com/blogs/2014/07/23/search-steven-thomas/.

[133] Ibid.

[134] Ibid.

[135] Ibid.

[136] Liza Frenette, "Trio Survives Marcy's Worst," *Press-Republican* (Plattsburgh), January 6, 1987.

[137] Ron Landfried, "Three Rescued From Mt. Marcy's Icy Grip," *The Lake Placid News*, January 8, 1987, accessed April 4, 2017, http://nyshistoricnewspapers.org/lccn/sn86033359/1987-01-08/ed-1/seq-2/.

[138] Tony Goodwin, "Accident Report," *Adirondac*, June 1989, 10.

[139] Laura Rappaport, "Survival Skills Kept Pair Alive," *Adirondack Daily Enterprise* (Saranac Lake), March 8, 1989, accessed April 4, 2017, http://nyshistoricnewspapers.org/lccn/sn86033360/1989-03-08/ed-1/seq-1/.

[140] Ibid.

[141] Ibid.

[142] Goodwin, "Accident Report," 10.

[143] "Autopsy Report Confirms Hypothermia," *Press-Republican* (Plattsburgh), April 14, 1991, 5, accessed April 4, 2017, http://nyshistoricnewspapers.org/lccn/sn88074101/1991-04-14/ed-1/seq-5/.

[144] "Australian Hiker Dies in High Peaks Wilderness," *Lake Placid News*, April 17, 1991, 2, accessed April 4, 2017, http://nyshistoricnewspapers.org/lccn/sn86033359/1991-04-17/ed-1/seq-2.pdf.

[145] Mike Lynch, "Lost Marcy Hiker Shares Survival Story," *Adirondack Almanack* (web log), January, 30, 2015, accessed March 3, 2017, https://www.adirondackalmanack.com/2015/01/lost-marcy-hiker-shares-survival-story.html.

[146] Dave Jackson, "Adirondacks & Panther Gorge," e-mail message to author, July 21, 2017.

[147] Colvin, *Seventh Annual Report*, 98 app.

[148] Will Roth, Facebook Messenger message to author, August 16, 2017.

[149] Emilie Drinkwater, "ADK Trilogy," e-mail message to author, August 6, 2017.

[150] Bill Schneider, Facebook Messenger message to author, June 26, 2017.

Figures:

i Verplanck Colvin, *Adirondack Survey 1873. Secondary Reconnaissance Sketch of Mount Marcy and the Sources of the Hudson River.* [map]. Scale not given. In: Verplanck Colvin. *Report on the Topographical Survey of the Adirondack Wilderness of New York for the Year 1873* (Albany: Weed, Parsons and Company, 1874), plate 20.

ii Conservation Commission, *Boundary and Type Map of the North West Part of TWP.48 T.& C.P. and the South One Half of OT 68 T.I & 2 OMT* portion of title illegible [map]. Scale not given. Albany, NY, 1920, Courtesy of Tony Goodwin.

iii Robert W. Carroll, Jr., *Horizontal "Grade-3 ½" Map of Marcy Cavern* [map]. Scale not given. In Robert W. Carroll, Jr. *Notebooks of Robert W. Carroll, Jr., 1941-2005*, 266, Courtesy of the Northeastern Regional Organization of the National Speleological Society and Chuck Porter.

The Chronicles of Panther Gorge

[1] Gerald D. Murray, "Panther Gorge," *High Spots*, July 1934, 20.

[2] Nolan Huther, "A Climbing Experience in Panther Gorge," *Pure Adirondacks*, n/a, accessed January 1, 2017, https://pureadirondacks.com/blogs/adirondack-field-notes/121368705-a-climbing-experience-in-panther-gorge.

Reference Plates

The following plates are provided to add context for routes discussed in this book; not all Panther Gorge routes are represented. Missing routes include those pioneered between 2002 and 2010. Route lines show the general path up the cliff. Names, grades, and lengths are listed. Rock climbing routes are red, ice climbing routes are blue and the first named ascent, the *Panther's Fang*, is orange. Landmarks are denoted with A, B, C, etc.

The Author on Fly By. Pencil sketch by Nolan Huther.

PLATE 2: MT. MARCY PANTHER DEN
1. Promised Land (5.8/410')
2. Cat on a Wet Tin Roof (5.8/200')
3. Climb After Slime (5.8/200')
4. Panther's Fang–ca. 1965 (5.8+/110')
5. You Moss Be Kidding Me! (5.7/110')
6. One for the Boys (5.9/75')
7. Belshazzar's Fate (5.8/100')
8. Castle Column (5.9/115')

A. Grand Central Slide
B. Chimney Wall
C. Overhang Slide

PLATE 6: MT. HAYSTACK
NORTH END ROCK ROUTES
1. For Whom the Lichen Tolls (5.9/40')
2. Eye for an Eye (5.8/60')
3. Less Than Zero (5.5/60')
4. All Battered Boyfriends (5.7/70')

A. Free-Standing Pillars
B. Ramp Wall

PLATE 7: MT. HAYSTACK NO MAN'S LAND
1. Paws Off (5.8/400')

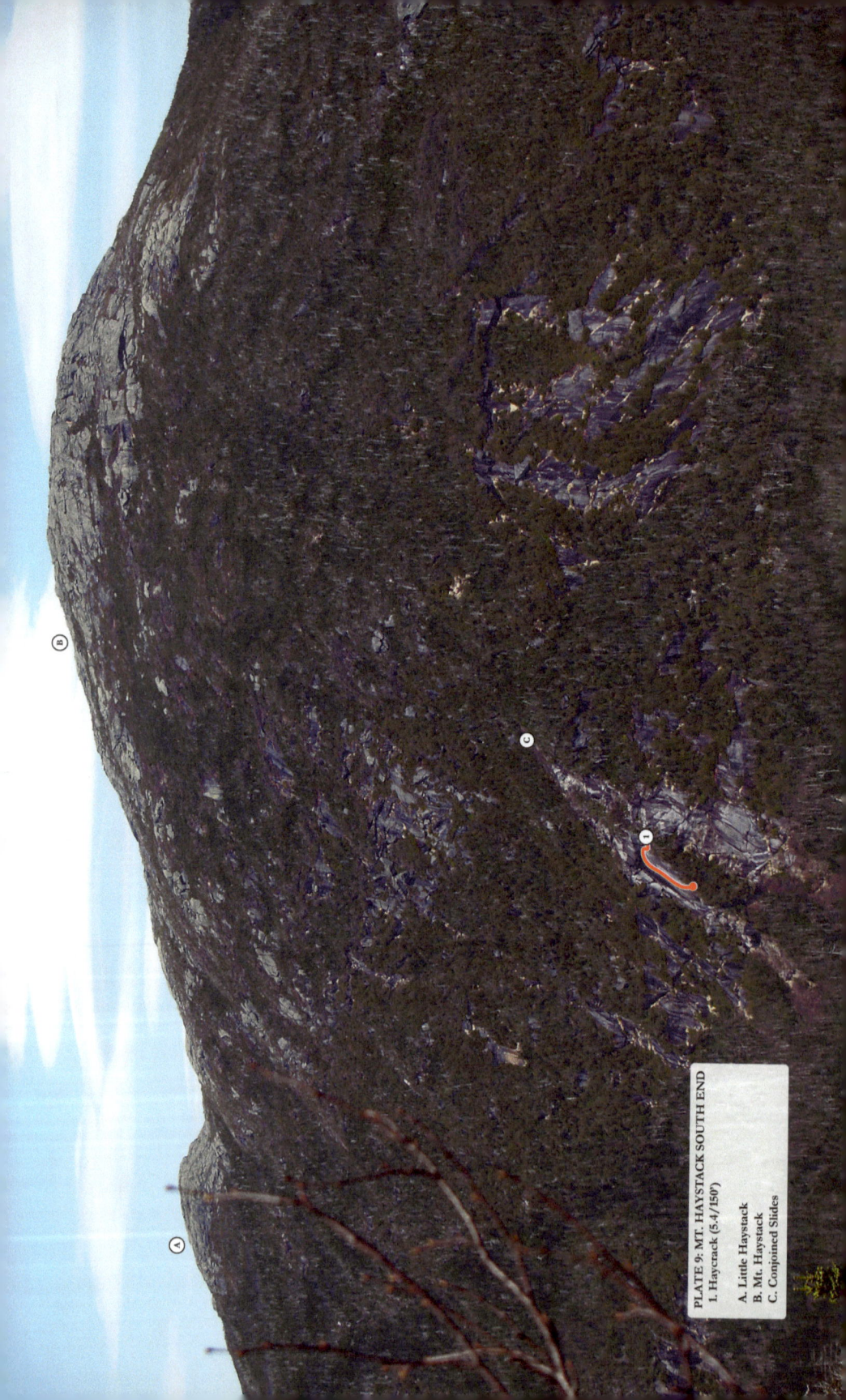

PLATE 9: MT. HAYSTACK SOUTH END
1. Haycrack (5.4/150')

A. Little Haystack
B. Mt. Haystack
C. Conjoined Slides

PLATE 10: MT. MARCY ICE ROUTES
(MINUS PANTHER DEN)
1. Panther Gorge Falls/Grand Central Slide
2. Spiritus Draconis (WI4+/90')
3. Apex Predator (WI4-5/160')
4. Pi Day (WI3-/260')
5. Charybdis (WI4/400')
6. Scylla (WI4/180')
7. Just Nickel and Iron (WI4-/575')
8. Agharta (WI4-/600')
9. Chimera (WI3-/275')
10. Sorry, Kevin (WI4/300')

PLATE 11: MT. HAYSTACK
NORTH END ICE ROUTES
1. Orson's Tower (WI3+/90°)
2. Kitty Cake (WI2/60°)
3. Fly By (WI3+/120°)
4. Skip the Lightning (WI3+/150°)
5. Ride the Lightning (WI5-/110°)

A. Free-Standing Pillars
B. Ramp Wall

Spiritus Draconis and Apex Predator as seen from the northern cliffs of Marcy.

Epilogue

Loren Swears and I marched into the Gorge on March 24, 2018. We lugged winter climbing packs over "Horse Hill" to the base of Little Haystack and into the depths of the Panther. This was a new approach relative to my other trips. The snowpack was unsupportive, and we logged an 18.5 hour day. In the end, we put up two ice routes: *John 3:16* and *PG-13* (see reference plate 8). We also scouted new lines for the winter of 2019.

Even as I write this, I contemplate future outings with a smile. What will they yield? What memories will we forge? The future is a blank slate, and the trip with Loren was as inspiring as my first. The uncertainties, trials, views, and thrills of the climb were everything I expected. I anticipate that trips during the coming years will be much the same. In this, I find hope.

I pray that other wilderness explorers will find the same joy in the backcountry as I have. I pray that they will adhere to the same environmental ethics. The Adirondacks must remain pristine and forever wild for future generations. My days of adventuring between Marcy and Haystack will someday wane, and I won't have seen all that I dreamed of seeing. Another will have to pick up the torch and begin their journey. As Don Mellor stated in the Foreword, "The Gorge is a big place. The shroud has been lifted, but only partly."

Index

The letter p following a page number denotes a photograph, the letter f denotes a footnote, the letter d denotes a drawing, the letter m denotes a map, and the letters pl following a page number denote a plate.

A

Adirondac, 64
Adirondack Cabin, An (Sidney), 21
Adirondack Explorer, 134
Adirondack Mountain Reserve (AMR), 38
Adirondack Outdoors, 97
"Adirondack Railroad Facts and Fancies," 30
Adirondack Research Library of Union College, 25
Adirondack Rock (Lawyer and Haas), 37, 47
Adirondack Survey, 25, 27, 43
Adirondack Trail Improvement Society (ATIS), 34
Adirondack Trilogy, 49, 195
Adirondack Wild, 114
Adirondacks Illustrated, The (Stoddard), 21, 87, 129
Adirondak Loj (Lodge)
    James, William, 32
    trailhead, 19, 43, 45-46, 54, 94, 189
Air Force, 44
Alderson Camp, 32
Alderson, Charles, 32
Alderson, William C., 38
Algonquin (Mt. McIntyre), 27
Ampersand Pass, 30
And Gladly Guide (Goodwin), 33
Anderson, Pop, 39
Armstrong, Thomas, 38
"At Panther Gorge with William James" (Shaw), 33

Ausable Lakes, 18, 22, 30, 32, 43
    Lower, 34
    Upper, 21, 22, 31, 45
Ausable Pass, 30
Ausable River, 18

B

Backpacker magazine, 64
Bald Peak, 27
Bartlett Mountain, 22
Bartlett Ridge, 14, 18, 21, 22, 28, 31, 34, 43
Basin Mountain, 28, 31, 33, 49, 64
Beard, Charlie, 51, 52, 53, 124
Beede, Charlie, 31
Benedict, Farrand, 26
Big Blow, 17, 80
Bill's Man-Cave, 126, 166
Blake, Mills, 43
Blin, Robert Scott, 20
Blue Lines 2 (Mellor), 47
Bockley, Walker Wolf, 51, 53, 163-66
Bureau of Criminal Investigations (BCI), 42
Bushnell Falls, 25, 54, 55m

C

Caribou Pass, 30
Carroll, Robert W., Jr., 16, 35, 39-41
Carson, Russell
    Peaks and People of the Adirondacks, 25
    Snow Climbing in the Adirondacks, 31
Castle Column, 24p, 25

caves (named)
- Haystack Boulder Cavern, 41
- Marcy Cavern, Mount, 16, 39-41
- Marcy Cavern II-III, 41
- Upper Panther Gorge Caves 1-5, 40

Champlain Watershed, 18

Chiarenzelli, Jeff, 175

Clarkson University, 40, 127

cliffs/areas
- *Agharta Wall*, 24, 34, 47p, 50, 52, 53, 54, 77p, 84-86, 88-90, 121p, 131-33, 140, 141, 144, 146-48, 206pl, 216pl
- *Beer Walls* (Chapel Pond Pass), 153
- *Chapel Pond Slab*, 69
- *Chimney Wall*, 52, 53, 54m, 55, 92, 175-79, 185-88, 192p, 207pl, 209pl
- *East Face*, 17, 19, 51, 52, 54, 54m, 55, 61-62, 68-70, 72-75, 153-57, 162p, 180-84, 210pl
- *Feline Wall*, 19, 50, 51, 52, 53, 54, 107-9, 121p, 139-42, 167-70, 206pl
- *Haystack North End*, 53, 86-87, 97-99, 127-30, 152p, 163-65, 182p, 211pl, 216pl
- *Haystack South End*, 52, 78-80, 214pl
- *Huge Scoop*, 19, 50, 52, 53, 54, 101, 104-6, 110-13, 135-38, 206pl, 215pl
- *Joshua Tree*, 177
- *No Man's Land*, 12p, 18p, 19, 53, 54m, 55, 212pl
- overview, 19, 54-55
- *Panther Den*, 19, 23, 25, 36, 50, 51, 52, 53, 54, 90, 101-3, 114-17, 118p, 123-26, 133-34, 143-45, 149-52, 163-66, 206pl, 207pl, 208pl
- *Panther's Shield (Shield Wall)*, 108, 120
- *Ramp Wall*, 50, 52, 53, 54m, 55, 98-99, 119, 171-74, 211pl, 216pl
- *Spider's Web, The* (Chapel Pond Pass), 137, 177
- *Twin Fracture Gully*, 51, 55, 101, 106, 138, 194-97
- *Upper Washbowl Cliff*, 172
- *V Wall*, 12p, 15, 19, 52, 53, 54m, 55, 81-83, 93p, 159-62, 213pl

Climber's Guide to the Adirondacks (Healy), 24

Climbing (magazine), 51, 144, 149

Climbing in the Adirondacks (Mellor), 37

Colangelo-Lillis, Jesse, 51, 52, 53, 124

Colden Interior Outpost, 46

Colvin, Verplanck, 14, 22-23, 25-30, 49, 60, 173
- leveling (rod and level), 22, 28-30, 43
- tower signal, 30
- *Winter Fauna of Mount Marcy*, 26

Cook, Mary, 21

Crofoot, Adam, 24, 37, 47p, 48, 50, 51, 52, 53, 81-100, 109, 110-13, 118-22, 131-34, 143-45, 175-78, 185, 189

"Crofoot Approach," 189

Courain, Aaron, 53, 189

D

Davis, Miles, 49

Department of Environmental Conservation (DEC), 42, 44

Descriptive Guide to the Adirondacks (Wallace), 16

DeShane, Jaryn, 53, 159-62, 175, 177-79, 186, 189-93

Dewey, Melville, 94

Dibble, Seth, 25

Dickens, Charlie, 49, 52

Dix Mountain, 27

Dobbs, Matt, 51, 52, 53, 124, 167-70

Dong of Death, 112

Drinkwater, Emilie, 49, 195

Dubay, Ronald, 36-38, 49, 52

Dudley Observatory, 27

Duncan, Laura, 51, 53, 169, 194-97

E

Edmund Fitzgerald, 86, 90
Elk Lake (Mud Pond), 14, 22, 40, 46
Elk Pass, 30
Elliott, Brent, 51, 53, 169, 194-97

F

Farkas, Devin, 51, 52, 123-26
Feldspar Brook, 50, 100
Ferguson, Doug, 51, 53, 129, 163-66
"Finding the True Height of Tahawus" (Phelps), 29
Forest Preserve Centennial, 34
Four Corners (Tip-Top Camp, Junction Camp, Summit Camp, Lake Tear Camp), 14, 22, 23, 28, 30, 45, 46, 122
Fracchia, Christian, 49, 52

G

Garden Trailhead, The, 19, 25, 54, 55m
geology
    chimney, 15, 25, 49, 51, 52, 91, 92, 102, 103p, 105p, 106, 117, 125, 132, 134, 147, 151, 52, 175, 177-79, 186, 195, 196p
    glacial erratic, 15, 17, 59
    pillar (column, needle, pinnacle, spire, tower), 15, 19, 23p, 24, 25, 50, 51, 52, 55, 86-87, 91p, 99, 102, 103, 127, 128p, 129, 130, 164, 177, 179, 185, 187, 188p, 211pl, 216pl
    trap dike, 15, 49, 57, 81-82, 160, 175-76
Giant Mountain, 23, 159
Gibbens, Alice (Mrs. William James), 32
Gifford (Edinburgh) Lectures, 32, 33
Gladd, Nic, 37, 52, 109
Goldmark, Pauline, 32, 33
Goodwin, Jim (James A.), 16, 33-35, 36, 39
    And Gladly Guide, 33
    climbing, 34, 48, 52

    guiding, 33-34
    trail cutting, 23, 33
Goodwin, Tony, 38
Gothics Mountain, 28
    James, William, 33
    North Face, 19, 49
    Rainbow Slide, 37
    Six Summits (Martin), 31
    South Face, 163
Gray Peak, 26m, 27
Great Britain, 38
Great Range, 31, 100
    James, William, 33
    rescue, 189
    state land purchase, 38
    traverse, 64

H

Haas, Jeremy
    Adirondack Rock, 37, 47
Hale, Ed, 34
Hamilton College, 146
Harvard University, 32
Haystack, Mount, 14, 15, 20, 23, 25, 142p, 170p, 211pl-14pl, 216pl
    bushwhack, 64-67
    cliff overview, 19, 55
    Conjoined Slides, 77-80
    survey bolt, 28
    first ice route, 51, 127-29
    Haystack Boulder Cavern, 41
    Johannsen Face, 67
    night hike, 76
    rescue, 46p
    Six Summits, 31-32
    state land purchase, 38
    trail cutting, 27

Healy, Trudy, 49
  Climber's Guide to the Adirondacks, 36, 37
Hebb, Ken, 53, 180
High Spots, 31, 35
Hodgson, Gary, 45
Hoffman, Andrea, 52
Hogback Brook, 111
Hopkins, Arthur S., 38, 39m
Horse Hill, 60, 83, 217
Hudson River, 27
Hunters Pass, 30
Hurricane Mountain, 27
Huther, Nolan, 7d, 10d, 51, 53, 99, 127-30, 135-38, 153-58, 205d

I

Indian Falls, 38, 43, 44
Indian Pass, 16, 20, 21, 22, 26, 30
Indian Pass, The (Street), 20, 162
Isham, Ed, 31

J

Jackson, Dave, 49, 52
James, William, 32-33
  Letters of William James, The, 32-33
  Varieties of Religious Experience, The, 32
Johns Brook, 25, 38, 54, 99p, 100
Johns Brook Interior Outpost, 36
Johns Brook Lodge, 25, 36, 54, 55m
Josten, Josh, 52

K

Kadlecik, Greg, 52, 60-67, 71
Keene Valley, 19, 25, 32, 33, 46, 54, 55m
Kennedy, Chad, 52

L

Lake Champlain, 18
Lake Colden, 19, 22, 26
Lake Placid, 22
Lake Tear of the Clouds (Lake Perkins, Summit Water), 14, 23, 27, 28, 45
Lamb, L.S. (Levi Scofield), 22
Lamb, Wesley, 31
LaRow, Fred, 45
Lauper, Cyndi
  "Time After Time," 152
Lawyer, Jim, 37, 47
  Adirondack Rock, 37, 47
Leave No Trace, 11
Letters of William James, The (James, W. and James, H.), 32, 33
Lewis, Will, 33, 39
Little Brook, 31f
Little Haystack Mountain, 12p, 31, 38, 76, 81, 83, 100, 129, 214pl, 217
Little Nippletop Mountain, 18
Loher, Colin, 52
Lombardi, Hunter, 52, 104-6
Loope, P. F.
  "Marcy via the Ausable," 34
Lowell, Mark, 56-59
Lower Wolfjaw Mountain, 38, 64
Lowrie, Walter, 31

M

MacLaren, Malcolm, 31f
MacNaughton Mountain, 129
Macomb Mountain, 27
MacKenzie, Deb, 90
MacKenzie, Kevin B. (MudRat), *passim*
Malcolm, Herbert L., 64
Marcy Brook, 17, 18, 20, 56, 57p, 62, 75, 76p, 78

Marcy Dam, 43
Marcy, Mount
    caving, 16, 39-41
    first winter ascent, 31
    first ice climb, 49
    first measurement, 26
    first technical rock climb, 34
    first trail, 21
    first women to summit, 21
    height, 27, 28, 30
    state land purchase, 38
Marcy Swamp, 45
"Marcy via the Ausable" (Loope) 34
Martin, Newell, 31-32
    Six Summits, 31
McDonnel, 18
Mellor, Don, 217
    Blue Lines 2, 47
    Climbing in the Adirondacks, 37
Merrill, Loyal A., 20
Moss Pond, 28
Mount Marcy Cavern, 16, 39-41, 71
Mountain Skills Climbing Guides, 129, 163
Mountain Wilderness Survival (Surviving in the Wilds) (Patterson), 38
Mullen, Jace, 53, 167-70
Murphy, Conor, 52
Murray, Gerald D., 35, 40, 120

N

Neilson, William G., 38
Newton, Fannie, 21
"New Trails to the Summit of Mount Marcy" (Phelps), 22
Northeastern Caver, 40
Northeastern Regional Organization of the National Speleological Society, 39

O

Olsen, Scott, 49, 52
Opalescent River, 49
Orebed Lean-to, 56
Orson Schofield Phelps Collection, 21, 22
Otis, John W., 31
Ouluska Pass, 30

P

Panther Gorge
    first named climb, 36-37, 49, 52, 90, 152
    first recorded climb, 34
    naming, 21
    ownership, 38
    railroad, 30
    remoteness, 19
    rock fall, 17, 61
    size, 13, 14
    state land purchase, 38, 39
Panther Gorge Camp, 22, 23, 24, 27, 28, 31
Panther Gorge Falls, 16, 17p, 33, 40, 49, 57, 66p, 119p, 195, 210pl
Panther Gorge Lean-to, 14, 15, 40, 45, 59, 62
"Panther Gorge Rocks" (Wechsler), 134
Patterson, Craig, 36-38, 49, 52, 90
    Mountain Wilderness Survival (Surviving in the Wilds), 38
Peaks and People of the Adirondacks (Carson), 25
Perkins, Frederick S., 21
Phelps, Ed, 22, 25, 31
Phelps, Orson Schofield (Phelps, Old Mountain), 21-25, 34, 50, 87, 129, 130
    "Finding the True Height of Tahawus," 29
    guiding, 20, 24, 26, 27, 28
    "New Trails to the Summit of Mount Marcy," 22
    Rivers and Brooks of the Adirondacks, 22
    trail cutting, 20, 21, 22, 25, 27, 28
Pikus, John, 53, 146-48, 159-62

Plateau Lean-to, 34, 43
  Lower, 44
Platt, Zephaniah, 38
Plumley, Dan, 52, 114-17
Point Balk, 80
Pond, Benjamin S., 31
Porter, Chuck, 39
Potsdam, 40, 127

R

Race, Willard, 49
railroad, 30
Revelation (Bible), 106
Revolutionary War, 38
Rivers and Brooks of the Adirondacks (Phelps), 22
Rooney, Allison, 50, 52, 53, 97-100, 118-22, 143-45
Roth, Will, 49
Round Trip, The, 22
routes, rock climbing
  All Battered Boyfriends, 52, 97-98, 211pl
  All Ryled Up, 53, 175, 179, 209pl
  All Things Holy, 52, 81-83, 161, 213pl
  Anorthofright, 53, 72, 180-84, 210pl
  Belshazzar's Fate, 53, 131-34, 206pl, 207pl
  Bushy Pussy, 52, 114
  Castle Column, 53, 206pl, 207pl
  Cat on a Wet Tin Roof, 52, 101-3, 124, 126, 150, 151, 206pl, 207pl, 208pl
  Cat's Meow, The, 52, 109, 114
  Climb After Slime, 53, 149-52, 206pl, 207pl, 208pl
  Cloudsplitter, 50, 52, 89, 133, 147, 148
  Cracks of My Tears, 53
  CrazyDog's Halo, 52, 88-90, 132, 133, 206pl
  Dacker Cracker (Chapel Pond Pass), 177
  Eye for an Eye, 52, 97, 99, 211pl
  For Whom the Lichen Tolls, 23p, 50, 52, 86-87, 99, 211pl
  Galaxy of Tears, 50, 53, 139-42, 206pl
  general information, 47
  grades (specific to each route), 48, 206pl-216pl
  Haycrack, 52, 77-78, 214pl
  Kat Nap, 52, 141
  Kitten's Got Claws, 52, 107-9, 114, 206pl
  Le Chat Noir, 52
  Less than Zero, 52, 97-99, 211pl
  Lioness Rampant, The, 53
  Marcy's Great Chimney (aka Empty Tomb), 49, 52, 175-79, 209pl
  Moonraker Runout, 53, 206pl
  One for the Boys, 53, 143-45, 206pl, 207pl
  Panther's Fang, 36-38, 49, 52, 90, 152, 206pl, 207pl
  Panther's Pinnacle, 53, 179, 185-88, 189p, 209pl
  Paws Off, 53, 212pl
  Pioneer Anomaly, 53, 131-34, 206pl
  Predatory Instincts, 50, 53, 135-38, 206pl
  Pride, The, 50, 52, 110-13, 206pl
  Promised Land, 52, 108, 114-17, 206pl, 207pl
  Psalm 23, 53, 159-61, 213pl
  Puma Concolor, 52
  Ranger on the Rock, 52, 72-75, 210pl
  Revelations, 51, 53, 72, 153-58, 180, 210pl
  Rumours of War, 52, 104-6, 112, 136, 206pl
  Slacker Cracker, 53, 175-77, 186, 209pl
  Tail of Redemption, 53, 146-48, 206pl
  Teddy's Trauma, 37
  Toma's Wall, 52, 89
  Watery Grave, 52, 88, 90, 206pl
  Weissner Route, 172
  Windjammer, 53, 159-62, 213pl
  Wreck of the Lichen Fitzgerald, 50, 52, 84-86, 113, 206pl
  You Moss be Kidding Me!, 53, 149-52, 206pl, 207pl

routes, ice climbing
- *Agharta (not Agartha)*, 49, 52, 89, 92, 120, 121p, 124, 148, 215pl
- *Apex Predator*, 53, 122p, 189p, 191p, 215pl, 217p
- *By Tooth and Claw*, 51p, 52, 102, 123-26, 163p, 165-66, 206pl, 208pl
- *Charybdis*, 51, 53, 101, 194-97, 206pl, 215pl
- *Chimæra*, 51, 53, 167-70, 206pl, 215pl
- *Fly By*, 53, 99, 127, 129-30, 165, 216pl
- general information, 47
- grades, 48, 206pl-16pl
- *Haggis and Cold Toast*, 195
- *John 3:16*, 53, 213pl, 217
- *Just Nickel and Iron*, 51, 52, 215pl
- *Kitty Cake*, 53, 163-66, 216pl
- *Multiplication Gully*, 195
- *Needle in a Haystack*, 51, 53
- *Orson's Tower*, 51, 53, 127-30, 164, 165, 216pl
- *Panther Gorge Falls*, 49, 210pl, 215pl
- *PG-13*, 53, 213pl, 217
- *Pi Day*, 51, 52, 92, 94-96, 120, 121, 215pl
- *Ride the Lightning*, 51, 53, 165, 171-74, 216pl
- *Scylla*, 53, 101, 194-97, 206pl, 215pl
- *Skip the Lightning*, 53, 99, 171, 174, 216pl
- *Sorry, Kevin*, 53, 116, 124, 169, 215pl
- *Spiritus Draconis* (Dragon's Breath), 53, 189-93, 215pl, 217p

S

Saddleback Mountain, 28, 49, 56, 64, 129
- James, William, 33
- *Six Summits* (Martin), 31

Sawyer, George, 22

Schneider, Bill, 37, 48, 50, 52-53, 101-3, 109, 110-13, 123-26, 135-38, 143-48

search, rescue, and recovery, 42-46, 50, 100, 129

Seidita, Anthony, 41p, 51, 52, 72-80, 94-96, 122, 153, 154

Shaw, Christopher,
- "At Panther Gorge with William James," 33

Six Summits (Martin), 31-32

Ski to Die, 56

Skylight, Mount, 32, 43, 60, 62-63
- state land purchase, 38

Slant Rock, 25, 31, 34, 54, 55m, 100, 153

slides
- *Back in the Saddle* (Saddleback), 56
- *Conjoined* (Haystack), 77-80, 214pl
- *Diagonal* (Giant), 159
- *Grand Central* (Marcy), 16, 17p, 18, 40, 49, 56-59, 60-61, 65, 67p, 68, 70, 71, 121, 154, 157, 183, 207pl, 210pl, 215pl
- *Margin* (Marcy), 52, 61, 68p, 69, 72, 73, 75, 121, 157, 210pl
- *Old (Southern)* (Marcy), 18, 20, 22, 26, 27, 34, 57, 62, 122
- *Overhang* (Marcy), 52, 55, 94p, 95, 120, 177, 207pl
- *Rainbow* (Gothics), 37
- Skylight rubble slides, 62-63
- *True North* (Gothics), 56

Snow Climbing in the Adirondacks (Carson), 31

state land purchase, 38

St. Huberts, 31

Stillwater Inlet, 18

St. Lawrence University, 123, 167, 175

Stoddard, Seneca Ray, 14, 24
- *Adirondacks Illustrated, The*, 87, 129

St. Pierre, Steven, 53, 180-88

Street, Alfred Billings, 17, 20-21, 187
- *Indian Pass, The*, 20, 162

Swears, Loren, 51, 53, 142, 153-58, 217

Szot, Joe, 49, 195

T

Tahawus Club of Plattsburgh, 22, 24
   "The Stroll of the Tahawus Club," 23
talus, 15, 16p, 35, 40, 41, 60, 70p, 71, 78, 117, 119p, 120, 126p, 158, 159, 166
Thalheimer, Justin, 52, 107-9
Thomas, Almon, 21, 38
Thomas and Armstrong Lumber Company, 38
"Time After Time" (Lauper), 152
Toso, Mark, 52
Toso, Willow, 52
Totten and Crossfield Purchase, 38
Touchy Sword of Damocles (TSOD), 40
Townships (45 and 48), 21, 38
trailheads
   Adirondak Loj, 19, 43, 45, 46, 54, 94, 189
   Garden, The, *passim*
   Rooster Comb, 67
   Upper Works, 19
trails
   1861, 21, 22, 28, 29
   cutting, 20, 21, 22, 25, 27, 28, 31, 33
   Elk Lake to Marcy, 17, 19, 38, 45, 46, 62, 118
   first trail up Mount Marcy, 20, 21
   Haystack connector, 31
   Phelps, 15, 19, 25, 38, 54, 55m
   Range, 31
   South Meadows, 40
   South Side, 68
   Van Hoevenberg, 19, 49, 54, 94, 189
Trilogy, The (or Adirondack Trilogy), 49, 195
Tropical Storm Irene, 17

U

Ulrich, Dustin, 50, 53, 139-42
University of Edinburgh, 32
Uphill Lean-to, 45

V

Van Hoevenberg, Henry, 32
van Laer, Scott, 68-71, 90, 183, 184
Varieties of Religious Experience, The (James), 32

W

Wallace, E.R., 14, 19, 57
   Descriptive Guide to the Adirondacks, 16
Wallface, 19, 24, 40
Warden's Camp, 34
Wechsler, Alan, 51, 53, 131-34, 149-52, 171-74, 189
   "Panther Gorge Rocks," 134
Wells, Sylvanus, 38
Whiteface Mountain, 22
"Wild Side, The" (MacKenzie), 97
wildlife
   bear, 28, 153
   beaver, 17
   bivalves, 28
   eagles, 28
   owl, 29
   panther (chat de montagne), 21, 26
   porcupine, 35
   raven, 28
   songbirds, 35
   woodpecker, 3-toed, 63
Winter Fauna of Mount Marcy (Colvin), 26

Y

Yosemite, 16, 33, 38

Courtesy of Karen Stolz, Vertical Perspectives Photography.

About the Author

Kevin MacKenzie, also known as MudRat, first came to the Adirondacks with his parents as an infant and later moved to the Lake Placid, New York area with his wife, Deb. He is a hiker, climber, explorer, and photographer as well as an Associate Registrar at St. Lawrence University in Canton, New York. Kevin is also a guide and serves as a volunteer for the New York DEC high-angle rescue team.

He specializes in exploring the most remote regions of the Adirondack backcountry where he pioneers new rock and ice climbing routes. He continues to write online trip reports about his adventures. His articles and photographs have appeared in various publications including *Blue Lines 2, Adirondack Rock, Climbing, Adirondack Life, Adirondac, Peeks,* and the *Adirondack Journal of Environmental Studies*. Additional information may be found at www.adirondackmountaineering.com.

www.ingramcontent.com/pod-product-compliance
Lightning Source LLC
Chambersburg PA
CBHW040302010526
44108CB00033B/9